Problem Solving and Programs with C
Second Edition

Christie I. Ezeife
Computer Science
University of Windsor

August, 2003

Dedicated

To

Dr. Anthony Ezeife, my loving husband, whose expertise as a science education professor I continue to tap from. Emilia, Doreen, Laura and Tony junior Ezeife, our cherished children, whose perspectives on topics enrich my presentation of course materials to my student audience.

PREFACE

Computer Science as a field embraces a broad area of tasks associated with designing and building the physical hardware and software components. The skills and knowledge needed to be proficient in these computer-related tasks are highly dynamic as new hardware technology, programming languages and concepts rapidly evolve. It is then paramount that training provides a solid and broad background in the concepts that enable efficient, adaptable problem solving and programming with computers.

One method for teaching a first-year programming language course is to use a fairly easy-to-grasp-programming language like PASCAL, which is also strongly data-typed and structured. This approach is adopted by many universities and is expected to achieve a high success rate in the art of learning the language syntax. A limitation of teaching first programming language with languages like PASCAL is that adapting programming skills to system-like and industry-wide used programming language C becomes difficult for students. A second method for teaching a first-year programming course is to make the language of study C. This enables students to learn programming in a language they will find useful when employed in the industries. Being skilled in C language programming also facilitates learning much used object-oriented languages like C++ and JAVA, which are built on top of the C syntax. The limitation of teaching C as the first programming language is that C is a robust and complex language, which is difficult to learn.

In both methods, many students get entangled in learning the programming language syntax, and less attention is paid to the art of problem definition, understanding, presenting different solutions, coding the solutions, evaluating the solutions, refining solutions and computing the overhead of adopting a solution.

A third method for teaching a first-year programming course eliminates many of the limitations from the two methods above by teaching a programming course which places emphasis on problem-solving skills and methods, discussing all important programming language concepts with little or no emphasis on any one specific programming language syntax.

Based on the third approach but using C programming language, this book teaches ways to define and discover problems representing a real world situation, how to understand a given problem by identifying its set of input and output data, how to define the transformations (algorithms, flowcharts and programs) needed to produce problem output from its set of input data, how to define alternative solutions for a problem, and how to evaluate and test problem solutions for accuracy.

Emphasis is placed on the use of top-down design approach to problem solving, which incorporates problem solving tools like structure charts, algorithms, and flow charts. The program logic structures (sequential, function calls, decision and repetition) and advanced data structures (arrays, files, binary trees, hashing and linked lists, etc.) are discussed. Standard algorithms are introduced with discussion of searching and sorting techniques.

Outline

Each chapter ends with a set of problems drawn from many real life environments, aimed at consolidating the concepts discussed in the chapter, a set of laboratory or tutorial exercises are also included.

Chapter 1 discusses an overview of computer systems to get students familiar with components of the computer systems, machine architecture, data storage and software components of the machine.

Chapter 2 presents problem solving methodology involving top-down design approach. Chapter 3 discusses basic programming language concepts of variables and constants, simple data types, algorithmic and C program structures as well as assignment instructions.

Chapter 4 discusses tools for top-down problem solving like structure charts, functions, parameters and flowcharts. In Chapter 5, sequential program logic structure is discussed with program testing and documentation.

Chapter 6 presents program decision logic structure with discussions on if/else and switch_case instructions. The Repetition logic structure, discussing the while, do-while, and for loop instructions is presented in chapter 7.

More advanced data type of arrays is discussed in chapter 8. String processing, sorting and search algorithms are also presented in chapter 8. An introduction to advanced data types like text files, stacks, linked lists and binary trees is presented in chapter 9. Chapter 10 presesents a recap of formats for using C instructions, declaring data type and writing a program, which is handy for revisions. Chapter 11 presents a comprehensive laboratory manual, statement on assignment exercises, sample past quizzes and sample past tests.

Positive Features of The Book

The book supports self study, class teaching and practice. It presents just adequate materials in each chapter to teach important concepts in problem solving and programming in a progressive easy sequence that is good for teaching the materials in class, and would allow many students understand much of the materials before classes. The book supports each chapter with adequate laboratory exercisesin the laboratory manual part in order to foster practice. This book does not replace the role of class teaching and excellence is only accomplished by attending classes, going through book chapters carefully and doing laboratory exercises in the laboratory manual part of the book.

The book simplifies the process of learning programming. The book de-emphasizes the stress of syntax chasing in a new programming language by first solving problems with English-like pseudocode algorithms at the early stages and then mapping the instructions of the algorithms to C language syntax. This makes the syntax learning process easier to handle.

The book emphasizes on top-down design approach to problem solving. Real life problem solving usually involves a team of experts working on complex problems that need to be broken down. This book takes the task of learning how to solve real life problems head on, with an early introduction of use of functions and teaching of all aspects of programming using functions, in a process called top-down design approach.

The book emphasizes on laboratory exercises to foster practice. This book includes a full laboratory manual, which encourages students working in groups of 2 each week to learn how to define solutions to problems, write programs to solve those problems and test the programs. A laboratory examination is also part of the laboratory manual, which is used to test students' individual abilities to write, edit, compile and run programs to solve problems with functions, arrays and necessary logic structures.

The book includes lecture slides, sample tests and quizzes. The book is good for teaching multiple sections of classes as it includes lecture slides, templates for sample midterm and final examinations as well as sample quizzes, giving both the students and the instructors templates to work with. It does not allow for a lot of discrepancies between testing mechanisms that could be adopted by different instructors teaching multiple sections of the same course.

The book uses a global teaching structure in a concise fashion. The book discusses all possible ways to use a programming instruction (e.g., decision if instruction or function calls) in a concise way with examples, leaving out unneeded details and producing a not too bulky document.

The book provides chapter and laboratory exercise objectives. The book provides objectives at the beginning of each chapter and laboratory exercises to help instructors and students develop a learning plan before getting into the materials.

The book provides a snapshot summary of formats for instructions, data types and program. This snapshot summary presented as a recap chapter is very handy for revisions and quick reference.

Supplementary Materials

This text book is supplemented by program files for all example programs in the book, which are made available to both instructors and students adopting this book, on demand or at a web site. Instructors also have access to electronic lecture slides, all laboratory solutions, solutions to sample quizzes and tests in the book as well as C programs for laboratory exercises. Solutions to end_chapter problems may be available to instructors only, as these problems may be used for term assignments. Author can be reached via cezeife@uwindsor.ca.

Book History

This book has emerged as a third edition of materials developed for a first year problem solving and programming class at the Computer Science Department of the University of Windsor, Windsor, Ontario, Canada. For many years, it was observed that enrolment in first year programming classes dropped suddenly after the first year classes in many universities and average performance was poor. Our department in 1996, followed the program recommendations of the acm (association for computing machinery) and replaced the first year programming course in the first semester of first year, with a course on problem solving and progrmming with only program level detailed pseudocodes. This course was usually then followed with a full C language course in the second semester. This method simplified the process of learning programming. Having developed this problem solving course and taught it for several years, the first book was written in 2000, that is based on detailed pseudocodes which mostly obeyed C language syntax but not strictly (the green book). In 2002, we decided to go back to teaching the course with full C language syntax and the materials in the 2000 green book needed to be translated into complete working C language syntax, and that gave rise to the orange book in 2002. To better maintain the level of interest and ease we managed with the green book and pseudocode teaching, there was need for a revision of the 2002 book to address some issues like introducing full self study-like laboratory manual, laboratory exam, and cleaning up the translation to update sections and remove minor errors from the orange book. This new book (2003 edition) is expected to be adequate as a course material although another reference material is always a plus with any course.

The <u>author</u>, Dr. Christie Ezeife has been teaching hundreds of students with versions of this book for a number of years and will welcome any comments on the book via email (<u>cezeife@uwindsor.ca</u>).

Acknowledgements: *I would like to thank many instructors, in particular, Pratap Sathi and students, Raymond Shum, Udechukwu Ajumobi, Zhang H., and Hu Cheng, who have done some work, including reviewing the book, implementing the book chapter and lab C programs, that contributed to the final state of this book.*

TABLE OF CONTENTS

TABLE OF FIGURES

1. OVERVIEW OF COMPUTER SYSTEMS

Today's computer equipment is affordable by private individuals (about $2,000 for the average personal computer), small in size (about same size as a home television), consumes low energy and is very fast (over 2200 MHz or 2.2 GHz processors in the market). A 2200 MHz (Mega Hertz) processor is able to execute 2200 million machine instructions per second. The advancement in the performance of the computer hardware is due to the success of the integrated circuit technology, which enables production of small size chips that accommodate complex electronic circuits for implementing various components of the computer.

Computers of the 1940's were very bulky, highly expensive (millions of dollars for one), and consume a lot of energy. Story had it that the first large-scale, general-purpose electronic digital computer, the ENIAC, completed in 1946 at the University of Pennsylvania, weighed 30 tons, occupied a 30 x 50 ft space (size of a house), and when first turned on, consumed so much energy that the whole city lost power. The electronic element used by ENIAC and other first generation computers was a vacuum tube (not integrated circuit chips). Figure 1.1 gives a comparative summary of features of computers in the 2000's and 1940's.

Computer	Size	Cost	Speed	Energy Consumed	Electronic element	Gener-ation	Owner
Today's (2000's)	Small (size of a TV)	Cheap (about $2000)	Fast (over 2200 MHz)	Low	Integrated circuit chip	4th and higher	Indivi-duals
1940's	Big (size of a house)	Expensive (about $1M)	Slow (a few instruct ions/s)	High	Vacuum tubes	1st	Organiza-tions

Figure 1.1:   Comparing Computers of 2000's and 1940's

The advancement in technology went through second generation, third generation, fourth and higher generations. A generation of computers is characterized by the dates they were built and used, type of electronic components they were built with, their memory, processor and programming capabilities. Figure 1.2 presents a summary of the basic electronic components used in building several generations of computers.

Computer Generation	Electronic Component	Reliability	Energy Consumption	Size	Programming allowed
First (1945-1955)	Vacuum tubes	Low	High	Huge	Wiring plug boards and machine language
Second (1955-1965)	Transistors	Relatively low	Relatively low	Small	High level language and stored program concept
Third (1964-1980)	Integrated circuit silicon chip	High	Low	Very small	Compatible software and family concept
Fourth (1980 – 2000s)	Large and very large scale integrated circuit chips	Very high	Very low	Very small	Massive support for networks, GUI, distributed and mobile computing

Figure 1.2:   Electronic Components for Generations of Computers

The processing power, memory capacity and programming capabilities of a generation of computers are highly tied to the electronic component they are built on. Vacuum tubes look like electric bulbs and can be used to represent decimal digits. Thus, in order to represent a 10-digit number on the computer, an array of 10 by 10 or 100 such bulbs, each of which can be set to on or off position is used. For example, a representation of the number 574 is given as shown in Figure 1.3 .

The process of adding two numbers in a first generation computer would need two arrays of vacuum tubes set to the values of the two input numbers respectively. Then, a plug board with switches for arithmetic operations is set to "Add" operation. The result of the operation is collected or obtained from a third array of vacuum tubes. Thus, 300 vacuum tubes are needed to represent three decimal numbers. Vacuum tubes are fragile and can break or easily become unreliable. The tubes are bulky, consume a lot of energy and emit a lot of heat. This made first generation computers bulky, expensive and unable to possess memories big enough to store computer programs.

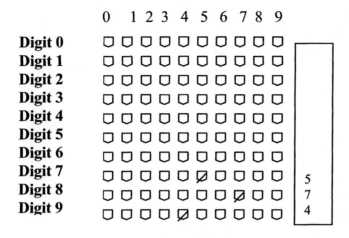

Figure 1.3:   A Representation of Decimal Number 574 With Vacuum Tubes

Computers of today belong to the fourth and higher generations. With first generation computers (1945-1955), programming was in machine language and by wiring up plug boards. Second generation computers (1955-1965) advanced to use of transistors as the basic electronic components. Transistors are more compact than vacuum tubes and more reliable. The stored program concept was supported making it possible for programming to be done in high level language using punched cards. Third generation computers (1965-1980) had the basic technology of integrated circuits (ICs) in use. This technology allows many transistors (tens to hundreds of them) to be packaged in a silicon chip. With the invention of chips, faster, cheaper and smaller sized computers could be built, e.g., IBM system 360. Fourth generation computers (1980-1990) allowed even smaller computers like personal computers to be built. Technology in use is large scale integration (LSI) which allows thousands and more transistors to be packaged in a single chip. There was support for network and graphical user interface. Higher generations of computer use very large scale integration (VLSI) technology allowing even more transistors to be packaged in a single chip to produce faster and more compact components.

1.1   Types of Computers

Modern-day computers belong to one of the following types, classified based on their size, processing power, and number of users it can communicate with simultaneously:

(1) Microcomputers - allow only a single user to connect and use the computer at any time, e.g., Macintosh PC, IBM PC, laptops. These computers are the smallest in size, least expensive and have the least processing power for supporting multiple users.

(2) Minicomputers - generally have more processing power and speed than microcomputers, allow multiple users to communicate simultaneously, generally bigger in size than the PC (although PC-sized minicomputers are being produced, causing many to regard workstations which are

13

minicomputers, as PC's). Most UNIX servers are minicomputers, e.g., the PDP II series, SUN's and SGI's workstations.

(3) Mainframes   - generally bigger in size than minicomputers, allow hundreds of users to be connected at the same time to one computer, e.g., IBM 370.

(4) Super computers - very powerful mainframes for high-performance number-crunching applications.

1.2   Components of the Computer System

All types of computers have the same basic components: hardware and software.

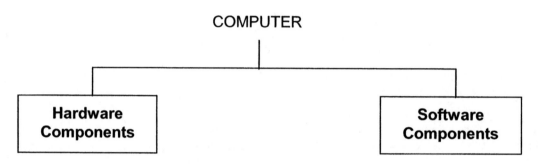

Figure 1.4:   *Hardware and Software Link*

1.2.1   Hardware Components

The hardware components are better seen and remembered through the functions they perform. Think for a moment, of a task you would like to accomplish with the computer. For example, you want to type up your assignment with the computer. You begin by pressing a key like "A" on the keyboard - an input device which converts the character "A" to a string of binary digits (representing that character) and sends the binary string to main memory (the primary storage device), where it is stored. The hardware unit responsible for receiving this input from the keyboard and storing it in memory is the Central Processing Unit (CPU). The CPU also executes instructions to allow us see what we have typed on the screen, terminal or printer (output device). Since we shall want to turn off our computer when done, we may not want to keep everything we have typed so far, currently stored in volatile primary memory, because the primary memory's contents are lost once the computer is powered off. We need to save our work on disk (secondary memory). Thus, the hardware components of the computer are:

(1)   Input Device: e.g., keyboard, mouse.

(2)   Central Processing Unit: also called CPU.

(3)   Main Memory: e.g., random access memory (RAM), and read only memory (ROM).

(4)   Secondary Memory: e.g., disks (floppy and hard), CD-ROM, tapes.

(5)   Output Devices: e.g., monitor, printer, speakers.

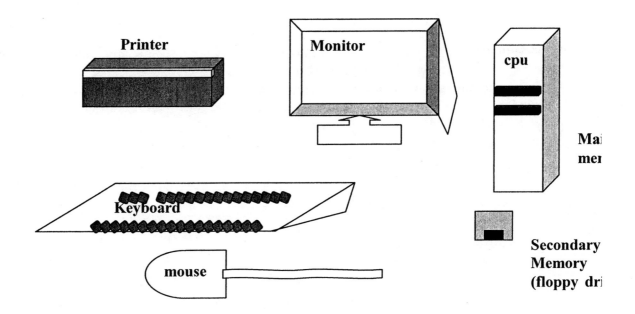

Figure 1.5   Components of a Computer

Input Devices: are the hardware components receiving input from the outside world to be fed into the computer. Examples are keyboard, mouse, joystick, light pen, etc.

The Central Processing Unit: (CPU) is the brain of the computer responsible for executing all machine instructions. It executes all arithmetic and logical operations as well as sequencing and branching. It is able to accept input from input devices, and to display data onto output devices. The power of the CPU is defined by its instruction set (the number of instructions it is able to encode) and its speed (the number of instructions it executes per second).

Main Memory: The primary memory of the computer, also called main memory, is used to store programs and data. There are two possible types of main memory: (1) RAM (random access memory), and (2) ROM (read only memory). RAM is volatile because it loses its contents when the computer is turned off. The part of the main memory used by general programs is called Random Access Memory (RAM), because it takes the same length of time to access every cell of the memory, irrespective of its location (unlike tape where cells at the beginning of the tape are accessed faster than those at the end of the tape). Read Only Memory (ROM), is the other type of main memory. ROM is not volatile because the programs stored on them (part of the operating system), are stored (hard wired in) during chip fabrication, and those programs can only be read by the CPU when the computer is turned on, and cannot be overwritten.

Organization of Main Memory

The next question that may be going through our minds is "Just how are data and programs stored in main memory?". Imagine a film theatre with 500 seats or an airplane with 200 seats, every seat has a unique label or address to enable people to be seated or removed from the seat. In the same manner, main memory is made up of a number of addressable cells. Cells have addresses 0, 1, 2, 3... $(2^n - 1)$ for a memory that is of capacity 2^n bytes. Each cell is capable of storing 8 binary digits (bits) of data or programs and a group of 8 binary digits is equivalent to one byte. Although for simplicity, a memory word is taken to mean the same as a memory cell in this book, with some computers, a memory word is made up of m cells (4 bytes or 4 cells for 32 bit computer and 2 bytes or cell for 16 bit computer). A memory with 1024 bytes or approximately one thousand bytes or cells is said to have a capacity of 1 kilobyte, a megabyte of memory has 10^6 or 2^{20} bytes, a gigabyte of memory has 10^9 or 2^{30} bytes and a terabyte of memory has 10^{12} or 2^{40} bytes.

Address	Content
0	0111 0110
1	
2	
.	
.	
.	
2^n-1	

Memory

Figure 1.6   Main Memory Cells.

A bit is a binary digit, which is either 0 or 1. Programs and data are stored in memory as patterns of bits. In order to represent a bit, the computer hardware needs a circuit device capable of being in one of two states, like a power switch, which can either be on or off, so that state "on" is represented as 1, while state "off" is represented as 0.

Representation of Data and Programs

How are data and programs represented as binary digits? Natural or positive numbers are converted from base 10 (decimal number system) to base 2 (binary number system) to get the bit pattern representation for each number.

For example, to be able to do 9 + 6, we need to convert both numbers to binary as follows:

$$9 = 2^3 + 2^0 = 8 + 1 = 0000\ 1001$$

$$6 = 2^2 + 2^1 = 4 + 2 = 0000\ 0110$$

This conversion is accomplished by breaking the decimal number to be converted to binary into a sum of numbers that are in powers of 2. For example, to convert 9 to binary, we look for the biggest whole number less or equal to 9 but which is a power of 2. The number in this case is 8, which is equivalent to 2^3. Next, we obtain the difference between 8 and 9 as 1. We again write this difference as a power of 2. The process continues until there is a zero difference. Finally, we write the original number 9 as a sum of the powers of 2 numbers (2^3 + 2^0) and write a 1 for every power of 2 position present in the sum of power of 2 numbers representing the original number, but we write 0 otherwise (that is, 0 is written for every power of 2 position absent in this sum of power of 2 number). Thus, for 9, we have:

2^7	2^6	2^5	2^4	2^3	2^2	2^1	2^0
0	0	0	0	1	0	0	1

Another way to convert a decimal number to binary is to keep dividing (integer or whole number division) it by 2 until the quotient becomes 0. Quotient is the whole number result obtained after performing a whole number division (excluding the remainder). For example, 7 divided by 4 has a quotient of 1 and a remainder of 3, while 2 divided by 5 has a quotient of 0 and a remainder of 2. Each time the remainder obtained is placed under the 2^{k+1} if not the first remainder, but placed under 2^0 if the first remainder (that is, k=0 the first time), where k represents the power of 2 position. The example below shows how the numbers 9 and 6 are converted to binary by continuously dividing each number with 2 until a quotient of 0 is left. Looking at the case for number 9, in the first round of division by 2, the power 2 position is k=0, 9 is dividied by 2 to obtain a quotient of 4 and the remainder 1 is placed under $2^k = 2^0$ bit position. The second round of division by 2 continues with the quotient of 4 (because it is not yet 0). When 4 is divided by 2, a quotient of 2 is obtained and the remainder 0 is placed under $2^k = 2^1$ (k is 0+1=1, this second time) bit position. In the third round, the last quotient of 2 is divided by 2 to obtain a quotient of 1 and a remainder of 0, which is placed under $2^k = 2^2$ bit position. The last quotient is 1 and this is divided by 2 to obtain a quotient of 0 and a remainder of 1 that is now placed under the $2^k = 2^3$ bit position. The division stops now that the quotient is 0 and the rest of the bit positions to the left are padded with 0 to make 1 byte.

For example:

powers of 2 2^7 2^6 2^5 2^4 2^3 2^2 2^1 2^0

```
2 | 9
2 | 4   R  1   =>                                             1
2 | 2   R  0   =>                                        0
2 | 1   R  0   =>                                   0
    | 0   R  1   =>   0   0   0   0   1

      9    =          0   0   0   0   1   0   0   1
```

128   64   32   16   8   4   2 1

1   1   0   0   1   0   0

Similarly:

powers of 2		2^7	2^6	2^5	2^4	2^3	2^2	2^1	2^0

```
 2 | 6
 2 | 3   R  0   =>                                    0
 2 | 1   R  1   =>                              1
   | 0   R  1   =>     0   0   0   0   0   1

     6   =                0   0   0   0   0   1   1   0
```

Note that once you obtain the binary equivalent of the number, to make up the 8 bits, we pad the positions up to the left-most bit positions with zeroes.

Converting a binary number back to a decimal number entails getting the sum of all products of each binary digit and its power of 2. For example:

$$0110 = (0 \times 2^3) + (1 \times 2^2) + (1 \times 2^1) + (0 \times 2^0)$$
$$= 0 + 4 + 2 + 0$$
$$= 6$$

Negative numbers are represented using either 2's complement, 1's complement, or sign and magnitude approaches. With 2's complement representation, the binary of its positive is flipped by changing all 0's to 1's, and all 1's to zeroes, and adding 1. With 1's complement representation, the positive binary equivalent is flipped and with sign-magnitude representation, the leftmost bit is treated as the sign bit, which has the value of 1 if the number is negative, and 0 if the number is positive. The rest of the bits in sign and magnitude representation, store the binary equivalent of its positive number.

For example, a computer that stores negative numbers using 1's complement in a 1 byte cell, will store the decimal number -15 as 11110000. Recall that the binary equivalent for +15 is 00001111. When this number is flipped, it becomes 11110000 (the 1's complement for -15). To store -15 using 2's complement, 1 is added to its 1's complement to obtain 11110001. The representation of -15 in sign and magnitude is 10001111.

Programs are made up of instructions, which are a combination of character strings. Thus, representation of programs and instructions is accomplished by representing the string of characters making up the program. Every character is represented using 8 bits or one byte. Characters are represented using standard codes. One code is ASCII (American Standard Code for Information Interchange), which uses seven bits to represent a character (See Appendix A). Another standard code used by some systems is EBCDIC (extended binary coded decimal interchange code) code.

Secondary Memory (Secondary Storage)

Some of the reasons why a computer system requires secondary memory devices like floppy disks, hard disk drives, CD-ROM's and tapes are:

1.   We may need to save our data and programs so that we can continue to work on them in the future.

2.   Main memory may not have enough storage space to keep all the programs we want to run.

3.   Many of the storage devices are detachable and we can carry data to another destination to be used on another computer, even if network data transfer is not possible.

Secondary storage devices are usually mounted on appropriate device drivers (e.g., floppy disk drive, CD-ROM drive) before data could be stored on or read from them. The secondary memory is used to store data and programs for later use.

1.2.2   The Software Components of the Computer System

A computer without software components is like a car without a driver. Computer software is a computer program, which is a sequence of instructions (much like a detailed cooking recipe) for solving a specific problem, or accomplishing a task. The software system drives the physical hardware components through a sequence of instructions.

There are many different software systems in a computer, based on the type of function they perform. The main classes of software systems are:

1. Operating Systems: These are programs that provide an interface between (i) other programs and the computer hardware, (ii) the user and other computer programs, (iii) the user and hardware. They are responsible for managing the hardware resources of the computer, e.g., queuing up job requests like "print" in the order they arrive and instructing the CPU on which job to run first for fairness. Part of the operating system is kept in the ROM part of memory to initiate the hardware and provide commands that users could issue to communicate with hardware once the computer is turned on. Some major operating systems software in the market today and in use are UNIX for mostly minicomputers, Windows 95/98/2000, Linux and NT for the PC's. Others include MSDOS, OS2, Apple OS, etc.

2. Translators or Compilers: These are programs, which are responsible for translating programs written in high-level languages (different from the machine language of 0's and 1's) to machine language so that the hardware system can execute (do what the instructions are asking) them. Compilers are also responsible for checking that program instructions conform to the language grammar rules (or syntax). There are many high-level programming languages available today and programs written in a high-level

language need the appropriate compiler to compile, or translate them to machine language code. Examples of compilers are C and C++ compilers, PASCAL, FORTRAN, COBOL, and JAVA compilers. Some languages have compilers that are simpler and more interactive, called interpreters.

3. Network Software: These software systems allow more than one computer to be connected together and share information. In this category are found telnet, ftp, communication protocol, software and Internet web browsers, like Microsoft Explorer, and Netscape.

4. Productivity Tools: These are software applications, which allow users to perform daily business and office operations in a more productive fashion. They are available for tasks related to word processing and desktop publishing (e.g., Microsoft Word and WordPerfect), spreadsheets (e.g., MS Excel and Quattro Pro), databases (e.g., MS Access, Oracle, Paradox, or DB2), slide and multimedia presentations (e.g., MS Power Point, Lotus Freelance, Aldus Persuasion).

5. Others: The list above may not be exhaustive as it is unclear which category some software systems may belong to. For example, utility software used for creating backup systems and disk error recovery, virus checking and recovery, etc. These other software systems are placed under this category.

1.3 Overview of Algorithms and Programming Languages

Every program or software, complex or simple, is made up of a sequence of instructions specifying the precise sequence of steps for solving the problem. One difference between an algorithm and a program is in the way and level of detail the sequence of steps, are expressed. Secondly, in an algorithm, the instructions are expressed in a pseudocode language (a combination of English and Math), but in a program, the instructions are expressed in a particular programming language syntax. A well-defined and detailed algorithm has each of its instructions directly and easily translated to only one instruction in the programming language. Of course, coarse level definitions of an algorithm may be used at some stage in problem solving, but in this case, one algorithmic instruction may not translate to only one program instruction. In this book, the final complete algorithmic solution of a problem is taken as the detailed version where each algorithmic instruction translates to a program instruction.

Example 1.1   Given the heights of 10 pairs of 15 year old children in the order, one girl's height, followed by a boy's height, write an algorithm to determine the number of boys taller than their girl partners, number of girls taller than their boy partners and number of pairs with the same height.

Solution:

We first try to present a solution by highlighting the set of input and output data to be used by the algorithm before defining steps for transforming the set of input to output data. In this solution, it is assumed that the given pairs of heights are surely those of 15 year old girls and boys. So, we do not need to cross-check that input data are valid.

Algorithm 1.1

Input: 10 pairs of girl_height, boy_height

Output: Number of girls' heights that are greater than boys' heights (girls_taller), Number of boys' heights that are greater than girls' heights (boys_taller), Number of pairs with same height (same_height).

Instructions of Algorithm 1.1:

Step 1:   Initialize cells for holding totals girls_taller=0, boys_taller=0, same_height=0
Step 2:   We know that we have 10 pairs, so initialize a counter to keep track, knt=1
Step 3: Begin
   Step 3.1:   Read the first pair of heights
               Read (girl_height, boy_height)
   Step 3.2: Check if girl_height is greater or smaller than boy_height
               If greater, add 1 to girls_taller counter;
               Otherwise if smaller, add 1 to boys_taller counter.
               Otherwise, add 1 to same_height counter.

               If girl_height>boy_height
                   then girls_taller=girls_taller+1
                   else if girl_height<boy_height
                       then boys_taller=boys_taller+1
                       else same_height = same_height + 1
   Step 3.3   Increment knt to process the next pair of heights: knt = knt + 1
   Step 3.4   If knt<= 10, Go to Step 3.1
   Step 4: Print out the number of boys taller than their girl partners, number of girls taller than their boy partners and the number of pairs with same height.

               Print (girls_taller,   "girls are taller than their boy partners")

```
Print (boys_taller, "boys are taller than their
girl partners")

Print (same_height, "boys and girls are of
equal heights and no group is taller")
```

Step 5:   End.

Computer programming languages fall into three main types:

1. Machine Language: Machine language programming instructions are represented as a string of bits corresponding to the programs and data in compliance with the particular machine architecture (internal organization of machine's circuits) the program is running. Programs in machine language run faster since they do not need to go through the translation or compilation stage. However, machine language programs are hard to understand or modify by human beings and not easily portable to computers with an architecture different from the computer they represent. For example, in a machine: A=A+5 may be represented as 00001001 01111111 00000101. The first binary code represents the encoding for the instruction "Add", while the second code represents the memory address called "A", and the third encoding stands for the binary representation for the decimal digit 5. The encoding says "Add 5 to memory location A".

2. Assembly Language: Assembly language is a symbolic form of machine language, which is still closely tied to the architecture of the machine. While it is easier for humans to understand than machine language, it is still not portable across other machines. An assembly language equivalent of the high level instruction A=A+5 given above in machine language is "Add A, =5".

3. High-Level Programming Languages: Instructions in these languages are easier to use, understand and modify by humans because they are closest to English and Math. They must go through a translation or compilation stage to be executed by the computer hardware, and thus, take up more computer time. They are more portable across different computers as a high level language program written on one computer can be run on another computer with a different architecture. Current programming languages fall into one of the following four programming paradigms:

    (a) Functional Languages: These languages view the process of program development as the construction of black boxes each of which accepts input at the top and produces output at the bottom. For example, in an early functional language, LISP, the process of computing the average of a list of numbers is accomplished with an instruction like (Divide(Sum Numbers) (Count Numbers)), meaning that the function average is defined with already existing functions, Divide, Sum and Count. The black boxes are given the input "Numbers". Examples of functional languages are LISP, ML and

Scheme. Although Miranda is not a full functional language, it is close to this category.

(b) Procedural/Imperative Languages: With this class of languages, programs are defined using the traditional approach, showing all step-by-step sequences for solving the problem. Examples of procedural languages are Machine and Assembly language, FORTRAN, COBOL, ALGOL, BASIC, Apl, C, PASCAL, and Ada.

(c) Object-Oriented Programming Languages: Programs written in these languages are largely procedural except that groups of data are bundled together with the operations for manipulating them. In other words, units of data are seen as active objects rather than passive units. A list of numbers as an object, for example, carries with it the ability to obtain its sum, product, sort, accept new members, delete existing members, etc. Languages in this category include Simila, Smalltalk, C++ and JAVA. Object-oriented languages can be either procedural or functional and their type is determined by the type of the language forming the basic building block for their methods or messages. For example, C++ and JAVA are procedural while object-oriented languages based on LISP are functional.

4. Declarative Languages: These languages declare a sequence of facts and the process of program writing becomes that of specifying a sequence of rules, which enable correct deductions to be drawn from the known facts. The approach is based on formal and predicate logic and logical deductions. For example, some facts may be:

> Mary is John's sister;
> Pete is Mary's son;
> A sister's son is a nephew;
> A mother's brother is an uncle;

With these facts, a program to find who Pete's uncle is, specifies the rules that will correctly deduce "John" given the facts above. Examples of languages in this category are GPSS and Prolog.

1.4 Introduction to C Programming Language

The programming language C, is a high level language, which provides a language syntax (grammar) that we can use to define the sequence of steps (program) for solving a problem. A program is a set of instructions for solving a problem defined in a specific programming language. The computer executes instructions of a program to produce desired output data (results) given the needed input data. The process of writing a correct program to be executed by the computer for purposes of solving a problem is called programming.

A written program is first typed and stored in a text file (also called ASCII file). Only a text editor like *Unix visual editor (vi), nedit,* pico or PC's *Window's Notepad* can be used to prepare a text file. Word processors (like *MSWord* and *WordPerfect*) are not used for preparing a text file like a C program. The file that contains the source program is called the source file.

A C source program file must be given a name with .c extension. For example, an appropriate name for a C program source file for calculating the class average is caverage.c. Since this program is not written in machine language, before it can be executed (run) by the computer, it has to be translated into machine language of 1's and 0's in a process called compilation. A C compiler is used to compile the C source program file to convert it first to machine code. The compiler also checks that the program follows the C language syntax (grammar). During compilation, instructions that do not conform to the C language syntax will cause a syntax error (bug) alert. Programs with syntax errors will not compile successfully, unless the syntax errors are first corrected in the source file. The process of correcting syntax errors is called de-bugging. Knowing the syntax of C language will provide the programmer with the skills needed to write error-free codes and to debug C programs. Some compilers come with a window-based text editor that programmers can also use to prepare their source files.

The translated machine code is next linked to include all external references (like other files and functions provided by the compiler and used by the program through an #include instruction). The machine code that is executable by the computer is in a.out file after compilation if program is being executed on a Unix system, and it is in .exe file if program is compiled with a PC window-based C compiler like Turbo C+ Lite.

The structure of a typical C program for solving a problem is:

```
#include <stdio.h>

void main (void)
     {
            /*  Input and output data variables are usually declared here */
            /*  Next valid program instructions like the following are placed */
            printf ("Hello World");
     }
```

A C program may have more than one #include statement, which is a pre-processor directive that serves to make available another C source file for use by this program. The #include files have .h extension for header files that contain statements which most programs would commonly use. For example, the <stdio.h> header file contains functions that enable programs to read data from the keyboard or print data to the monitor. This directive #include <stdio.h> is used by most programs and is always the first line in a program. Other #include files like <math.h> may be placed in addition if mathematical functions are to be used by the program. Other necessary header files to be included when processing string or character data will be introduced in the appropriate sections.

void main (void) is used to mark the main C program block (containing the sequence of instructions to be executed). The opening { and closing } curly brackets are used to mark the beginning and end of the set of instructions defining the main program. The printf ("Hello world"); is an example of a valid instruction for printing the string "Hello world". Every valid C instruction ends with a semi-colon. Comments in a C program are text placed in between the comment marker characters /* and */. Comments are not executed by the computer, but are useful for program readability.

For more complex programs, many more instruction blocks (called functions) could be used in solving a problem. When more than the main function is used, the simple structure of a program is changed to accommodate additional complexity. Also, many more valid program instructions can be used in each function block marked by an opening and closing curly brackets. The use of these more complex constructs will be discussed in the appropriate chapters.

Process of Executing a High-Level Language Program

Before a program written in a high-level language is executed by the CPU, it needs to be compiled, linked and loaded into memory in a process called compilation and linking. Thus, to obtain expected output from a program, we need to do the following:

1)   Type the source program in a high-level language (usually typed with the help of an ASCII or text editor like Unix vi, edit or PC-based notepad). Some window-based compilers like Turbo C++ Lite also come with their own text editor, which can be used to prepare the source program file.

2)   Compile the program to get object program in machine language. For example, on Unix system, to compile a C program, saved in file c140.c we use the command

```
cc c140.c
```

This converts the program in c140.c to machine language and keeps this object module in a file called a.out, which is an executable file. On PC-based Turbo C++ Lite, select Compile Menu, then Build All Option, and then Run (note that Build and Run on this kind of PC-based system here are similar to link and run step).

3)   Link to get load module to run. This is the process of including all functions needed and used by this program by resolving all address references before loading the program into memory. On Unix-based systems, all of the linking might be done automatically in step 2 before producing a.out and to load and run a compiled C program, we simply type

```
a.out
```

A sample C program version of Algorithm 1.1 is given below:

```c
#include <stdio.h>
void main (void)
 {
        float girl_height, boy_height;
        int knt=1, girls_taller=0, boys_taller=0, same_height=0;

        while (knt<=10)
                {
                scanf("%f %f", &girl_height, &boy_height);
                if (girl_height>boy_height)
                        ++girls_taller;
                else if (girl_height<boy_height)
                        ++boys_taller;
                else ++same_height;

                ++knt;
                }

        printf("%d girls are taller than their boy partners \n", girls_taller);

        printf("%d boys are taller than girl partners  \n", boys_taller);

        printf("%d girls and boys  have the same heights \n", same_height);
 }      /* end of program  */
```

Figure 1.7:   C Program Equivalent of Algorithm 1.1

1.5   Exercises

1.   Angela, your neighbour, would like to buy a computer and consults you to advice her on what components to buy.   She lives with her grandson, who wants to type assignments and get on the Internet.
a) Outline all components she needs to buy.
b) What type of computer would you recommend for her (Mainframe, Mini, or PC), and why?
c) Explain in detail the functions of all computer parts you are recommending that she would buy.

2.   How are ROM and RAM related to the CPU?
a) Give two differences and two similarities between ROM and RAM
b) How are programs and data represented in memory?
c) Convert each of the following decimal numbers to binary:
     i) 128   ii) 59   iii) 32
     iv) 18   v) 121   vi) 78
d) Convert each of the following binary numbers to decimal:
     i) 01101101   ii) 10010011   iii) 10000000
     iv) 10000111   v) 00001111   vi) 01111111
e)   Show how the following instructions will be represented literally using ASCII:
     i) A = A + B;
     ii) ++a;
     iii) while (i <= 10)

3.   Show the conversion of the following negative numbers to binary in
a) 1's complement   b) 2's complement and   c) sign and magnitude
The numbers are:
     i) -128   ii) -59   iii) -32
     iv) -18   v) -121   vi) -78

4.   Your friends bought 256 megabytes of main memory.   How many cells or bytes does this memory contain?
a) What is a byte?
b) What are memory addresses?   What range of addresses are defined for this memory?
c) Is this memory bigger or smaller than a 256 gigabyte hard disk?
d) Why would you need a hard disk?

5.   What functions do the following perform?   Give an example of each that you have used or know.
a) Operating systems
b) Compilers
c) Productivity Tools

6.   How are algorithms different from programs?

a) Write an algorithm, which finds the biggest of any three numbers.

7. Write an algorithm to find the largest common divisor of two positive integers.

8. Write an algorithm to convert a given binary number to decimal. Assume the number is a positive whole number (no fractional part).

9. Write an algorithm to convert a given decimal number to binary. Assume number is a positive whole number.

10. Write an algorithm to convert a given negative decimal number to its 2's complement equivalent.

11. Type, compile and run the C program equivalent of Algorithm 1.1 given as Figure 1.7. Hand in your source program file, the input data and the output of your run. Use the following set of input data:

5.1	4.3
4.2	4.5
5.3	5.2
5.7	6.0
4.1	4.3
5.0	5.3
5.2	5.3
5.6	5.5
4.8	4.8
4.9	4.9

1.6   References

J. Glenn Brookshear, "Computer Science - An Overview", 5th ed., Addison Wesley, 1997.

Nell Dale/Chip Weems, "PASCAL", 3rd ed., Heath, 1991.

H. M. Deitel/P. J. Deitel, "C How to Program", 2nd ed., Prentice Hall, 1994.

Kris Jamsa, "Jamsa's C Programmer's Bible – The Ultimate Guide to C Programming", first edition, Onword Press, Thomson Learning, 2002.

Elliott B. Koffman, "Turbo PASCAL" 5th ed., Addison Wesley, 1995.

Maureen Sprankle, "Problem Solving and Programming Concepts", 3rd ed., Prentice Hall, 1995.

Uckan Yuksel, "Problem Solving Using C – Structured Programming Technique", 2nd edition, WCB McGraw-Hill, 1999.

2. PROBLEM SOLVING STEPS

2.1 What is a Problem?
2.2 Steps in Solving a Problem Using Top-down Design Approach
2.3 Exercises
2.4 References

Before discussing the steps for solving a problem, it is good to have a clear understanding of what a problem is. Problems to be solved fall into two broad categories namely (1) algorithmic problems or (2) heuristic problems.

For algorithmic problems, a detailed sequence of steps can be found that produces the desired solution, while for heuristic problems, correct solutions will only emerge if a sketchy and non-detailed sequence of steps is combined with previous or common sense knowledge and experience, and some trial-and-error procedures. Examples of algorithmic problems are baking a cake or adding two numbers, while examples of heuristic problems are winning a tennis match, or making a speech at a ceremony. Note that some problems may not be clearly heuristic or algorithmic.

In this book, we are mostly concerned with algorithmic problems since computers are good at solving such problems. Heuristic problem solving (getting the computers to speak English or recognize patterns, e.g., faces) is the focus of Artificial Intelligence (a field of Computer Science). In the early chapters, this book adopts the convention of defining an algorithmic solution to a problem first before defining an equivalent C program for the solution.

2.1   What is a Problem?

A problem has some given input data and some desired output data and we are interested in defining a sequence of steps for transforming its input data to the desired output data (algorithmic solution and program). Input data are given while output data are the results of the processing.

Example 2.1: Management wants to see the patterns in
    absenteeism across its two departments, dept1 and dept2
    for one week. It is interested in knowing the total
    absenteeism in each department in the one week it
    collected data. The question is to identify the input
    and output data of this problem and attempt to define an
    algorithm and a program.

Solution:

Input data: Number of employees absent in `dept1` for each of the five work days,
Number of employees absent in `dept2` for each of the five work days
(integers)

	dept1	dept2
day1	numberabsent	numberabsent
day2	""	""
day3	""	""
day4	""	""
day5	""	""
totalabsent	output	output

Output data: total number of employees absent in `dept1`,
total number of employees absent in `dept2` (integers)

The next thing is to define an algorithmic solution for the problem and the main steps involved are presented next.

2.2   Steps in Solving a Problem Using Top-Down Design

Top-down design approach to solving a problem breaks a big problem into a set of simpler, smaller problems which can be solved independently and simultaneously. The solution to the original problem is made up of the integration of the solutions of the sub problems. A more detailed discussion of the tools for solving problems using top-down design approach is presented in chapter 4. This section presents the overall sequence of steps for solving a problem. If the problem is simple, then, the step for breaking it down into sub problems is omitted.

The steps for defining an algorithm for future translation to a program are:

1.   Defining the Problem Requirements

Knowledge of the real world helps in understanding a given problem environment (e.g., a problem to compute students' GPA, which does not provide grade points attached to each grade will send you asking for this important information in this problem domain). Many problems are also so wordy that a lot of work needs to be done to state them clearly and unambiguously.

Example 2.1 already has Step 1 taken care of, but one question that may arise here is whether this a five or seven day work week.

2.   Identifying Problem Components

Here, we outline the problem   (a) inputs; (b) outputs, and; (c) any relationships between input and output data that can be expressed in formulae. Also specified here are data constraints. The data type for these data are also specified.

From **Example 2.1**:

Input data: `absent_day1_dept1, absent_day1_dept2`
`absent_day2_dept1, absent_day2_dept2`
`absent_day3_dept1, absent_day3_dept2`
`absent_day4_dept1, absent_day4_dept2`
`absent_day5_dept1, absent_day5_dept2 (integers)`

Output data: `total_absent_dept1, total_absent_dept2`
`(integers)`

Relationships:

`total_absent_dept1= absent_day1_dept1+ absent_day2_dept1+`
`absent_day3_dept1+ absent_day4_dept1+ absent_day5_dept1`

`total_absent_dept2= absent_day1_dept2+ absent_day2_dept2+`
`absent_day3_dept2+ absent_day4_dept2+ absent_day5_dept2`

Constraints: No constraints.

3.   Breaking Problem Solution into Small Problem Modules
This is the step that represents top-down design. Top-down design solves a big problem by first breaking it down into small problems (called module or functions). The solutions to the sub problems can only be integrated into overall solution of the problem through the main sub problem called the main or control module. Events begin and end in the main module, which is responsible for calling in the other sub modules when necessary. Sub modules called by the main module can in turn call other sub modules.

This step (for breaking a problem into sub problems) may not be necessary for very small problems, but is extremely important for code reusability and cooperative work needed in bigger problems. The objective is to come up with a solution structure that allows functions to solve small parts of the problem, which are later integrated to obtain the main solution. The software development tool used to break problem solutions into smaller parts (sub problems) is called a structure chart.

With Example 2.1, one way to structure the solution is to define a separate module that reads all data about a department, then calculates and prints the total. This structure is shown in Figure 2.1. Other correct structures for the same problem exist.

An alternative structure is to have everything in the main module since this is a small problem.

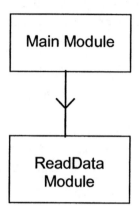

Figure 2.1: *A Simple Structure Chart for Example 2.1*

In breaking down the problem, it is a good design practice to weigh and compare alternatives and go with the approach which seems efficient and easy to read.

4.   Designing the Algorithm to Solve the Problem

In this step, we define algorithmic solutions for all modules in the structure chart from step three above, starting with the main or control module. The main module drives the solution, meaning that execution of the overall problem solution starts in instruction 1 of the main module, although control is transferred to and from other modules through function calls.   In writing an algorithm for a problem, valid instructions are used to clearly specify the action to be performed by the CPU in the correct sequence. The normal logical sequence for presenting a problem solution in an algorithm requires that input and output data variables and their types be declared first. Then, data values are read into input variables before appropriate instructions are used to assign values to output variables. Finally, output variables are printed.

Using **Example 2.1**, assuming we choose for now, to define a solution in one control module, the algorithmic solution is:

```
Main Module
a) Begin
   /* Declare Input and Output variables         */
   Input data:   absent_day1_dept1,  absent_day1_dept2
                 absent_day2_dept1,  absent_day2_dept2
                 absent_day3_dept1,  absent_day3_dept2
                 absent_day4_dept1,  absent_day4_dept2
                 absent_day5_dept1,  absent_day5_dept2 (integers)
   /*Note that this is the list of input data as in step 2 */
```

Output data: `total_absent_dept1, total_absent_dept2`
`(integers)`
`/* Note that this is list of output data as in step 2 */`
`/* Next, define instructions by first reading     */`
`/* data values into input variables.              */`

```
b) read (absent_day1_dept1, absent_day2_dept1,
   absent_day3_dept1, absent_day4_dept1,
   absent_day5_dept1);
c) read (absent_day1_dept2, absent_day2_dept2,
   absent_day3_dept2, absent_day4_dept2,
   absent_day5_dept2);
```

`/* Now, use input data values to obtain values for */`
`/* output variables.                               */`

```
d) total_absent_dept1=
   absent_day1_dept1+absent_day2_dept1+
   absent_day3_dept1+absent_day4_dept1+absent_day5_dept1;
e) total_absent_dept2=
   absent_day1_dept2+absent_day2_dept2+
   absent_day3_dept2+absent_day4_dept2+absent_day5_dept2;
```

`/* Next, print the output data values for the user. */`

```
f) Print (total_absent_dept1, total_absent_dept2);
g) End
```

Other software development tools like flowcharts can also be used in this step to present a solution. As an alternative, we can choose to use top-down design approach here, which allows us to define a function Readdata to implement steps (b) and (c) above. Then, the main module will invoke Readdata function in one call at this point in the algorithmic solution.

5. ## Implementation or Coding

    Coding is the process of translating an algorithm into a program in a programming language such that the computer can compile and execute this program to produce the required result. Once the algorithm is tested and confirmed to have correct logic, process of coding it into a program in a programming language is easy if programmer is familiar with the syntax of the language. During implementation or coding stage, the algorithmic solution defined in step 4 of the problem solving steps is translated into the desired high-level language code to obtain an equivalent program.

    ### Algorithm Coding and Syntax Errors
    A program written in any specific language has to be clear and unambiguous to be accepted by the computer. In other words, programs have to obey the syntax

(grammar rules of the particular language). A program statement represents coding of an instruction and any violation of the language syntax is an error called a bug. A bug needs to be found and corrected in a process called debugging. Syntax errors lead to many bugs that must be corrected before the program can be executed. Another type of error that may arise during the execution of the program is logic error (error that is caused by incorrect algorithmic solution). There may be several correct solutions to a problem but some may be more efficient than others. The third type of error encountered in programs is run time error. Run time error is an error that is caused by a program instruction doing an illegal operation like dividing by zero. While syntax and run time errors may cause discontinuation of processing of the program by the computer, a program with logic errors still runs to completion but produces incorrect results, making the process of finding the bug more challenging.

Implementing the above algorithmic solution in C language yields the following program:

```
#include <stdio.h>

void main (void)
{
/* Input and output data are declared first in a program*/

    int     absent_day1_dept1, absent_day1_dept2, absent_day2_dept1,
            absent_day2_dept2, absent_day3_dept1, absent_day3_dept2,
            absent_day4_dept1, absent_day4_dept2, absent_day5_dept1,
            absent_day5_dept2;
    int     total_absent_dept1, total_absent_dept2;

/*Now present the sequence of instructions*/

scanf ("%d %d %d %d %d", &absent_day1_dept1,
        &absent_day2_dept1, &absent_day3_dept1, &absent_day4_dept1,
        &absent_day5_dept1);
scanf ("%d %d %d %d %d", &absent_day1_dept2,
        &absent_day2_dept2, &absent_day3_dept2, &absent_day4_dept2,
        &absent_day5_dept2);
total_absent_dept1 = absent_day1_dept1 + absent_day2_dept1
            + absent_day3_dept1 + absent_day4_dept1 +
            absent_day5_dept1;
total_absent_dept2 = absent_day1_dept2 + absent_day2_dept2
            + absent_day3_dept1 + absent_day4_dept1 +
            absent_day5_dept2;
printf ( "Number of people absent in dept1 is %d and Number
        of people absent in dept2 is %d\n", total_absent_dept1,
        total_absent_dept2);
}
```

6.   Test and Verify the Solution

This step uses a set of test input data (either given or made up by the designer) to go through the sequence of steps in the defined algorithm or program. The objective is to compare the result produced by evaluating the algorithm/program with the actual correct result (not the one from the algorithm/program) as previously calculated by hand. If there are any errors identified at this stage, the algorithm and program in step 5 are corrected.

Continuing with **Example 2.1**, assume we have the following test data:

Input data:

	absent_dept1	absent_dept2
Day 1	5	2
Day 2	3	1
Day 3	0	4
Day 4	1	0
Day 5	2	2

We can test and verify our program as given in step 5 above either manually, by executing the sequence of instructions in the program with test input data (hand tracing the program), or test automatically by executing the program with a complete set of test data. The following discussion demonstrates how to test and verify manually.

Executing the program, the declared variables cause memory locations to be set aside for the variables absent_day1_dept1 to absent_day5_dept1 as well as the variables absent_day1_dept2 to absent_day5_dept2. Memory cells are also set aside for the output variables total_abaset_dept1 and total_absent_dept2.   The first executable instruction, **scanf ("%d %d %d %d %d", &absent_day1_dept1,**
&absent_day2_dept1, &absent_day3_dept1, &absent_day4_dept1,
&absent_day5_dept1);
has the effect of reading the 5 data values (5, 3, 0, 1, 2) in the first column for dept1 into the reserved memory cells called absent_day1_dept1, absent_day2_dept1, absent_day3_dept1, absent_day4_dept1, absent_day5_dept1 respectively. Note that the scanf instruction expects the user to type these values at the keyboard in the order the variables are listed in the instruction. Executing the next program instruction
scanf ("%d %d %d %d %d", &absent_day1_dept2,
&absent_day2_dept2, &absent_day3_dept2, &absent_day4_dept2,
&absent_day5_dept2);
reads into those memory cells, all values in column two for dept2 (2, 1, 4, 0, 2). Executing the third instruction of the program stores in `total_absent_dept1`, the value 5+3+0+1+2=11.   The fourth program instruction has the effect of placing the

value 2+1+4+0+2=9 into memory cell labeled `total_absent_dept2`. The last program statement is

printf ("Number of people absent in dept1 is %d and Number
       of people absent in dept2 is %d\n", total_absent_dept1,
       total_absent_dept2);

This last instruction has the effect of printing the string literal with the values of the memory cells total_absent_dept1 and total_absent_dept2 to display "Number of people absent in dept1 is 11 and Number of people absent in dept2 is 9". The beginning { and ending } curly brackets are used to mark normal begin and end of the main program.

The program also contains some comments, which are not part of executable instructions, but are used to make the program readable and maintainable. Comments in C programs are text inserted in between the start comment marker characters /* and the end comment marker characters */.

Difficulties with Problem Solving

Some of the reasons for obtaining unsatisfactory output from problem-solving are:

1. Failing to define the problem correctly because there are still some ambiguous facts.
2. Failing to consider all possible ways to solve the problem in order to choose the most efficient solution.
3. Failing to use a logical sequence of steps in the solution.
4. Poor evaluation or testing of the algorithm for correctness because not all possible cases are tested. For example, it may work for positive, but not negative data values.
5. Failing to remember that the computer does not see and cannot predict errors in a solution it is executing. It does only rote processing, and needs to be given all details about what to do.

2.3   Exercises

1.   Given the length and width of a rectangular yard in meters, write an algorithmic solution and a C program to compute and print

(a) the area of the yard;
(b) the perimeter of the yard;
    Show all six problem-solving steps in developing your solution.

2.   Given the lengths and widths of two rectangular yards in meters on a street as well as the lengths and widths of the houses located in the yards, and knowing that parts of the yards not holding the houses are covered with grass, write an algorithmic solution and a C program to determine the area of each property that has grass.   Show all five problem-solving steps.

3.   Write an algorithm and a program that outputs the temperature in degrees Fahrenheit (°F), when given the temperature in degrees Celsius (°C) (hint: °F = (9/5 * °C) +32).

4.   You are given the number of hours worked in a week by Peter and his wage per hour, write an algorithm and a program to compute his weekly salary before deductions.

5.   Given that a circular skating stadium has an outer circle for the entire stadium and an inner circle used for skating. Spectator area lies between the outer and the inner circles. Given the radii of both the outer and the inner circles of the stadium, that each 9 square meters of spectator area holds 15 seats and the average cost of a seat for an event is $20.00, write an algorithmic solution and a C program that (a) computes the spectator area in the stadium in square meters, (b) computes the number of seats in the stadium and (c) computes the amount of money realized in the stadium for each skating event.

6.   (a) Discuss the differences between syntax, run-time and logic errors in programs.
      (b) Give the meaning of the terms coding and debugging.
      (c) What is top-down design approach to problem solving?
      (d) Explain what is involved in the process of testing or evaluating a program/algorithm.
      (e) Discuss the six problem solving steps.

2.4 References

H. M. Deitel/P. J. Deitel, "C How to Program", 2nd ed., Prentice Hall, 1994.

Kris Jamsa, "Jamsa's C Programmer's Bible – The Ultimate Guide to C Programming", first edition, Onword Press, Thomson Learning, 2002.

Elliott B. Koffman, "Turbo PASCAL" 5th ed., Addison Wesley, 1995.

Maureen Sprankle, "Problem Solving and Programming Concepts", 3rd ed., Prentice Hall, 1995.

Uckan Yuksel, "Problem Solving Using C – Structured Programming Technique", 2nd edition, WCB McGraw-Hill, 1999.

3. TYPES OF ALGORITHMIC AND PROGRAM INSTRUCTIONS

3.   Some Programming Language Concepts

We are now ready to discuss some concepts used in writing programs, which are applied when writing algorithms as well. Since the objective is to learn how to define efficient algorithms for coding into programs, there is a need to give detailed algorithms, and this chapter discusses the possible types of instructions used in both an algorithm and a program.

3.1.1 Variables and Constants

Variables and constants are names for storage locations (memory cells), that hold data values processed by the computer. Recall that memory cells are identified internally using their integer addresses. However, in a high-level language program, the address of a memory cell we want to store some data in, or read some data from, is renamed by our program. The cell name or label assigned by our programs/algorithms is called a variable name. Variable names are usually alphanumeric characters beginning with a letter and unlimited number of characters may be allowed in a language (e.g., C), but limiting the length of a variable name to 15 for clarity is a good programming practice.

A constant name is a name given to a memory cell, where you assign a data value only once in the solution, (done generally, when you are defining the constant). A constant cell can only be read but not written to, or changed by any instruction in the algorithm or program. In some programming languages, constants are referred to as "constant variable names" to distinguish this use of the word from the use where the singular word constant refers to a direct data value, like 2,3*8, "I am happy".

In both cases, variable and constant names are chosen such that it is obvious what data they hold. Thus, use of meaningful variable/constant names is encouraged. In both an algorithm and a C program, all input and output data represented by their variable/constant names are first declared before they are used in a program instruction. Declaring a variable entails specifying its data type in front of the variable name before the semicolon ending the declaration. The format for declaring variables in both an algorithm and a C program is:

```
datatype    variablename[,variablenames];
```

An equivalent expression for the format given above for declaring variables of type *datatype* is :

```
datatype    variablename1, variablename2, ......,variablenamen;
```

The format for declaring constants in both an algorithm and a C program is:

```
const  datatype    variablename= value[,variablenames=values];
```

In specifying the format for an instruction or declaration, the symbols [ ] are used to indicate terms or items which are optional and included only if needed. The format above states that the datatype of a variable must be written first, followed by at least a blank space and one variable name and ended with a semi colon. However, the optional square brackets indicate that following the first variable, a list of other variables separated by commas could be used in the declaration. A constant name can also be defined using the #define preprocessor directive using the format:

```
#define  constantname   value
```

For example, to declare a constant name for 100 students with this directive, at the beginning of the program, we insert:
#define numstudent 100

Throughout the book, the algorithms are used to show more clearly the meaning of the corresponding programs. Since the difference between an algorithm and a program is that the program must stick to the syntax of the programming language, an algorithm contains English descriptions of instructions and keywords. To make it easier to learn programming in C, the book adopts the convention of bringing the format of algorithmic instructions close to the format of C instructions, while still using English words like Input/Output variables, Read, Print in algorithmic instructions to represent variable declaration sections that are for input/output data, scanf, printf in the equivalent program code. In the examples that follow, both the algorithmic and program solutions are given.

Example 3.1:   An elementary school is organizing a summer camp for children and would like to know what activities to provide. They have surveyed 200 children, asking them to select only three out of the following activities: skipping, swimming, jogging, roller-blading, mountain climbing, tennis, singing, drawing, basketball, and walking. Question: what variable or constant names do you need to solve this problem?

Solution:

```
Algorithm
Input data for each child:
Variables:  integer   skip, swim, jog, roller, mount, tennis,
                      sing, draw, basket, walk;
Constant:   integer   numkids = 200;

Output data:
Variables:  integer      Skipknt, swimknt, jogknt, rollerknt,
               mountknt,    tennisknt,   singknt,    drawknt,
               basketknt, walkknt;
```

```
Alternative Solution:
Input data: Variables for each child are
        string  Choice1, Choice2, Choice3;
Output data:  integer      Skipknt, swimknt, jogknt, rollerknt,
          mountknt, tennisknt, singknt, drawknt, basketknt,
          walkknt;
```

C Program Solution of Example 3.1:
Solution 1: /* Note that no distinction is made here between input and output variables*/

```
int     skip, swim, jog, roller, mount, tennis,
               sing, draw, basket, walk;
const int     numkids = 200; /*Note how this constant is declared*/
int             Skipknt, swimknt, jogknt, rollerknt, mountknt, tennisknt, singknt,
          drawknt, basketknt, walkknt;
```

Alternative Solution of Example 3.1 in C Program

```
char  Choice1[10], Choice2[10], Choice3[10];
int   Skipknt, swimknt, jogknt, rollerknt, mountknt, tennisknt, singknt, drawknt,
          basketknt, walkknt;
```

Example 3.2: You need to find out the number of students who have completed Assignment #1. There are 250 students in the class. What variables and constants are needed?

Algorithm Solution:

Input:
Variables for each student: logical/Boolean assign_done;
Constant: integer   num_student = 250;

Output:
Variables: integer   number_done_asn1;

C Program Solution of Example 3.2
int   assign_done, number_done _asn1;
const int num_student=250;

Example 3.3:   Find the sum and product of 2 numbers. List the
        needed variables and constants.

Algorithm Solution:

Input:
Variables: integer   num1, num2;
Constants: none

Output:
Variables: integer   sum, product;

C Program Solution of Example 3.3
int   num1, num2;
int   sum, product;

In forming variable names, programmers should avoid choosing keyword names that have been reserved for use by the C compiler. A list of such keywords to avoid is given in Table 3.1.

Table 3.1:   *The C Keyword List Not Used as Variable Names*

auto	break	case	char	const	continue	default	do	double	else	enum
extern	float	for	goto	if int	long	register	return	short	signed	
sizeof	static	struct	switch	typedef	union	unsigned	void	volatile	while	

Programmers define data relevant to a problem as constants or variables and these form building blocks for equations and expressions used in problem solving. Both variables and constants have specific data types.

3.1.2 Data Types

Algorithms and programs accept input data (e.g., num1, num2) and produce output data (e.g., sum, product). Every data processed belongs to a particular type. The different simple types that any data can assume are discussed below.

1.   Integer Data Type (called int in C):

Integers are positive or negative whole numbers which do not contain decimal points. The biggest or smallest integers that can be represented in a program vary depending on the language and machine. It generally depends on the number of bits used to represent an integer value. If 32-bit representation is used, the biggest integer is $2^{(32-1)}$-1; while the smallest integer is $-2^{(32-1)}$ when negative numbers are represented in 2's complement. Examples of types of program or problem data that can be represented as integers are: ages of people in a room (10, 70, 16), number of students, and number of assignments handed in, and negative numbers like (-1577). Arithmetic operations can be performed on this data type. In C, integer data are of type int and example declarations of data that are of type int are:

int   age, sum;
int   product;

A long integer value can also be declared with the keyword long int. New C compilers use 32 bits (4 bytes) to represent an int value. Thus, integer that is larger than can be represented in 4 bytes can be stored as long int. Thus, an example declaration of long int value is:
long int onemillion;

2.   Real Data Type (called float or double in C)

A real number is a numeric value which has both an integral and a fractional part separated by a decimal point. These can be used to represent data values like a person's height (5.65), rate of pay per hour (12.68), and negative real numbers (-15.752, -112.95).

In some languages, scientific notation is used to represent very big and very small real numbers. For example, the real number 0.000145 can be represented as 1.45E-4, because it is equivalent to 1.45×10^{-4}. Similarly, the real number 257899 can be translated as 2.57899E5 (meaning 2.57899×10^{5}). Arithmetic operations can be performed on this data type. A value's precision defines its degree of accuracy. In C, float and double are used to declare real data with single and double precisions respectively. A real data with single precision (float) provides six to seven significant digits of precision, while a double precision real data (double) provides 14 to 15 significant digits. For example,
float precisef = 1.12345678978521553;
double précised = 1.12345678978521553;
will end up printing a not too precise number like 1.1234567870041833 for the float variable precisef and a slightly more precise number like 1.12345678978521432 for the double variable précised.

43

3. Character Data Type (called char in C)

The character data type is used to represent an individual character value, which can be a letter, a digit, or a special symbol, usually surrounded by quotation marks (single quotes are used in this book and in C for characters). Problem or program data that can be represented as character are letter grades ('A', or 'B'...), categories of students in a competition ('1', '2', '3'), all vowels ('a', 'e', 'i', 'o', 'u'), and special symbols, like '+', '/', '&'. All single characters in the ASCII (American Standard Code for Information Interchange) set, which have codes between 0 and 127 (as shown in Appendix A) can be stored in variables of char type. Arithmetic operations cannot be performed on this data type, but characters can be compared, read and printed. They can also be concatenated to produce string type. A comparison between characters 'A' and 'B' as in 'A' < 'B' produces a result *true* because the ASCII code for 'A' is 65, which is less than the ASCII code for 'B', which is 66. Example declarations of variables of type character in C are:
char initial = 'B';
char lettergrade, code;

4. String Data Type (char variablename[ ] in C)

A string is a sequence of characters enclosed in double quotations. Many programming languages now make this type available as a primitive type although some programming languages, like C, still consider string type as an array of characters. Problem input data like name, student number, phone number can be represented as string. Examples of string data are "Randy", "8561", "519-111-2345". String data can be compared and concatenated. In C, a string variable is declared as character variable with a specified number of characters enclosed in square brackets. A string variable is declared in C as an array of characters using the format:

> **char   variablename[number_of_characters];**

The use of square brackets in this format and in other arrays are not optional. The brackets are part of the declaration. Example declarations of string data in C are:
char lastname[15];
char choice1[15], choice2[15], choice3[15];

5. Boolean or Logical Data Type (Implemented as int with values 0 or !0 in C)

The Boolean data type has only two possible values, true and false. This data type can be used to represent conditional data like whether grade is an 'A' or not. In C, data of logical type are implemented with int data type, where a value of 0 represents false and any other value not equal to 0 represents true. Example declarations of logical data in C are:
int   absent = 0;
int   gradeA, happy;

Each data type has a data set, the set of values from which any datum of that data type is specified. Table 3.2 gives a summary of the data set for the five primitive types.

Table 3.2   Data Types and their Data Sets.

DATA TYPE	DATA SET	EXAMPLE DATA
Integer (int)	All whole numbers between -2^{31} to $(2^{31}-1)$	`1999, -67`
Real (float/double)	All real numbers (whole and decimal part)	`1999.0, 2.58E5, 0.00581`
Character (char)	All letters and special symbols	`'A', 'B', 'b', '1', '8', '+'`
String (char variable[ ])	Combination of more than one character	`"Atlas", "956"`
Boolean (int)	True , false	`True (!0), false(0)`

Rules Guiding Use of Data Types

1. Data types cannot be mixed. For example, character data cannot be placed in a variable memory location designated as numerical (int, float or double). C provides a method, called cast for converting an expression of a different type to the type of a variable on the left hand side of an assignment instruction. For example, cast can be used to convert an integer expression to real before assigning to a real variable (average) as follows:
   average = (float) (sum/3);

2. Data defining the value of a variable or a constant will be one of the five data types: integer (int/long int), real (float/double), character (char), string (char variable[ ]) or Boolean (int with value 0 or !0).

3. The use of any data outside the data set of the data type results in an error.

4. Only valid operations on a data type are allowed. For example, numbers designated as string type cannot be used in calculations.

3.2   Algorithmic/Program Structure and Algorithmic/Program Instructions

Since an algorithm/a program is a sequence of instructions, we are ready to discuss the type of instructions that can be used in defining both an algorithm and a C program. In strongly-typed languages, like C, and PASCAL, every data value to be processed in an algorithm or program has a data type which must be declared at the beginning of the program. In keeping with the general structure of programming, the structure of an algorithm has the input and output variables and their data types declared at the beginning following the keyword character { which marks the beginning of an algorithmic/program block. Other intermediate variables are also declared. Next, the executable instructions of the main driver (main block) or the control module are defined as a sequence of instructions ending with the keyword character }. Figure 3.1 gives a concise presentation of the structure of an algorithm, while Figure 3.2 presents the general structure of a C program. The function declarations are included only if there are other modules (functions) in the solution and this is why it is enclosed in square brackets [], which indicate an optional component. Declaration of function prototypes are done globally before the beginning of the main module, when needed. Other input and output variables may also be declared globally. While the structure of an algorithm and that of a program are similar, the program instructions (statements) pay fine attention to syntax and must be written in exact syntax of C language or syntax error may result. English-like instructions are used in algorithms to clearly relay the meaning of the corresponding program instructions and operations.

```
[Global Input/Output Variables/Constants and their types]
[Function Prototype list: type and parameters]


Mainalgorithm
{
Input:  Variables/Constants list and their types.
Output:  Variables list and their types.
Intermediates: Variables/Constants list and their types.



/* Now the body of the main Driver or Control Module follows */


        Instruction 1;
        Instruction 2;
              .
              .
              .
        Instruction n;
}

/* Now include the definition for each function   */

[function definition 1]
[function definition 2]
        .
        .
        .
[function definition n]
```

Figure 3.1:   An Algorithmic Structure

The next question to address is defining the form and structure of each type of algorithmic instruction. An algorithmic instruction can be one of the following types: read/print instruction, assignment instruction, a function call, a decision instruction, or a repetition instruction. We shall conclude this chapter with a discussion of assignment instructions, while function calls, decision and repetition instructions will be discussed in subsequent chapters.

```
#include  <stdio.h>

/* Optional global variable and function prototype declarations*/
[Input/Output variable declarations]
[Function prototype list: type and parameters]

void main (void)
{
 variable declarations;

 /*Now the sequence of executable instructions*/
 Instruction 1;
 Instruction 2;
 ....
 ....
 Instruction n;
}

/*Present the definition of each function*/
[Function definition 1]
[Function definition 2]
....
....
[Function definition n]
```

Figure 3.2:   The General Structure of a C Program

3.2.1   Read/Print Instructions (scanf/printf Instructions in C)

Read instructions in an algorithm are instructions that get input data from the keyboard (data typed by the user) or from data file, while print instructions display the value of a variable or an expression on the screen or printer. There are many variations of instructions for reading data and printing data in a C program. However, the basic C instruction for reading data from the keyboard is scanf, while that for printing data on the monitor is printf. The formats of both the algorithmic read/print instructions and the C program scanf/printf instructions are provided next with examples. These instructions are used for reading data from the standard input device (the keyboard) and writing data to the standard output device (the monitor).

Format of Algorithmic read and print instructions are:

Read (variable1, variable2, ..., variable*n*);   Print (variable1, variable2, ..., variable*n*);

e.g., `Read (num1, num2);`   e.g., `Print ("Sum is ", sum);`

Note that string literal or constant, e.g., "Sum is", can also be printed using an algorithmic *Print* instruction and each parameter of the *Print* instruction can also be a constant name, constant value or an expression. A *Read* instruction like Read(num1, num2) has the effect of taking the first number typed in at the keyboard by the user and placing that number in the memory cell called *num1*. Then, the second number typed in by the user is stored in the memory cell called *num2*. The user can mark the end of each number by hitting the "return" key or the space bar. A *Print* instruction like Print("Sum is", Sum) has the effect of writing on the monitor first the string literal "Sum is". Then, on the same print line, the content of the memory location called *Sum* is printed. Assume the location called Sum has value 90. This instruction would print:

`Sum  is   90`

In order to print the next item on the next line, a special variable called newline (for printing the return character and going to a new line) is used in the print instruction. For example, the instruction, Print ("Sum is", newline, Sum) would print:

`Sum   is`
`90`

The general format of C program scanf and printf instructions are:

`scanf("format specifiers", &variable1, &variable2, .. ,&variablen);`

`printf("format specifiers", variable1, variable2, .. ,variablen);`

Both scanf and printf instructions accept a number of parameters (arguments). A parameter or an argument provides information regarding the variable name we want to read data into or print data from, its data type, the format for reading or printing data. A parameter could be a variable name, an expression or a string literal enclosed in double quotes. While a printf instruction can accept an expression or a variable name where ever a variable argument is specified in the general format above, a scanf instruction can only accept variable arguments following its first string argument. Example scanf and printf instructions are given next.

scanf ("%d %f %c", &num1, &num2, &letter);

printf("Numbers are %d %f and letter is %c", numint, numeral, letter);

The first parameter of a scanf or printf instruction is a string literal enclosed in double quotes. This string literal should include the format specifiers (e.g., %d for int variable, %f for float and double variable, %c for character char variable, %s for string variable) for each variable to be read or printed in the order the variables are listed in the instruction. This first parameter can also include any other string literal (words, spaces and \n (the newline character for going to next line)) for printf. For the scanf instruction, format specifiers can be separated by blank spaces. This first parameter string literal, usually excludes punctuation characters and special characters that mean something else to C. There are ways to include punctuation marks in scanf/printf string parameter when necessary. The special character should be preceded by a backslash \ to indicate that this character is part of the literal string. Following the first parameter of scanf and printf is the list of variable names to be read or printed given in the exact order the format specifiers have been submitted in the first string parameter. The format specifier %d is used to indicate an integer variable is to be read or printed, %f is used to tell the compiler that a real data of type float or double is to be read, %c is used for character data, while %s is used for string data and %ld is used for long integer data. In listing the variables for scanf instruction, the address operator & is usually, written in front of each variable name if the type of the variable is not string. A string variable is read with scanf without the address operator (&). Thus, if Name is a string variable, it can be read with scanf("%s", Name).

In the scanf example given above, the first parameter is the string "%d %f %c". When this instruction executes, the program displays a cursor on the monitor and waits for the user to type in an integer at the keyboard so that it will store that integer as num1. Once that integer is typed in as, say 56, it will continue and now wait for the real number (e.g., 35.8) to be typed in by the user and next it will prompt for the character data (e.g., G) to be typed in and it goes to the next instruction. If the example printf is the next instruction to execute, it will display:

Numbers are 56 35.8 and letter is G

Other valid examples of scanf and printf instructions are:
scanf ("%d", &num1);
scanf("%d %d", &num1, &num2);
printf ("Sum is %d", 10+15);
printf ("%d %d \n", num1, num2);
printf (" %d", num1 + num2);
print ("* * * * \n It is a good day");

Output Formatting with printf
With appropriate format specifiers printf can print an integer data value in other number base systems, like base 8 (octal with specifier %o), base 16 (hexadecimal with specifier %x for small letters and %X for uppercase letters).
E.g.,
     printf (" Number %d in octal is %o\n", 255, 255);
     printf (" Number %d in hexadecimal is %x\n", 255, 255);
     printf (" Number %d in hexadecimal is %X\n", 255, 255);

An integer variable declared as unsigned integer can be printed with %u specifier. An integer variable declared as long integer and initialized with big L at its end is displayed with %ld specifier. For example,
     long int one_million = 1000000L;

printf ("%ld\n", one_million);

To display a floating-point number in exponential format, printf uses the %e (for small e) or %E (for capital E) format specifier.
For example, with pi = 3.14159,
printf ("%e\n", pi*10);
will print 3.14159e01, while
printf ("%E\n", pi*10);
will print 3.14159E01.

A pointer address can be displayed with %p specifier. To display a plus or negative sign in front of a numeric value, place plus (+) or negative (-) as appropriate after the % sign of the format specifier, e.g., %+d, %+f, %-d, %-f.

An integer value can be formatted with printf to specify the minimum number of columns that printf should use to display the value, by placing the number following the % sign of the format specifier. For example, to print the value 25 using only 5 columns, the specifier is %5d, while it is %4d if we intend to use 4 columns. The integer data is usually printed in this number of columns right justified. With the following printf instructions
printf ("%3d\n", 25);
printf ("%4d\n", 25);
printf ("%5d\n", 25);

output data lines (not including the first line for column numbering) are:
column 1 2 3 4 5
    2 5
      2 5
        2 5

To zero pad (preceed these output with leading 0's), we place a 0 (zero) immediately after the % in the format specifier prior to the desired number of digits (e.g.,"%03d" for printing 025, and "%04d" for printing 0025).

To format a floating-point or real output, we specify two values. The first gives the minimum number of columns to use for writing this data, while the second specifies the number of digits to be displayed to the right of the decimal point. For example,

printf ("%8.1f\n", 3.14159);
displays
    3.1
while
printf ("%8.4f\n", 3.14159);
displays
  3.1415

Exponential output can also be formatted the same way floating-point is, with say, %10.2e, %10.1e, %5.3e specifiers.

To override the right-justification of output such that output is left-justified, place a negative sign (-) immediately after the % sign and before the number of columns to use, e.g., "%-5d".

3.2.2   Assignment Instructions

An assignment instruction is the simplest type of instruction in an algorithm or a C program. It has this form:

$$variable = expression;$$

where *variable* is a variable or constant name, and expression is an *expression* that evaluates to data of the same type as the variable name on the left-hand side of the equation sign (assignment operator).   The effect of this assignment instruction is that the value of the expression on the right hand side of the equality sign, is assigned to the memory cell, which has *variable* as its name or label. Usually, only one variable is allowed on the left hand side of an assignment instruction.

Examples of assignment instructions are:

```
a=b;
a=b+5;
totalmark = (as1+as2+as3)/3;
testwritten=true;
category ='1';
check = strcpy(studentname,"John");
a= SQRT(y); (where SQRT and strcpy are  builtin functions)
```

We can see that an expression can be of many types.

What is an expression?

An expression is either a variable, a constant, a literal or a combination of these connected by appropriate operators (e.g., +, -, /, *, >, <, =). Functions returning a valid value can also be part of an expression. Examples of expressions are:

```
b+5
b
(total/3)*5
'A'<'B'
grade != 'A'
```

Operators

Operators are used to tell the computer how to process data. They are used to connect data (operands) in expressions to produce a result. There are three basic types of operators, namely, arithmetic, relational and logical operators provided by many programming languages. C language provides additional operators including bitwise operators (<<, >>, &, ^, |, ~), address operator (&), indirection operator (*), increment operator (++), decrement operator (--), operators for arithmetic assign (+=, -=, *=, /=, %=), bitwise assign (<<=, >>=, &=, |=, ^=) and conditional operator (?:). Other C language operators are for function call ( ), array subscript [ ], component selection (.), indirect component selection (->), cast (type), sizeoftype (sizeof) and comma (,). The three basic types of operators are discussed next in more detail.

Basic Types of Operators

1.   Arithmetic operators in C

The arithmetic operators are: addition (+), subtraction (-), multiplication (*), division for both integer and real data (/), modulus division (remainder after integer division, %). Arithmetic operators need integer or real operands. The division operator / returns an integer result if its operands are integer, but returns real result if its operands are real.

For example, how many whole weeks has Peggy worked if she worked 13 days during the month in a 5-day work week?

Answer: 13 / 5 = 2 whole weeks   (this is integer division)

If the daily wage is computed at a different rate from the weekly salary, how many days do they need to apply the daily wage for her this month?

Answer: 13 % 5 = 3 days   (this is remainder after dividing 13 by 5)

The desired answer for the first question is a whole number, which is obtained using a whole number division. A whole number or integer division gives the quotient as the result, disregarding the remainder after division. On the other hand, the integer modulus division returns the remainder after integer division as the desired integer result, while disregarding the quotient. For example, 13 % 5 computes the whole number remainder after dividing 13 by 5, which is 3, while 13 / 5 computes the whole number quotient resulting from dividing 13 by 5, which is 2. While integer division and modulus division require integer operands, and produce integer results, real division requires real operands and produces a real result. Expressions formed with arithmetic operators are called arithmetic expressions.

2.   Relational operators in C

The relational operators are = = (equals), < (less than), > (greater than), <= (less than or equal to), >= (greater than or equal to), != (not equal to). These operators are used to program decisions and need data operators of any type, except that the two operands must be of the same type. The result produced by a relational operator is a Boolean value (true or false). For example, 31>5 operands as integers, but the result is a Boolean value, true. Relational operators are used in both decision instructions and repetition instructions for making decisions regarding which sequence of instructions to execute.

For example:
```
        if (mark>90)
                grade = 'A';

while (num_student <=100)
  {
        scanf("%d", &mark);
        printf ("%d", mark);
}
```

Expressions formed with relational operators which produce Boolean results are called relational expressions. For example, (mark > 90), num_student <= 100 are relational expressions.

3.   Logical operators in C

Logical operators are NOT (! in C), AND (&& in C), OR (|| in C). These operators are used to connect relational expressions.
For example, if a student's grade in a course is 'A' and the student has attended all classes, give them special course recognition.
```
        If ((grade=='A') && (attendance==100))
                printf("Student merits special recognition");
```
Logical operators have operands that are Boolean type and they produce Boolean results as well. The following provides meaning of logical operators.

NOT (!)		AND (&&)				OR (||)		
A	! A	A	B	A && B		A	B	A || B
t	f	t	t	t		t	t	t
f	t	t	f	f		t	f	t
		f	t	f		f	t	t
		f	f	f		f	f	f

Figure 3.2   Meaning of Boolean Operators

Precedence Hierarchy of Operators in C

A precedence rule dictates the order in which different operators are executed in an expression. An associativity rule states the order in which multiple occurrences of the same operator(s) at the same hierarchy level are applied. Expressions sometimes contain more than one operation, some of which may belong to any of the categories. In this case, there is a need to execute the operators in a specific order to produce correct results. This specific order is determined by the precedence hierarchy of operators, similar to that adopted and used in mathematics. The hierarchy rule for basic operators (arithmetic, relational and logical) says that the first operators to be evaluated in an expression are the brackets, then function calls before logical NOT (!). Following these will be multiplication, division and modulus (remainder after integer division, %) at the same level, followed by addition and subtraction before the relational operators (in the order, all other relational operators before == and !=). Then, the logical operations in the order: AND (&&) before OR (||), are followed in the hierarchy order. The hierarchy is shown below in Figure 3.3.

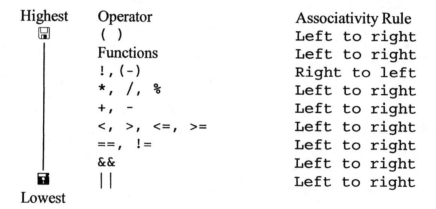

Highest	Operator	Associativity Rule
	( )	Left to right
	Functions	Left to right
	!, (-)	Right to left
	*, /, %	Left to right
	+, -	Left to right
	<, >, <=, >=	Left to right
	==, !=	Left to right
	&&	Left to right
	||	Left to right
Lowest		

Figure 3.3   Basic Operator Precedence Hierarchy

Operator Precedence and Association in C

Although many of the C language operators are yet to be discussed, a quick discussion of C's increment, decrement, bit operators, sizeof, cast and operator assign operators is presented here before providing the complete table of operator precedence and association used by C.

C's Increment and Decrement Operators

A common program instruction is that which increases the value of a variable by 1. For example, the instruction:

Numstudent = Numstudent + 1;

is used to add 1 to the current value of the variable Numstudent. C provides a shorthand method for incrementing the value of a variable by 1. This is done with the increment operator ++. With the ++ operator, the above instruction, can be written as:

Numstudent ++;   /* postfix form */

The increment operator as used in the last instruction is the postfix form (after the variable). It can also be used in the prefix form (before the variable) as:

++ Numstudent;   /* prefix version */

With the Numstudent currently having the value 20, if the postfix form, *Numstudent++;* is executed, the effect is that the current value of 20 is used before Numstudent is incremented to 21, while if the prefix (++ Numstudent;) is executed, C will add 1 to Numstudent first to obtain 21 before using the variable as in a printf instruction. For example, consider the following program:

```
#include <stdio.h>
void main (void)
{
 int Numstudent = 20;
 printf ("With Postfix %d\n", Numstudent++);
 Numstudent = 20;
 printf ("With Prefix %d\n", ++Numstudent);
}
```

The output printed are:
With Postfix 20
With Prefix 21

Similarly, the C's decrement operator (--) is used to subtract one from the value of a variable such that the program instruction
count = count – 1;
can be written as:
count --;   /* postfix */
or
-- count;   /* prefix */

For example, with count = 35 before executing each of the two following printf instructions:
printf ("With Postfix count is %d\n", count--);
printf ("With Prefix count is %d\n", --count);

The printed output is:
With Postfix count is 35
With Prefix count is 34

The effect of the increment or decrement operator when used in the prefix form on a variable, is to include all modifications to the same variable specified in the instruction (including multiple modifications) before using the variable. For example, with count = 35, printf("%d, %d\n", ++count, count++) will print 37, 35 because total of modifications to count in this instruction is +2, which is added ahead of time to count in the first case, but added after using count in the second instance.

Bit Operations in C

An integer number like 5 is usually stored in memory in bits (binary digits) in one or more bytes of memory. A byte can hold eight bits. The number 5 in bits stored in 1 byte of space is 0000101, while the number 4 is 0000100. Bit operations are used to manipulate data at the bit level and may be used in some situations to increase performance of a program.

These are six main operations that can be performed on bit data namely:

1. Bitwise OR operation (|) : Given two bits, this returns 1 as result if one or both of them is 1, but 0 otherwise.

    E.g.   5   0000101   OR (|)
           4   0000100
                0000101

2. Bitwise AND operation (&) : Given two bits, this returns 1 as result if both input bits are 1, else it returns 0.

    E.g.   5   0000101   &
           4   0000011
                0000001

3. Bitwise Exclusive OR operation (^) : Given two bits as input, this returns 1 as result if either input (not both) is 1, otherwise it returns 0.

    E.g.   5   0000101   ^
           4   0000100
                0000001

4. Bitwise Inverse operation (~) : Given a bit, it returns 1 if input is 0, but returns 0 if given input is 1.

    E.g.   5   0000101   (~)
                1111010

5. Bitwise Left Shift operation (<<) : This operation is used to shift a value a given number of bits to the left. For example, given 0000101, we can shift this value 2 bits to the left with the expression 0000101 << 2 to obtain 0010100. This has the effect of moving away the two leftmost zeros. However, since the value has to be stored in eight bits, the remaining six bits (00101) are padded on the right with two zeroes to obtain 0010100.

6. Bitwise Right Shift operation (>>) : This operation shifts a given value a given number of bit positions to the right. For example, the expression 0000101 >> 2 asks that the value 0000101 be shifted 2 bits to the right. The result of this operation is 00000001. Here, two most significant bit positions that are empty after the right shift are padded with 0 because this number is positive. If we right shift a negative number, the most significant bit positions are padded with 1. For example, 11111011 >> 2 will result in 11111110. In this case, the most significant 2 bits are padded with 1 (not 0).

The C compiler also provides the functions that allow bits of a data value to be rotated left, _rotl (variable, numberofbits) and to be rotated right, _rotr (variable, numberof bits).

C's Sizeof Operator

The sizeof operator returns the number of bytes a variable or type requires. For example, sizeof (int), sizeof (float) would return 4 and 4 respectively.

C's Cast

The cast operator is a unary operator that accepts an expression as its operand and it converts the type of the operand to the type specified by the cast operator. The form of the cast expression is:
(Type)Expression
For example,
Totalmark = (int)(average * 150);

C's Operator Assign Operations

C provides short form for writing various kinds of assignment instructions including arithmetic assignment and bitwise assignment instructions. These instructions have an arithmetic (+, -, *, /, %) or bitwise (<<, >>, ^, ~, |, &) operator preceding an assignment operator (=). The form of these instructions is:

> | **variable operator= value;** |

This boxed instruction is equivalent to:
variable = variable operator value;

For example,
total += 40 is equivalent to total = total + 40
product *=5 is same as product = product * 5
average /= 10 is same as average = average / 10
knt -= 2 is same as knt = knt – 2
Rem %= 15 is same as Rem % 15
Number <<= 2 is same as Number = Number << 2
Number >>= 2 is same as Number = Number >> 2
Number &= 10 is same as Number = Number & 10

When a combination of several operators appear in an expression, the precedence and association rule applied by C is shown in Figure 3.4.

Operators	Names in Order	Association Order
(), [ ], ., ->	function call, array subscript, component selection, indirect component selection	left to right
++, --, +, -, *, &, !, ~, (type), sizeof	increment, decrement, unary plus and minus, indirection, address of, logical not, bitwise inverse, cast, sizeof	right to left
*, /, %	multiplication, division, modulus	left to right
+, -	addition, subtraction	left to right
<<, >>	right shift, left shift	left to right
<, <=, >, >=	less than, less or equal, greater than, greater or equal	right to lift
==, !=	equals to, not equal to	left to right
&	bitwise AND	left to right
^	bitwise Exclusive OR	left to right
|	bitwise OR	left to right
&&	logical AND	left to right
||	logical OR	left to right
?:	conditional operator	right to left
=, +=, -=, *=, /=, %=, &=, ^=, |=, <<=, >>=	simply equal, assign sum, assign minus, assign product, assign division, assign remainder, assign AND, assign Exclusive OR, assign OR, assign left shift, assign right shift	right to left

Figure 3.4:   C Operator Precedence and Association Order (From Highest to Lowest)

3.3   Exercises

1.   Write an algorithm and a C program that reads three integer numbers from the user and displays both their sum and product.

2.   Write an algorithm and a C program to print out a cheerful message enclosed in a rectangular box. For example, the output looks like:

```
* * * * * * * * * * * * * * * * * * *
*                                   *
*  What  a  Nice  Day!  *
*                                   *
* * * * * * * * * * * * * * * * * * *
```

3.   Evaluate the following expressions,

```
B/A,  A/B,  B%A,  A%B
```

given the following values of A and B respectively:
    a)   6, 21   b)   3, 21
    d)   8, 18   d)   -3, -16

4.   Write an algorithm and a C program to evaluate the following mathematics equations:

    a) $j = \dfrac{kA(P_1 - P_2)}{M}$

    b) $q = \dfrac{z^3/4c^3}{n^2}$

5.   Evaluate the following expressions:

    a)   true && false
    b)   true || true && false
    c)   ! (true) || true
    d)   40 % 5
    e)   5 % 40 / 8
    f)   ! false
    g)   15 < 1
    h)   100 > 15

6.   a)   What is the difference between an expression and an assignment instruction?
      b)   With A = 15, B = 3, C = 6 and D = 3; evaluate the following equations:
            i) F = A+B/C-D*D

ii) $F = (A+B)/C-D*D$

iii) $F = A+B/(C-D*D)$

iv) $F = (A+B) \% C$

v) $F = (A+B) / D*D$

vi) $F = 5*(A+B)-4*B(D+6)$

vii) $F = A-2>B$

    c)   For each equation in (b) above, state the data type of F.

7. With the initial value of the variable count=52 and that of total=120 before the execution of each instruction, give the result of the following instructions:
   a)   printf("%d %d", count++, --total);
   b)   printf("%d %d", ++count, total--);
   c)   printf("%d %d", ++total, total++);
   d)   printf("%d %d", --count, count--);
   e)   total += 30;
   f)   total /= 4;
   g)   total -= count;
   h)   count += 10;
   i)   count *= 2;

8. Given the two bit values bitone=01101011 and bittwo=00010111, give the result of the following C expressions:
   a)   bitone << 3
   b)   bitone & bittwo
   c)   bitone | bittwo
   d)   bitone ^ bittwo
   e)   ~ bittwo
   f)   bittwo >> 4

3.4 References

Kris Jamsa, "Jamsa's C Programmer's Bible – The Ultimate Guide to C Programming", first edition, Onword Press, Thomson Learning, 2002.

Elliott B. Koffman, "Turbo PASCAL" 5th ed., Addison Wesley, 1995.

Uckan Yuksel, "Problem Solving Using C – Structured Programming Technique", 2nd edition, WCB McGraw-Hill, 1999.

4.   PROBLEM SOLVING TOOLS USING TOP-DOWN DESIGN AND FUNCTIONS

In Chapter 2, we discussed steps in solving a problem with little emphasis on the use of top-down design approach in problem solving. The top-down design approach to problem-solving is based on the principle of "divide and conquer", which basically breaks up the problem to be solved into smaller problems and the solution to the big problem comprises integration of solutions to the sub-problems (functions). One of the software development tools used to break down problems into sub-problems or modules is the structure chart and in this chapter we shall discuss the use of structure charts, definition of algorithms and programs from structure charts and the use of flowcharts. Each solution to a sub problem represents a function. A function, like a program, is a sequence of instructions for solving a problem. A program can be written using a number of functions that are called by the main driver.

Some of the common questions regarding the top-down design approach have to do with "how do I make decisions on what constitutes a sub-task? or function?", "how do I integrate the functions to ensure they eventually work together towards solving the main problem?"

The answers to these questions come from the fact that when breaking down problems, the objective is to create functions that (1) are cohesive, because they are able to perform independent tasks, and (2) can be coupled with other functions in the sense that they can be connected to other functions through an input and output data interface. With the coupling ability, a function is able to accept input data from a calling function, use it to do its processing and arrive at a result to be either displayed or sent back to this calling function it worked for.

Thus, top-down design is achieved through cohesion and coupling. Cohesion enables us to break down the problem into independent sub problems while coupling ensures that solution of each sub problem (function) contributes to the overall solution of the main problem. For example, given a problem to compute the areas and perimeters of all the yards on a street, it can be seen that through cohesion, a sub problem (function) that computes the area of any given yard can be created, and another sub problem (function) that computes the perimeter of any given yard (length and width of yard are given) can also be created.

Coupling ensures that these two problem functions are made to work together. The coupling goal is accomplished through (1) the coordinating function, which at the highest level is the main driver, and (2) the input and output interface used by the coordinating function to communicate with the sub problem functions. Figure 4.0 provides a C program solution for computing the area and perimeter of any yard given its length and width that applied top-down design approach.

```
#include <stdio.h>
/* function prototypes follow */
float ComputeArea (float, float);
void ComputePerimeter (float, float, float *);

void main (void)
{
/*Declare variables*/
 float   ydlength, ydwidth;
 float   ydarea, ydperimeter;

 /*Now the executable instructions*/
 scanf ("%f %f", &ydlength, &ydwidth);
 ydarea = ComputeArea (ydlength, ydwidth);
 ComputePerimeter (ydlength, ydwidth, &ydperimeter);
 printf ("The area of this yard is %f\n", ydarea);
 printf ("The perimeter of this yard is %f\n", ydperimeter);
}

/*Now we provide the definition of the functions ComputArea and ComputePerimeter*/
float ComputeArea (float ydlength, float ydwidth)
{
 float area;
 area = ydlength * ydwidth;
 return (area);
}

void ComputePerimeter (float ydlength, float ydwidth, float *ydperimeter)
{
 *ydperimeter = 2 * (ydlength + ydwidth);
}
```

Figure 4.0:   C Program Solution of the Yard Example

Thus, with this yard example, there are three functions: (1) the main driver (called Main or Control function) which has the objective of finding the area and perimeter of all yards, (2) the ComputeArea function for finding the area of any given yard and (3) the ComputePerimeter function for finding the Perimeter of any given yard. The ComputeArea and ComputePerimeter functions never get involved in solving this problem unless they are called by the main function to contribute through coupling. In order to solve this problem, main will begin by obtaining the length and width of the yard from the user through the keyboard, then would call ComputeArea and next would call ComputePerimeter giving these functions the yard length and width for doing the job. Finally, main will print the computed area and perimeter of the yard. In this example, calls to the two functions by main are done in two different ways. The first call, which is made to ComputeArea involves only two call-by-value input parameters, while the second call, which is made to ComputePerimeter uses two call-by-value input parameters and a call-by-reference output parameter. This example, merely serves to introduce the concept of solving a problem using functions through top-down design approach. Proper techniques for using the necessary tools to solve problems by breaking them down into functions in top-down design approach, are presented in subsequent sections with more examples.

The top-down design (breaking a big problem into smaller subproblems) approach has many advantages, some of which are:

1. Increased productivity because many programmers can work on a large problem since different programmers working on different modules simultaneously would produce faster results.
2. Finding working solutions is easier because it is easier to write and test many small functions than a single one.
3. It is easier to maintain existing solutions because it is easier to modify structured and small functions.
4. Reusability: a defined function can be used several times by any function including itself and this avoids repetition of code.

4.1   Structure Charts

A structure chart is a software development tool used to graphically show the sub problems in a problem and the links between them. Since control always begins and ends in the coordinating main driver (control function), it is at the top of the chart.

Example 4.1   Write a solution that inputs three different integers from the keyboard and then prints the sum, average and product of these numbers. Use top-down design approach and functions.

In solving this problem we go through the problem solving steps:

Step 1: The Problem requirements are clear and we proceed.
Step 2: Identifying the problem components

Input data are:
    first number (num1, data type is integer)
    second number (num2, data type is integer)
    third number (num3, data type is integer)
Output data are:
    sum (data type is integer)

```
average (data type is real)
product (data type is integer)
```

Relationships are:
```
sum = num1 + num2 + num3
sverage = sum/3
product = num1 * num2 * num3
```

Step 3: Breaking problem-solution into smaller modules

Here, we use the structure chart, which has each function or subtask represented as a rectangular box. The main or control function is the top-most function. Every function is linked to the function underneath it with straight lines. An example structure chart for problem Example 4.1 is given as Figure 4.1.

A module processes only tasks directly below and connected to it by making function calls to those modules located below it. For ease of reference, in this book, functions are given unique number labels, based on their level with top-level being 0000. The number of digits used for function numbering may increase as the number of sub problems increases.

Although there is no hard and fast rule about what types of functions should be defined, we want to create functions that are cohesive and can be coupled and we want the best or most efficient solution. Some common types of functions that can be identified in many problems are:

a) Control function or Main Driver: which shows the overall flow of the problem and uses or calls other functions. Executing the program entails executing the instructions of the control function. Thus, any other defined module (or function) has to be called directly inside the control function or indirectly by a function called in the control function, to be executed.
b) Init function: may be needed if a large set of variables like array elements and others need to be initialized e.g.; `sum=0, knt=1`
c) Read Data function: may be needed if a large set of variables like array elements needs to be read into memory. Data validation may need to be done in this module as well.
d) Calculation functions: are used for arithmetic calculation, string manipulations like sorting, etc.
h) File Maintenance functions: could be used for adding, changing or deleting a record in the file.
f) Print Result function: for printing ouput of the program.
g) Wrap-up function: may be used for closing files and giving messages to mark normal end of program.

This classification of function types merely serves as a guide as the number and type of functions created while breaking down a problem is also determined by the nature of the problem. In some cases, the duties performed by a number of the functions given above are combined in one function. While there are lots of advantages in breaking problems down using top-down design approach, it may be inefficient to include more functions than are necessary because the overhead of saving parameters and switching between functions could increase substantially with the use of too many functions.

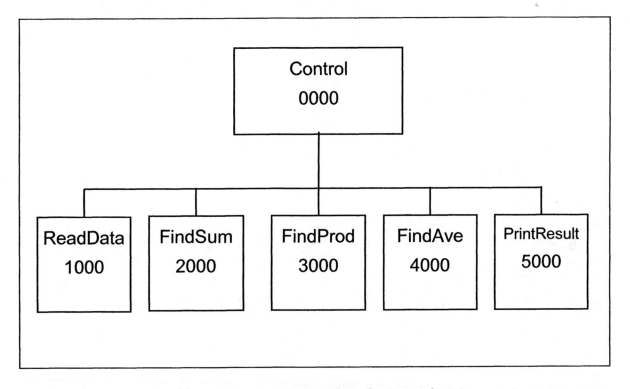

Figure 4.1: *Structure Chart for Example 4.1*

The break down of Example 4.1, shown in Figure 4.1 has many functions. An alternative top-down design break down of the same problem is shown below as Figure 4.2.

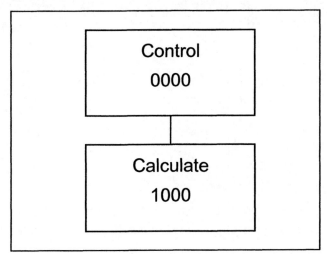

Figure 4.2: *Alternative Structure Chart for Example 4.1*

4.2   Functions, Algorithms and Programs

Once a number of functions has been defined in our structure chart, we shall proceed to define an algorithm and then a program for each of the functions in the structure chart. The type of each function and the types of its parameters (function prototype) is specified globally before the definition of the main driver as shown in Figures 3.1 and 3.2 (the overall structures of an algorithm and a program respectively). However, the full definitions of the functions are provided after the definition of the main driver (control function).   Function parameters are variables for passing input and output data into and from the function. The structure of an algorithm is the same as the structure of a corresponding program. However, while the program is written in C syntax, the algorithm is written in pseudocode (English-like language) for clarity.   In some cases, it is convenient to write the program straight without first presenting its algorithm and this is the case in later chapters when people are more familiar with the logical presentation of a problem solution in a program.

The structure of each function definition is similar to that of the control module, except that the function header has a data type for the value the function returns (at the beginning of the function header) and also has a list of function parameters for accepting input into the function as well as communicating output.   Intermediate variables used within the function for communicating output are called the function's local variables.   The function's local variables are declared inside the function block for local processing of instructions.   The body of a function consists of the sequence of instructions specifying the processing tasks to be performed by the function.   Thus, the general structure of a function prototype and its definition are given below. Since most C compilers need to know a function return type and its parameter types before the program calls the function, function definitions can be placed in front of their function callers without the need for function prototype definitions. However, having function prototypes before the main driver eliminates the need to keep track of what order function definitions are presented in a program.

A function prototype is used to tell the compiler the types of return results to expect from the function, the types of function parameters (input and output) and in what order to expect them.   The general format for defining a function prototype in both an algorithm and a program is given as:

function_return_type   functionname (type for parameter1, type for parameter2, ..., type for parametern);

> e.g., for the FindSum module of **Figure 4.1**, the function prototype becomes:
>
> int   FindSum (int, int, int);

This is because FindSum takes three input data num1, num2, num3 as its input parameters, all of type integer, and computes their sum, also of type integer, which it returns to the calling main function.

In both an algorithm and a program, the function definition is structured as follows:

```
function_return_type functionname ([type parameter1],
    [type parameter2], ..., [type parametern]);
        {
                [local variable declaration];
                instruction1;
                instruction2;
                .
                .
                instruction;
                [return (output variable or expression or 0)];
        }
```

4.2.1   Parameter, Local and Global Variables

There are three main approaches for communicating data between functions called coupling techniques. These approaches are explained with a simple example of writing a program to compute the difference between two numbers:

1. Use of parameters in functions: Through parameters, input data to be processed by the function are sent in. Output data from the function can also be specified using a parameter that can be changed within the function. There are two types of parameters that a function can use, namely, (i) call-by-value parameter for sending only input data to a called function and (ii) call-by-reference parameter for sending data (that the function can change) to a called function.

```c
#include <stdio.h>
/* function prototypes follow */
float   FindDiff (float, float);
void main (void)
{
/*Declare variables*/
 float Num1, Num2;
 float diff;
/*Now the executable instructions*/
 scanf ("%f %f\n", &Num1, &Num2);
 diff = FindDiff (Num1, Num2);
 printf ("The difference between Num1 and Num2 is %f\n", diff);
}
/*Now we provide the definition of the functions FindDiff*/
float FindDiff (float first, float second)
{
 float differ;
 differ = first − second;
 return (differ);
}
```

C Program to Find Difference Using Only Call-by-Value Parameters

The above program has only call-by-value parameters as only copies of input parameters, Num1 and Num2 are sent to FindDiff function by the main driver during the function call, diff = FindDiff (Num1, Num2);. Also note that because all input to this function are through call-by-value parameters with no accompanying call-by-reference parameter for the output, the function has to send the result back to the calling function using a function return instruction. The following program gives a C program solution of the same problem to find the difference between two given numbers, using only call-by-reference output parameters.

```
#include <stdio.h>
/* function prototypes follow */
void FindDiff (float, float, float *);

void main (void)
{
/* Declare variables */
 float Num1, Num2;
 float diff;

 /* Now the executable instructions */
 scanf ("%f %f\n", &Num1, &Num2);
 FindDiff (Num1, Num2, &diff);
 printf ("The difference between Num1 and Num2 is %f\n", diff);
}

/* Now we provide the definition of the functions FindDiff */
void FindDiff (float Num1, float Num2, float *differ)
{
 *differ = Num1 – Num2;
}
```

C Program to Find Difference Using a Call-by-Reference Parameter, &diff

Note that in the program above, the result, diff, in the function call made by main, FindDiff (Num1, Num2, &diff); is a call-by-reference parameter and thus, its address is passed using the address operator, &, to get its address. The function definition for the FindDiff function in this case, has no return instruction. Also the function call is not an assignment instruction as in the case with the call-by-value example.

2. Use of a function return value for sending one output back to a calling function: With this approach, calling a function will lead to the value of the variable it returns in its function definition being placed at the point of call. The first program example in section 4.2.1 uses a return instruction. A function is able to return only one data value through a return instruction. The general format of a *return* instruction in C which sends back a value is:

```
return   expression;
```

A function may also return no value to the called function, but passes execution control back to the called function using a return instruction that sends back no value in the following format.

```
return;
```

3. **Use of global variables:** Following the C language convention, global variables to a function are defined outside the function and before the opening curly bracket { of the function. Functions can use their global variables in their instructions. Global variables of a function are declared above the function definition in the algorithm and program. Variables declared within a module or function block are its local variables and are not accessible to other functions. A slightly different variable scoping rule, which allows variables declared in an algorithmic/program block to be visible to functions underneath them in the structure chart is adopted by languages like Pascal. However, the C convention is adopted in this book. Generally, variables that are global to all functions can be read and modified by all of them as they please. Examples on the use of global and local variables will be provided later.

Call-by-Value and Call-by-Reference Parameter

When a function like, main, calls another function like FindDiff (to obtain the difference between 2 float values), the calling module provides the actual data values (for the 2 float values) in the calling module's (main's) memory space (see first program in section 4.2.1 above). These are the input data to the FindDiff function. Since these 2 input data belong to main and FindDiff function is not required to change the values of these input data, when making the call, main provides the values of these input data through call-by-value technique. This means that it simply gives a copy of the values in its own memory space to the called function FindDiff as depicted in the table below.

main function memory		FindDiff function memory	
Actual parameter	value	Formal parameter	value
Num1	20.0	first	20.0
Num2	15.0	second	15.0
diff	? (value returned)	differ	5.0

Call-by-value made by main to Calculate

With this call-by-value, where only a copy of the actual input data value is given to the called module to store in its own memory space, the called function cannot change the values of the actual parameters in the memory space of the calling function. The called function (FindDiff) can only change the values of its formal parameters, its local or global variables. Thus, call-by-value parameters are used for passing input data to called functions. The result of the computation in the function, FindDiff, stored in its local variable, differ, has to be sent back to the calling main function, using a return instruction. This result is placed in the main's variable, diff. A called function can return only one data value. Sometimes, we may require a function to compute more than one output data. For example, a function is required to compute both the sum and product of any three given numbers. In this case, we can choose to pass all the input data through call-by-value, but we can only return the value of one output data like sum. Thus, another technique is needed for sending back computed results from a function other than through a return instruction. That alternative method is call-by-reference.

A second method for bringing back the results of calculations (e.g., difference) to the called function (main) is call-by-reference, since call-by-value would not allow FindDiff function to change directly, the value of the output parameter, diff, in the main's memory space. Call-by-reference technique passes the address of the actual output parameter to the called function (not its copy as done during call-by-value). Once the address of a memory space is passed to a function by a calling function, the called function has direct access to this memory space that does not belong to the called function. Thus, the called function can change this specific memory space of the calling function, directly with the called function's own instructions. The next table below shows how call-by-reference made by main to FindDiff using the diff output parameters (as shown in the second program of section 4.2) is used to change main's variable, diff, without a return instruction. To make the function call, the address of the variable is passed as the actual parameter in the instruction: FindDiff(Num1, Num2, &diff). In the function definition of FindDiff, the corresponding formal parameter for diff is a pointer variable declared as float *differ. Then, within the function, FindDiff, the value of diff in main, pointed to, by pointer variable differ is obtained as *differ with the instruction, *differ = Num1 – Num2. The next discussion gives the format for declaring a pointer variable, assigning an address to it and using this pointer variable to access the data value it points to.

Main function memory		FindDiff function memory
Actual call-by-reference parameter	Data in main changed by FindDiff	Formal call-by-reference parameter
address of diff (&diff)	value of diff (called *differ in FindDiff and diff in main)	pointer to main's diff (*differ)

Call-by-reference made by main to FindDiff

Address Operator (&), Pointer Variable and Indirection Operator (*)

A pointer variable is a variable that can store or hold only memory addresses as its value. Like other variable types (int, float, char), a pointer variable has to be declared first before it is used in a program instruction.

To declare a pointer variable requires specifying the type of value, the pointer variable points to, (e.g., int, float, char), and an asterisk is placed before the variable name. The format for declaring pointer variable is:

data_type_pointed_to　　　*variablename;**

Assume the following memory set-up for the second FindDiff program in section 4.2.1:

	main		FindDiff	
diff	5.0		addr (diff)	differ
Num1	20.0		20.0	Num1
Num2	15.0		15.0	Num2

70

The formal parameters in FindDiff are (float Num1, float Num2, float *differ). While Num1 and Num2 are call-by-value parameters, differ is a call-by-reference formal parameter that needs to hold the address of the actual parameter, diff, from main. Thus, to declare the pointer differ in FindDiff, which points to a float data, we use:

   float *differ;

This is how the formal parameters are declared in the function header for FindDiff or any other function, when the parameters are call-by-reference parameters that receive addresses as their actual parameters. In the function header, call-by-reference parameters are declared as pointer variables using the format given above for declaring a pointer variable. The call-by-value and call-by-reference calls made to the function FindDiff in the program in section 4.2.1 can also be described using the memory addresses of the actual parameters in the function call *FindDiff(Num1, Num2, &diff)*. Assume that the addresses of the variables Num1, Num2 and diff in the function main are 0560, 0564 and <u>0556</u> respectively.

	main			FindDiff
diff (0556)	5.0	◄	0556	differ
Num1 (0560)	20.0		20.0	Num1
Num2 (0564)	15.0		15.0	Num2

Like all variables, a pointer variable needs to be assigned a value (an address) before it can be used. The address operator (&) is used to obtain the address of an already existing variable like (diff of main) so that this address can be stored in the formal parameter differ of FindDiff as:

   differ = &diff; (assigns address of diff of main to differ of FindDiff)

In the function call FindDiff(Num1, Num2, &diff); in the main function, the third actual parameter, &diff is the address of diff, which corresponds to the third formal parameter, differ in the function definition of FindDiff, declared as the pointer, float *differ. The effect of this function call is assigning this address &diff to pointer variable differ in FindDiff. Though the formal parameter differ points to diff of main by holding its address, the actual value of diff is what it needs to change. By having diff's address, differ has exclusive permission through call-by-reference, to change diff's value. However, since differ is a pointer variable, a simple assignment like

   differ = Num1 - Num2;

does not store the difference between the two numbers in differ or diff (but either stores this value (e.g., 7) as an address of a memory location where the result is, or is an invalid operation). Thus, the above assignment is an incorrect operation for this solution since differ is a pointer variable and not a simple float variable.

To store this difference as the value pointed to, by differ, the dereference or indirection operator (*) is used to obtain the value pointed to, by a pointer variable (like differ). For example, to store the difference between the two numbers as the value of diff in main pointed to, by differ, we use the indirection operator in FindDiff as follows:

   *differ = Num1 - Num2;

Generally, the value of data pointed to, by a pointer variable with name, pointervar is, obtained through the pointer variable with the expression *pointervar.

The algorithmic solution of Example 4.1 using the structure chart of Figure 4.1, where the same problem is solved with 5 functions, is given below as Figure 4.3 , while the C program for this same algorithm and structure chart is given as Figure 4.4.

```
/*Now define 5 function prototypes                   */
     void ReadData (int*, int*, int*);
     int FindSum (int, int, int);
     int FindProd (int, int, int);
     float FindAve (int, int);
     void PrintResult (int, int, float);
Module 0000
void main (void)
{
     Input variables: int num1, num2, num3;
     Output variables: int sum, product;
                       flaoat average;
/* Now write the instructions of the control module */

     ReadData (&num1, &num2, &num3);
     sum=FindSum(num1, num2, num3);
     product=FindProd(num1, num2, num3);
     average=FindAve(sum,3);
     PrintResult(sum, product, average);
end


/*Now begin the definition of each of the 5 functions */
Module 1000
void ReadData(int *num1, int *num2, int *num3);
     {
         read (num1, num2, num3);
     }


Module 2000
int FindSum(int first, int second, int third);
     {
     local variable: sum integer
         sum = first + second + third;
         return sum;
     }


Module 3000
int FindProd (int num1, int num2, int num3)
     {
         return num1 * num2 * num3;
     }
```

```
Module 4000
float FindAve (int sum, int knt)
    {
        return sum/knt;
    }


Module 5000
void PrintResult(int sum, int product, int average)
    {
        print (sum);
        print (product);
        print (average);
    }
```

Figure 4.3   Algorithmic Solution of Example 4.1 Using Structure chart 4.2

```
#include <stdio.h>

void ReadData (int*, int*, int*); /* fn prototypes */
int FindSum (int, int, int);
int FindProd (int, int, int);
float FindAve (int, int);
void PrintResult (int, int, float);

void main (void)
{
        int    num1, num2, num3, sum, product;
        float  average;
 /* Now write the instructions of the control module */
        ReadData (&num1, &num2, &num3);
        sum=FindSum(num1, num2, num3);
        product=FindProd(num1, num2, num3);
        average=FindAve(sum,3);
        PrintResult(sum, product, average);
}
/* Now begin the definitions of the 5 functions */
void ReadData(int *num1, int *num2, int *num3)
    {
        scanf ("%d %d %d", num1, num2, num3);
    }
int FindSum(int first, int second, int third)
    {
        int sum;
        sum = first + second + third;
        return sum;
    }
```

```
int FindProd (int num1, int num2, int num3)
    {
          return (num1 * num2 * num3);
    }
float FindAve (int sum, int knt)
    {
          return (float)sum/knt;
     }
void PrintResult(int sum, int product, float  average)
    {
        printf("%d\n", sum);
        printf("%d\n", product);
        printf("%f\n", average);
    }
```

Figure 4.4   C Program Solution of Example 4.1 Using Structure chart 4.2

In the example, the function prototypes are included for each function or module. The prototype is used to indicate the type of "return" result being expected from the function as well as the types of its parameters in the correct order they are defined and called. There are no global variables in this solution.

Function Parameters and Function Calls

Function parameters are variables, which hold input and output data going into and coming from functions. The function parameters are specified in the definition of the function (these are the formal parameters) and in the function call (these are the actual parameters). The order of the parameters and their types are important and actual parameters in the function call have to be submitted in the exact order the formal parameters are specified in the function definition. Formal parameters are place holders for actual values used during function calls. The variable names used for corresponding actual and formal parameters do not have to be the same, but the correct order and data type must be preserved. The actual parameters consist of variables already declared in the calling module and may have some data values stored in them before the function call.

For example, in the program in Figure 4.4, the first instruction in the main driver `ReadData(&num1, &num2, &num3)` is a function call, which is asking the function `ReadData` to read data into the variables `num1, num2,` and `num3 of main.` These are call-by-reference parameters that allow the memory cell of the passed variables to be modified by the called function. When it is a call-by-reference parameter, the address of the variable is passed. Thus, the address operator & is used to pass the addresses of num1, num2 and num3 to ReadData. In this function call, the actual parameters are &num1, &num2, and &num3, while the formal parameters are in the function definition specified as *num1, *num2, *num3. Here, the formal parameters have the same variable names as the actual parameters, but are preceded by "*" to indicate that these formal parameters are pointer variables that hold addresses and can be used to modify corresponding variables of the calling module (main) directly within the ReadData module (call-by-reference). Also, in the function call in main, the actual parameters are preceded by & to show that they are call-by-reference parameters. Once a function call is made by a function (main), execution control jumps to the function definition of the called function, where the instructions of this function will execute before the next instruction in main is executed. Thus, the result of the call, ReadData(&num1, &num2, &num3) is that the function definition for ReadData is jumped to. The first instruction in this function is scanf("%d %d %d", num1, num2, num3); This instruction has the effect of reading from the keyboard, the values to be placed in these three variables. Note how the scanf variable parameters in this case are not preceded by & because these variables are already holding addresses of num1, num2 and num3 respectively. Since this is the only instruction in this function, execution control goes back to main, where the second instruction sum=FindSum(num1, num2, num3) is executed. This again is a function call that jumps to the function FindSum, copying the values of num1, num2, num3 of main to the formal parameters, first, second and third of FindSum respectively.

This second instruction of the control module, sum=Findsum(num1, num2, num3), is a function call that returns a data value at the point of call. Thus, this function call is part of an expression. Also, the formal parameters in the definition of FindSum are first, second, and third, corresponding to the actual parameters num1, num2, and num3 respectively. The type of call made in this case is call-by-value, which means that copies of the values of the variables num1, num2, and num3 are placed in the local variables first, second, and third, of this function. The implication of call-by-value is that, even if any changes are made to first, second, and third, these changes will not affect the actual variables num1, num2, and num3 in the calling function. This will not be the case with call-by-reference parameters, where, because addresses of the actual variables are passed to the function, changes made by the function to the actual parameters remain visible in the calling function. The sum of the three numbers are obtained according to the instructions of the function, FindSum and this sum is returned as the value of sum in the main module because of the assignment instruction. The next instruction to execute in main is the function call average=FindAve(sum,3), which shows how a data constant can be used as an actual parameter in a function call. This causes control to be passed to function definition of FindAve, where the average is computed as the sum/knt and returned to main to be placed in the main's variable, average. Now, that all the needed results have been computed, the last function call in the control module passes the actual parameters for sum, product and average to be printed by the function PrintResults. A distinction needs to be made between what constitutes a function prototype declaration, a function definition and a function call.

A function prototype is used to inform the compiler what types of input and output parameters to expect for a function. A function definition specifies how to carry out the operations performed by the function by giving the sequence of instructions for the function (its algorithm). A function call is used to get the function involved in solving the problem. A function that is defined but never gets called never contributes to the solution of the problem just as an electrician included in the initial plan for building a house never contributes to the building if the overall contractor never calls him to complete his part of the project.

Local and Global Variables

Variables declared within a function are the function's local variables, while variables declared outside a function's block and above a function in the algorithm/program are this function's global variables. Instructions in a function can only use variables that are this function's local variables, global variables or its formal parameters. The difference between local variables and global variables is in their scope (where and in which functions their values are allowed to be used). While local variables may be used only inside the function that it is declared, global variables can be used by any function below it in the algorithm or program.

```c
#include <stdio.h>
/*variables global to main and fn1*/
int a = 0, b = 0, c = 0;
float x = 17.0;

int fn1 (int, float);     /*function prototype*/

/*main function next*/
void main (void)
{/*variables local to main*/
 int e = 5, f = 10;
 float g = 30.0;

 /*instructions of main can only use its local or global variables*/
 g = x;
 a = e + f;
 b = fn1 (a, g);
 printf ("%d %d %d %d %d\n", a, b, c, e, f);
 printf ("%f %f\n", x, g);
}

float y;         /*variable global to only fn1*/

int fn1 (int a, float g)
{/*variables local to fn1*/
 int d;
 printf ("%f\n", g);
 d = a * 20;
 return d;
}
```

Figure 4.5:   C Program Example on Use of Global and Local Variables

76

Formal function parameters are local to the function in which they are declared. However, while the formal parameters are declared in the function parameter list in its header, the function local variables are declared in the body of the function after the beginning curly brace. The scope of a global variable starts at the point it is declared and terminates at the end of the program. The scope of a function local variable or formal parameter starts at the point it is declared in the function and terminates at the end of the function. Figure 4.5 illustrates the scope of variables, identifying which variables are global and which are local in each function.

The following table shows which variables are global, local and formal parameters to the different functions in Figure 4.5.

Function	Global variables	Local variables	Formal parameters
main	a, b, c, x	e, f, g	none
fn1	a, b, c, x, y	d	a, g

The table below also shows the scoping of variables in the example program on computing the sum, product and average of any three given numbers in figure 4.4.

Function	Global variables	Local variables	Formal parameters
main	none	num1, num2, num3, sum, product, average	none
ReadData	none	none	num1, num2, num3
FindSum	none	sum	first, second, third
FindProd	none	none	num1, num2, num3
FindAve	none	none	sum, knt
PrintResult	none	none	sum, product, average

Use of global variables as a coupling technique has some shortfalls some of which are:

1. Possibility of Side Effects: A global variable, can easily be modified accidentally by an incorrect or malicious module because there is no data protection. Every module has access to the same memory cell.
2. No Duplication of Variable Names: If a variable is intended to be used as global, but a local variable with the same name is declared in a function, all changes to this local variable are no longer reflected on the global variable leading to undesired program results. Some programming languages do not allow duplication of variable names in functions to prevent this problem from occurring.

FindSum has a local variable sum. So, any change made to sum by FindSum is local but may be sent out to another function only through a return instruction to be effected or used. Variables num1, num2, num3, sum, product, and average are local to the control function and can only be accessed (used) by instructions in the body of the control function. The variables first, second, and third are parameters, which are local to the module `FindSum` and cannot be accessed by any other function. There are no global variables in Figure 4.4.

Example 4.2   Write a program to find the sum, product and average of three integer numbers using only global and local variables (no parameters passed).

```c
#include <stdio.h>
int      num1, num2, num3, sum, product;
float average;

/*       Prototypes            */

      void ReadData (void);
      void FindSum (void);
      int FindProd (void);
      float FindAve (void);
      void PrintResult (void);

void main(void)
{
/*         Body of Control       */
      ReadData ();
      FindSum();
      product=FindProd();
      average=FindAve();
      PrintResult();
}
void ReadData (void)
      {
               scanf ("%d  %d  %d", &num1,  &num2,
&num3);
      }
void FindSum (void)
      {
               sum = num1+num2+num3;
      }

int FindProd (void)
      {
      int product;  /* local variable */
               product = num1*num2*num3;
               return (product);
      }
float FindAve (void)
      {
```

```
            return (float)sum/3;
    }
void PrintResult(void)
    {
            printf  ("%d   %d   %f\n",sum,  product,
average);
    }
```

The following table shows the global and local variables of the functions in the solution for Example 4.2, as well as their parameters.

Function	Global variables	Local variables	Formal parameters
main	num1, num2, num3, sum, product, average	none	none
ReadData	none	none	none
FindSum	none	none	none
FindProd	none	product	none
FindAve	none	none	none
PrintResult	none	none	none

The solution of Example 4.2 above uses only global variables and made no parameter calls. Note how the address operators are again used in the scanf instruction inside the ReadData function because there are no actual parameters (addresses) passed in to this function by main as in the case of the solution for Example 4.1 given in Figure 4.4. In Figure 4.4, the addresses of Num1, Num2 and Num3 are passed through call-by-reference into the function ReadData by main, and since the scanf instruction requires these addresses which are already stored as the formal parameters, the names of the formal parameters are directly used in the scanf instructions without the address operators. A combination of both parameter calls and use of global variables may be adopted as well in solving problems. A slightly modified version of Example 4.2, which makes some parameter calls is given as Example 4.2a.

Example 4.2a: Solve the problem of finding the sum, product
    and average of three integer numbers using global and
    local variables as well as parameter calls.

```
#include <stdio.h>
int     num1, num2, num3, sum;


/*       Prototypes         */

    void ReadData (void);
    void FindSum (void);
    int  FindProd (void);
    float FindAve (void);
    void PrintResult (int, float);
```

```c
void main(void)
{   int product;
    float average;
/*        Body of Control        */
        ReadData ();
        FindSum();
        product=FindProd();
        average=FindAve();
        PrintResult(product, average);
}
void ReadData (void);
        {
                scanf ("%d %d %d ", &num1, &num2, &num3);
        }
void FindSum (void)
        {
                sum = num1+num2+num3;
        }
int FindProd (void)
        {
        int product;   /* local variable */
                product = num1*num2*num3;
                return (product);
        }

float FindAve (void)
        {
                return (float) sum/3;
        }
void PrintResults (int product, float average)
        {
                printf ("%d %d %f",sum, product, average);
        }
```

Example 4.3: Write the C program of the problem of finding the sum, product and average of three integer numbers using the structure chart of Figure 4.2.

```
#include <stdio.h>

/*Now define  function prototypes  */
void Calculate (int, int, int, int *, int *,float *);

void main (void)
{       int num1, num2, num3, sum, product;
        float average;

                scanf ("%d %d %d", &num1, &num2, &num3);
                Calculate(num1,num2,num3,&sum,&product,&average);
                printf ("%d %d %f",sum, product, average);
}


        /* Now begin the definition of the function */
        /* calculate                                          */

void Calculate(int first, int second, int third,  int *sum,
                        int *product, float *average)
    {
            *sum = first + second + third;
            *product = first * second * third;
            *average = (float) *sum/3;
    }
```

Figure 4.6:   Algorithmic Solution of Example 4.3 Using Structure Chart of Figure 4.2

4.3   Built-in Functions

As discussed in Section 4.2, a function is a set of instructions that performs specific tasks and can return a value. Functions contribute towards the solution of a problem by making the solution of a big problem more efficient because they can be reused, more elegant because it is structured, and easier to read. Many languages provide a variety of built-in functions in their standard library which are pre-defined in the language and user programs can call these functions without providing a function definition as part of the program code. The common classes of built-in functions are:

1. Mathematical functions: In C, there are two categories of mathematical functions, those that take arguments (parameters) of type double and return values of type double, and those that accept and return only values of type int.   In order to use any of these mathematical library functions, kept in the <math.h> and <stdlib.h> header files, we must include in the program, the directives #include <math.h>.   Available mathematical functions are summarized below.

Function	Description	Example
sqrt(x)	Square root of x	sqrt(25.0) is 5.0
exp(x)	exponential function e^x	exp(1.0) is 2.72
log(x)	natural logarithm of x (base e)	log(2.72) is 1.0
log10(x)	logarithm of x (base 10)	log10(1.0) is 0.0
fabs(x)	absolute value of x (for x real)	fabs(-15.3) is 15.3 fabs(5.0) is 5.0
Abs(x)	Absolute value of x (for x int)	Abs (-245) is 245
ceil(x)	rounds x to the smallest integer not less than x	ceil(7.1) is 8 ceil(-6.3) is -6
floor(x)	rounds x to the largest integer not greater than x	floor(7.1) is 7 floor(-6.3) is -7
pow(x,y)	x raised to the power of y (x^y)	pow(2,3) is 8 pow(16,.25) is 2
sin(x)	trigonometric sine of x (x in radians)	sin(0.0) is 0.0
cos(x)	trigonometric cosine of x (x in radians)	cos(0.0) is 1.0
tan(x)	trigonometric tangent of x (x in radians)	tan(0.0) is 0.0

2. String Functions

These functions are used to manipulate string data, e.g., used to copy part of a string into another variable. The string manipulation functions of the string handling library in C, are declared in the header file <string.h>. Thus, to use these functions, the directive, #include <string.h> must be included in the program. Available string functions in C include strcat, strchr, strcmp, strcpy, strcspn, strlen, strtok and more details on C string functions are provided in section 8.3 of the book.

3. Character Handling Functions

A number of character handling functions are available in the C standard library in the header file <ctype.h>. The preprocessor directive #include <ctype.h> needs to be included in the program for these character functions to be used. Some useful character handling functions from the C character handling library are:

Function	Description	Example
isdigit(c)	returns a true value (non zero) if c is a digit and 0 otherwise	isdigit('A') is 0
isalpha(c)	returns a true value (non zero) if c is a letter and 0 otherwise	isalpha('A') is 1
isalnum(c)	returns a true value (non zero) if c is a letter or digit and 0 otherwise	isalnum('+') is 0
islower(c)	returns a true value (non zero) if c is a lowercase letter and 0 otherwise	islower('c') is 1

`isupper(c)`	returns a true value (non zero) if c is an uppercase letter and 0 otherwise	`isupper('a') is 0`
`isspace(c )`	returns nonzero if c is whitespace char and 0 otherwise	`isspace('a') is 0`
`ispunct(c)`	returns nonzero if c is punctuation char and 0 otherwise	`ispunct(';')is 1`
`tolower(c)`	returns c as a lowercase letter	`tolower('A')is 'a'`
`toupper(c )`	returns c as an uppercase letter	`toupper('b') is 'A'`

4. Conversion Functions

In C some string conversion functions found in the <stdlib.h> header file are given below. Programs using these functions should include the directive #include <stdlib.h>.

Functions	Description
atof (s1)	Converts s1 to double
atoi (s1)	Converts s1 to int
atol (s1)	Converts s1 to long int

5. Utility Functions
Some general utilities found in the header file <stdlib.h> are:

Functions	Description
rand ()	Returns a random number between 0 and Rand_Max (a constant >= 32767)
srand (seed)	Uses *seed* as a seed for a new sequence of random numbers in subsequent calls to function rand

Other utility functions in the <time.h> header file are:

Functions	Description
clock_t ()	Returns the processor time used by the program. Called at the beginning and end of program to determine CPU time in clocks. CPU time in seconds is obtained by dividing this time by constant CLOCKS_PER_SECOND.

4.4   Flowcharts

We have seen how the solution to a problem can be organized into functions using structure charts, and the algorithmic solution or program to a problem requires defining an algorithmic solution/program for each function in the structure chart with appropriate function calls and parameter set ups. Defining an algorithm is one intermediate way to present a solution to be translated into a program code. An alternative approach is the use of flowcharts. Every algorithmic definition has a corresponding flowchart definition. A flowchart is a graphical representation of an algorithm. It shows the sequence of execution of instructions using special boxes. A flowchart always starts at the top of the page and uses straight and neat connecting flow lines. The specific types of boxes used to represent the different types of algorithmic and program instructions and connectors are given in Figure 4.7.

Type of Instruction	Symbol
Start, End, Exit instruction, Enter, Return	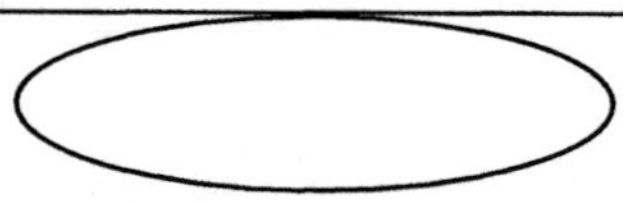
Read or Print Instruction	
Assignment instruction	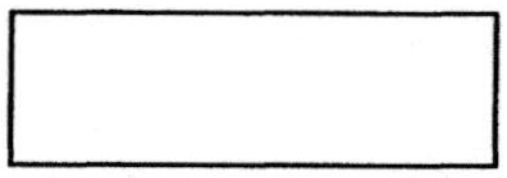
Function Call (not part of assignment instruction)	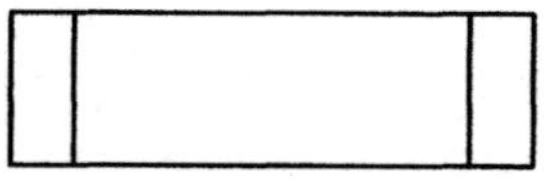
Automatic counter repetition loop[start s, incr i, end e]	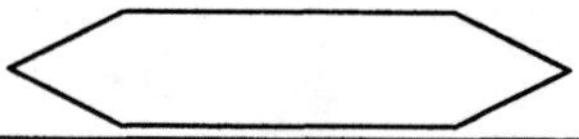
On-page connectors	
Off-page connectors	
Flow lines	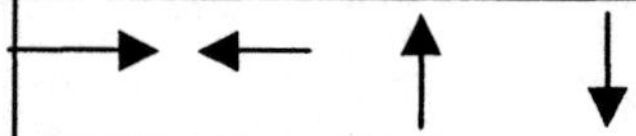
Connecting Parameters to a function	

Figure 4.7   Flowchart Symbols

Example 4.3   Provide the flowchart solution to the problem of finding the sum, product and average of three integer numbers using parameters (similar to the solution in Figure 4.3 above).

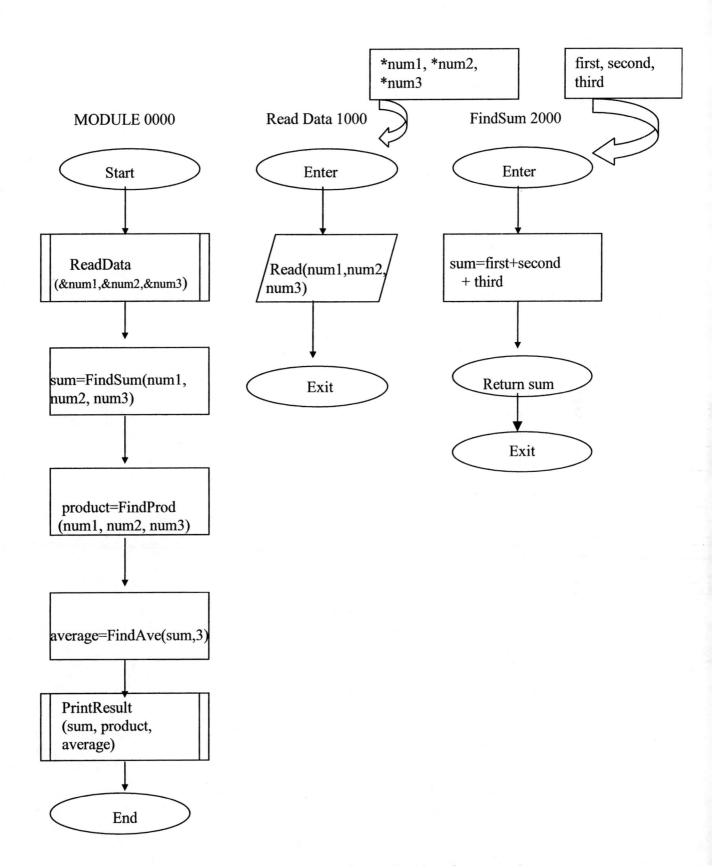

Figure 4.8: Flowchart Solution to Example 4.1 (continued next page)

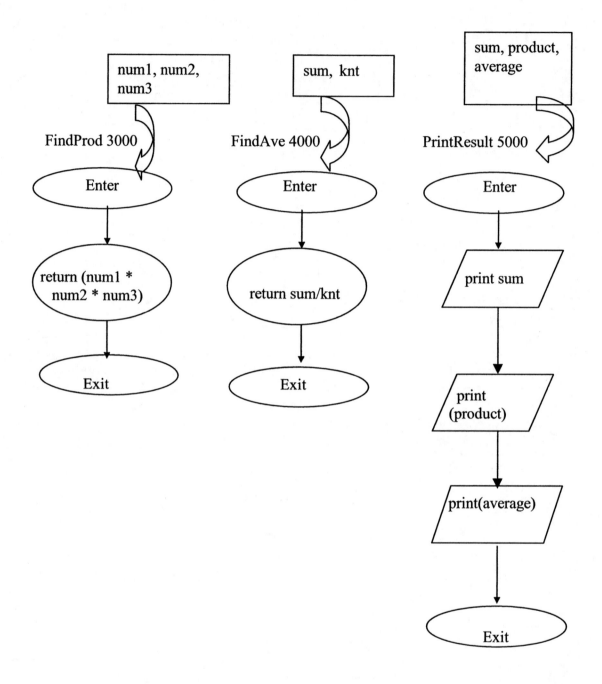

Figure 4.8a: Continuation of Figure 4.8

4.5 Exercises

1. What are the differences between the following pairs of terms?
   a) local and global variables
   b) a function prototype declaration and a function definition
   c) a function definition and a function call
   d) call-by-reference and call-by-value
   e) cohesion and coupling
   f) structure chart and flowchart
   g) formal and actual parameters

2. a) What is meant by the scope of a variable?
   b) Give the C variable scoping rules.
   c) Why is the use of parameters preferred over the use of global variables?

   Use the top-down approach for the following:

3. Using top-down approach to problem-solving, write a C program that returns the fewest number of coins in change from a purchase of under five dollars, given a five dollar bill. The coins to be returned may include only toonies (two dollars), loonies (one dollar), quarters, nickels, and pennies. (Assume you can use a built-in function to convert a real n to an integer n.)
   Example: purchase is 51 cents
        change is $4.49
        Coins: 2 toonies
            1 quarter
            2 dimes
            4 cents

4. Your instructor evaluates student performance based on the 6 assignments, 2 quizzes, a lab mark, a midterm test and a final examination mark. While 10% of the total course mark of 100% is for the 6 assignment marks, 15% of the total is assigned to the quizzes, 10% of the total is reserved for lab mark, the midterm test is worth 20% while the final weighs 45%. Given a student's assignment marks, quizzes, labs, midterm test and final examination marks, write a program to compute the final course mark of the student. Hint: all input marks should be out of 100. For example, assignment marks for a student could be 65 (meaning 65 out of 100%).

5. Write a program that reads in the starting time and the ending time of a phone call, then computes and prints the cost of the phone call. The phone company uses the following billing method:
   - The regular rate for a call is $0.25 per minute
   - Any call started after or at 6.00p.m. (1800) and before 8.00am(800) is discounted 50%

- Any call longer than 120 minutes will be billed only for 120 minutes.
- The cost of all calls include the GST (7% of the cost) and the PST (8% of the cost) taxes.

Note: For simplicity, assume that the starting and ending times for a call are integers, e.g., 5.35pm is 1735 and 9.45am is 945. Give the programs and flowcharts including internal documentation. Test your solution on the two input sets: (1937, 2027) and (2330, 0301).

6. Given the following program, show the values of the variables a, b, c, x, y, z in the main function after each function call to module2. Also, show the values of a, b, c in module2 immediately after executing each function call to module2.

```
#include <stdio.h>

/*    function prototype declaration for Module2    */
void module2(int, int, int *);

void main(void)
{
int a=3, b=4, c=5, x=7, y=8, z=10;

/*    body of main    */
  module2 (a, b, &c);      /* a first call to Module2    */
  module2 (x, y, &z);      /* a second call to Module2    */
}


/*    definition of Module2    */
void module2 (int a, int b, int *c)
{
  a += 4;
  b += 4;
  *c += 4;
}
```

7. Using top-down design approach, write a program to display the following:

```
****      *****      *****      *****
*   *     *          *          *    *
*   *     *****      *****       *    *
*   *     *          *          *    *
* ***     *****      *****      *****
```

4.6   References

Kris Jamsa, "Jamsa's C Programmer's Bible – The Ultimate Guide to C Programming", first edition, Onword Press, Thomson Learning, 2002.

Elliott B. Koffman, "Turbo PASCAL" 5th ed., Addison Wesley, 1995.

Maureen Sprankle, "Problem Solving and Programming Concepts", 3rd ed., Prentice Hall, 1995.

Uckan Yuksel, "Problem Solving Using C – Structured Programming Technique", 2nd edition, WCB McGraw-Hill, 1999.

5. PROGRAM LOGIC STRUCTURES ---SEQUENTIAL

5.1 Sequential Logic Structure
5.2 Program Testing and Documentation
5.3 Exercises
5.4 References

The logic structure of a program dictates the sequence of execution of instructions in the program. The common logic structures found in programs and algorithms are

i)   Sequential logic structure and function calls
ii)   Decision logic structure and
iii)   Repetition logic structure.

The default logic structure is sequential and programs are usually executed from beginning to end, starting with instruction 1, followed by instruction 2, ... , followed by instruction *n*. However, any of the instructions may be sequential, function call, decision or repetition type. In this chapter, sequential logic structure is discussed.

5.1   Sequential Logic Structure

Although every program has a sequential logic structure, a distinction can be made between a program that is totally sequential and those that include some branching due to a decision or a repetition instruction. A program or algorithm is said to be totally sequential if none of its instructions changes the sequential order of execution of instructions. The sequential instructions are Read (e.g., scanf), Print (e.g., printf), Assignment (e.g., sum=sum+Num) and Function calls (e.g., FindSum(Num1,Num2, &Sum)). Since function calls return to the next instruction in sequence, we also group them for simplicity with sequential instructions. In reality, function calls cause a branch or jump to the memory location where the first entry instruction of their definition is stored. When the instructions of the function are all executed, then, control of the program execution is returned to the next instruction following the function call in the calling function. The structure of a totally sequential program is:

```c
#include <stdio.h>

void main (void)
{

Input variable list and types;
Output variable list and types;
        instruction 1;
        instruction 2;
        .
        .

        instruction n;
}
```

Here, instruction i can only be a Read type (e.g., scanf), Print type (e.g., printf) instruction or an assignment instruction (e.g., A=A-B), or a function call (e.g., FindSum(x, y, &sum)).

Example 5.1:Monique has some money to spend on work clothes. The type of skirt suit she likes costs $320.00, a pant suit costs the same amount. She has enough money to buy two suits. She also wants to buy a number of shirts, which cost $45 each with money left. How many shirts is Monique able to buy? Assume input data is always greater than or equal to $640.00.

Solution:

```c
#include <stdio.h>
#include <math.h>

void main(void)
{
   float Available_Cash, Money_left , Suit_Cost = 640.00;
   int Num_Shirts;

/* body of the main */
        scanf ("%f", &Availble_Cash);
        Money_left = Available_Cash – Suit_Cost;
        Num_Shirts = floor( Money_left / 45.00 );
        printf ( "Monique can afford %d warm
            shirts in addition to the suits", Num_Shirts);
}
```

Note that this program involves only sequential instructions.

5.2   Program Testing and Documentation

Program testing requires drawing a complete input test data and executing the instructions of the program to produce some results. The results produced by the program are compared with the expected results to verify the correctness of the program. The expected results can be pre-computed using a calculator or other means. Errors and inconsistencies can also be identified more easily by executing a program with hand during testing and verification. Thus, hand tracing of a program is also a method for testing and verifying program correctness.

The test data has to be selected in such a way that all possible classes of input data are represented. This is necessary because a solution may be working for a class of input data (e.g. input data >0), but fails to produce correct results when input data is less than zero. Test data should be selected to test all possible situations that may arise.

Testing and Verifying Example 5.1

First step is to draw our test data since they are not given. The data needed to be formed is the input data, Available_Cash. Since from the problem, we are told that she always has enough money to buy 2 suits which cost $640.00, it means Available_Cash should never be less than $640.00. The only data categories to be represented now and tested are:

(i) when Available_Cash is exactly $640.00 (e.g., with test data $640.00), and

(ii) when Available_Cash is greater than $640.00 (e.g. with test data $1000.00, $720.00).

We now have the test data $640.00, $1000.00 and $720.00 which we want to submit to our program during its execution to confirm that the program is working correctly.

Pre-computation of correct result

From the problem,
Number of shirts Monique can buy =
(amount of cash available – cost of two suits)/45.00 [number has to be whole number]
cost of two suits = $640.00

(a) if Available_Cash = $640.00
    then, number of shirts = lower whole number of [(640.00-640.00)/45.00]
                                    = 0.0/45.00
                                    = 0.0
                                    = 0
(b) if Available_Cash = $1000.00
    then, Number of shirts = lower whole number of [(1000.00-640.00)/45.00]
                                    = 360.00/45.00
                                    = 8

(c) if Available_Cash = $720.00

    then, number of shirts = lower whole number of [(720.00-640.00)/45.00]

$$= 80.00/45.00$$
$$= 1$$

Hand Simulation (Tracing) of the Program

The next thing is to execute each instruction of the program using the test data, to see if the results we obtain are the same as the ones computed above (which is the expected result). The purpose of this test is to see if the program is correct and produces the right results.

    Input data is $640.00.

Instruction 1 of the program reads 640.00 into variable Available_Cash, constant Suit_Cost was initialized to 640.00 in the declaration part. Instruction 2 of the program stores (640.00 –640.00) = 0.0 in the variable Money_left. The variable Num_Shirts is made equal to integer number lower than (0.0/45.0) which is 0. Last instruction prints 0 as the number of shirts. This executes correctly for this class of test data. For the class of test data greater than 640.00, we go through the C program with test data 1000.0.

    Declaration has the following variables/constants and their contents.

Available_Cash	Num_Shirts	Suit_Cost	Money_left
		640.0	

Then the effects of instructions of the program after sequential execution with hand, to the contents of the variables/constant are illustrated in the following figure:

Instr 1	Instr 2	Instr 3	Instr 4
1000.00	360.00	8	640.0
Available_cash	Money_left	Numshirts	Suit_cost

These are some of the two ways to verify (evaluate) the correctness of your program. If there is a logical error in the program, the result from this evaluation will reveal that, giving you the opportunity to go back and correct the instructions of the program that, are the cause of the error.

Algorithm and Program Documentation

Algorithm/program documentation has two main types, namely internal and external documentation. The internal documentation is for the benefit of the programmers, evaluation team or maintenance team. The purpose of the internal documentation is to enable the reader of the program understand the intentions of the instructions, the meaning of the variables/constants and the data links between modules of the program. Understanding how the program code works, makes it possible for the program to be modified or improved. Thus, internal documentation consists of comments included inside the algorithm or program. Comments are included generally at the beginning of each function to say what the function does, where its inputs are coming from and the output of the function. Other functions called by this function should also be indicated. A small variable dictionary is also included as part of each function's comments to explain what data each of its variables holds. In this book, the beginning of every comment line is marked with /* and its ending with */.

The objective of internal documentation is to make program easily readable, maintainable and expandable by either the original programmer or another programmer.

External documentation consists of manuals written for the user to understand how to use the program. It is a separate documentation not part of the program, which describes what the program does, its input data, its output data and their types. Objective of the external documentation is to describe how to prepare input to be accepted by the program, how to run the program (any special commands or files involved in running the program need to be specified), and in what form to expect the output data.

```
Example 5.2: Write a program that inputs the numbers of
    seconds a marathoner takes to cover a 3 miles distance.
    The program is expected to print this time in hours,
    minutes and seconds.
```

```c
#include <stdio.h>
void main(void)
{

/* These comments are part of internal documentation */
/* This program inputs integer number representing time in seconds and   */
/* outputs the time in  (hours, minutes and seconds).           */
/* Variables used are:                                    */
/*      second for input time in second              */
/*      hour  for  output time in hour               */
/*      minute for output time in minutes            */
/*      o_second for output time in seconds          */

int second, hour, minutes, o_second;

/* This is the body of the program              */
/* To obtain the numbers of hours, time in second    */
/* is divided by 3600 sec and the remainder */
/* is divided by 60 to get the number of     */
/* minutes while the rest become the output   */
/* second                                       */


        scanf("%d", &second);
        hour = second / 3600;
        minute = (second % 3600) / 60;
        o_second = (second % 3600) % 60;
        printf( "%d seconds is equivalent to %d hours %d minutes %d  seconds", second,
                hour, minute, o_second);
}
```

External Documentation for Example 5.2

This manual shows how to use the program for converting numbers of seconds to hours, minutes and seconds.
Input to the program is an integer representing the number of seconds to be converted.

Output from the program is a sentence giving the number of hours, minutes and seconds it converts to. To run the program, in UNIX at shell prompt (assuming source program code is in file timeconvert.c), type

  cc timeconvert.c
then
  a.out

Output of the program is displayed on the screen.

5.3   Exercises

1.   a) What are internal and external documentations.
        b) Discuss three logic structures found in programs with examples.
        c) List all sequential logic instructions with examples.

2.   Write a program and a flowchart that inputs the radius of a circle and outputs the
        circle's   diameter, circumference and area. (Hint: pi=3.14159, diameter =2r,
        circumference = $2\pi r$ and area = πr^2). Use only sequential logic structure. May also
        use top down design approach. Include internal documentation.

3.   Write a program and a flowchart to print the following message using only
        sequential logic structure.
```
        ****        *            *           ***
        *          *   *        *   *        *   *
        *   ***    *   *        *   *        *     *
        *     *    *   *        *   *        *     *
        *****       *            *           ***
```

4.   Write a program and a flowchart which reads a four digit integer (e.g., 3059) as one
        number and prints each of the digits making up the integer starting with first digit,
        second digit, then third digit and finally fourth digit. Use only sequential logic
        structure. With input 3059, output is 3   0   5   9.

5.   Write a program and a flowchart to compute both solutions for the quadratic
        formula, where

        Use only sequential logic structure.

5.4   References

H.M.Deitel /P.J. Deitel, "C How To Program ", Second edition, Prentice Hall, 1994.
Eliot B. Koffman, "Turbo Pascal", Addison Wesley, 5th edition, 1995.
Maureen, Sprankle, "Problem Solving & Programming Concepts", Third Edition,
       Prentice Hall, 1995.

6.   DECISION LOGIC STRUCTURE

The default control structure (order for execution of programs and algorithmic instructions) is sequential, meaning that once the CPU finishes executing instruction 1, the next instruction executed is instruction 2 and so on. This rule is true only if all instructions are sequential type (Assignment, Read, Print or Function call). Many problems will require a solution that includes other types of instructions, which have the power to dictate an execution order that is different from sequential. One such class of instructions is decision instruction.

Decision instructions have decision logic structure. A decision instruction evaluates a Boolean expression first and based on the value of the expression, specifies a sequence of instructions to be executed next. In a decision instruction, there may be more then one execution path, one of which must be chosen based on the value of "decision Boolean expression". The two main decision instructions are "if instruction" and "switch-case instruction".

6.1   if/else Instruction

The *if* instruction is the most common decision logic structure which conforms to the way humans reason. There are many variants of this instruction. However, all forms of the *if* instruction fit into the general form of the instruction given below for C programs. Note that the general form of *if/else* instruction in C skips the "then" keyword that is included in many other programming languages.

```
if (decision Boolean expression is true)
              {
                        sequence of instructions
                            to execute  if expression is TRUE;

              }
          else
                {

                        sequence of instructions to
                            execute if expression is FALSE;

              }
```

In the *if* instruction, if only one instruction is enclosed in the curly brackets, the brackets can be omitted. If there are no instructions to execute when the *if* decision expression evaluates to false, there is no "else" part and the general *if-else* instruction reduces to an *if* form. When the instruction to execute is another *if* instruction in the "True" part, then, the general *if-else* instruction becomes nested *if-else* form of the instruction (negative logic form). Similarly, when the instruction to execute in the "else" part, is another *if* instruction, then, the general *if-else* instruction becomes a nested *if-else* instruction (positive logic form). It is also possible to have an *if* instruction in both the "True" part and the "else" part.

Shown in a flowchart, the general form of the *if* instruction is:

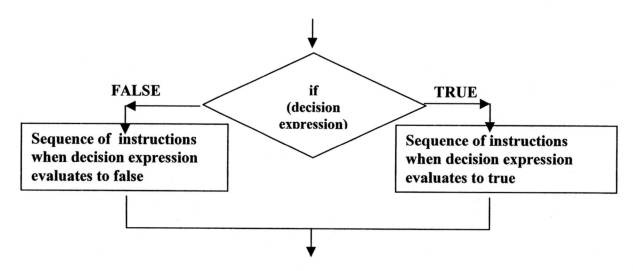

Figure 6.1 Flowchart structure for if /else decision instruction

Example 6.1: Write decision instruction to tell a beginner driver when to proceed at a traffic light intersection with green, yellow and red lights each of which can be either on or off.

Solution
Assume input data green, yellow and red are Boolean types with values already set to true if on, but false if off, output data Go is also Boolean type.

```
if (green)
{

        printf ("Go Ahead ");
}
else
        /* Means light is either red or yellow */
        {

        printf (" Wait until green light goes on");
        }
```

98

6.1.1 if/else form

This is one form of the *if* instruction which is used when there is/are action(s) to be taken if the decision expression evaluates to true and there is/are other action(s) to be taken when decision expression evaluates to false. Example 6.1 is a problem that can be solved using this form of *if*.

Example 6.2: A retail store allows part-time workers a rate of $8.00 an hour for a maximum of 20 hours of work in a week. However, a part-time worker earns $10.00 an hour for each additional hour exceeding the initial 20 hours. Write a decision instruction to compute a given part-time worker's wage for a week.

Solution

Assume input data Num_hours worked (real), is read and output data is Week_wage(real), C program instruction is:

if (Num_hours –20) >0
      Week_wage = (20*8.0)+(Num_hours –20)*10.0;
else
      Week_wage = Num_hours*8.0;

This form of *if* instruction is efficient because only one set of instructions is executed following the test for decision expression. In measuring efficiency of a program, the lower the number of instructions executed in order to arrive at the correct solution, the better the program response time. Also, the lower the number of tests executed, the better the performance of the program. With example 6.2, there is only one test and a total of 2 instructions executed irrespective of what value Num_hours has. For a complete test data set, we can test to see what happens when Num_hours is < 20, =20, and >20. We shall try to rewrite this example using other forms of *if* instruction and check the performance of this form against the other types later.

6.1.2 The *if* form

In the general decision instruction structure shown in figure 6.1 above, the TRUE set of instructions must consist of at least one instruction. However, the FALSE set of instructions may have zero instruction. The case where the FALSE part has no instruction, reduces to an *if* instruction since there is no ELSE part. The *if* instruction just specifies the actions to be taken if the decision expression evaluates to TRUE. Many problems that can be expressed using the *if/else* structure can also be expressed using one or more *if* instructions. Generally, if only one *if* instruction can be used to correctly express an *if/else* instruction, then, the *if* instruction is likely a better choice in this case. However, when more than one *if* instruction is needed to simulate an *if/else* instruction, then the *if* instruction in this case will lead to worse performance. Using only *if* instruction to solve decision problems is sometimes referred to as straight-through logic. Some problems can only be solved with a series of *if* instructions in sequence. A series of tests on different variables not related to each other needs a series of *if* instructions in sequence to implement it.

Example 6.3: Write the program segment for example 6.2 using only C's *if* instructions.

Solution

if   ((Num_hours –20) > 0)
        Week_wage = (20*8.0) +(Num_hours-20)*10.0;

If   ((Num_hours –20) ≤ 0)
        Week_wage = 20*8.0;

Analysis

How many tests and how many instructions are executed when Num_hours has a value > 20, and when it has a value =20, and when it has a value < 20 ?

If Num_hours >20, two test instructions are executed and a total of 3 instructions executed. If Num_hours =20, 2 tests and 3 instructions are executed. Similarly, if Num_hours <20, 2 tests and 3 instructions are executed in total. Thus, whatever the value of Num_hours is, all instructions are executed. This has worse performance than the *if/else* solution.

Example 6.4: Assume you want to assign a number of passengers(P) to different flights such that each aircraft takes only 150 passengers and once you have got 150 passengers for one aircraft, you initialize P back to 0. Similarly, the flight attendants(F) for attending to passengers in the flights are assigned 5 to each aircraft and once you have got 5 FA's assigned, you initialize F back to 0. Write decision instructions for initializing both P and F to 0.

Solution

```
if      (P == 150)
                P = 0;
if      (F == 5)
            F = 0;
```

With example 6.4, only straight through *if* logic solution is meaningful with the problem because the two *if* instructions are used to test two different variables.

6.1.3   Nested *if/else* Form

Nested *if/else* form is the *if* instruction where in the general form shown in figure 6.1, either the TRUE sequence of instructions (negative logic form), or the FALSE sequence (positive logic form), or both sequences contain another "*if*" instruction. In other words, a nested *if/else* instruction may have the form:

```
if      (decision expression 1 is true )
        if      (decision expression for expression1-true is true)
                instructions for when expression of expression1-true is true;
                else
                instructions for when expression of expression1-true is false;
        else
                if      (decision expression for expression1-false is true)
                   instructions for when expression of expression1-false is true;
                else
                instructions for when expression of expression1-false is false;
```

Note that this is the case when both the "True" and "else" parts contain "*if*" instructions. It is still a nested "*if* instruction" when only the "True" part or the "else" part contains an "*if* instruction". The inner "*if* instruction" may also consist of more decision instructions.

Example 6.5: In a city, the monthly bus fare for seniors 65 years or older is half the normal rate of $45.00 for adults while fare rate for kids under the age of 18 is one-third the normal adult rate. Write an If instruction to determine what fare to charge a person given his/her age.

Conditions	Actions
Age >= 65	½ * 45.00
18 ≤ Age < 65	45.00
Age <18	1/3 *45.00

For problems involving nested *if* instructions in only the "Then" or "else" part of an *if* instruction, there are two ways they can be expressed:

(1)   Using positive logic or
(2)   Using negative logic.

These two approaches will be discussed next.

(1) Positive Nested *if* Logic

The positive logic nested *if* instruction basically writes the instruction in such a way that commands the CPU to process some instruction (not decision) when the decision expression evaluates to TRUE but to process another decision when it evaluates to FALSE. This means that with positive nested *if* logic structure, there is a nested "*if*" instruction in the "else" part of the outer "*if*" instruction but not in its "True" part. Another way to remember positive logic is that it consists of a sequence of "*if, else-if*" combinations.

Positive logic nested *if* instruction must be in the form:

```
if      (expression is true)
            instruction (non-decision);
    else
            Decision instruction;
```

Providing a solution to Example 6.5 using Positive Logic Nested *if* gives the following:

Solution 6.5.1

```
if      ( Age >= 65)
            Fare = (0.5 )*45.00;
    else
            if      ( Age >= 18)
                        Fare = 45.00;
                else
                        Fare = 0.33 *45.00;
```

Note: Using the condition/action table is a process that clearly defines the problem and facilitates the solution process. Once a condition/action table is defined, two positive solutions can be defined for the problem. One solution starts with conditions at the top of the table and works downward, while the second solution starts with the condition at the bottom of the table and works upward.

Flowchart solution for the above algorithmic solution is :

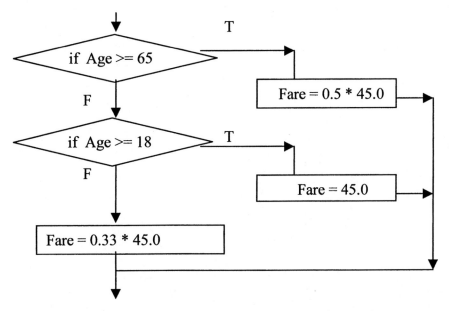

Positive logic is easy to read and understand since it is similar to the way most humans reason.

(1)   Negative Nested *if* Logic

Negative nested *if* logic writes the decision instruction in such a way that it commands the CPU to process a set of instructions (non-decision) when the *if* Boolean expression evaluates to FALSE, but process another decision when the condition evaluates to TRUE. Negative logic is the opposite of positive "if logic". Although, it is sometimes more difficult to read, it may lead to a decrease in the number of instructions and tests needed to solve a problem. This means that with negative "*if* logic", the "nested *if* instruction" is in the "True" part of an outer *if* instruction, not in its "else" part. Negative *if* logic can also be described as a sequence of "if-, if-, ..., if, else, else, ..., else" combinations.

For negative nested logic if instruction, it must be in the form:

    if   (expression is true)
            decision instruction;
      else
            Instruction (non-decision);

103

A negative logic solution to Example 6.5 is discussed next.

Solution 6.5.2

```
if      (Age < 65)
        if      (age < 18)
                Fare = (1/3)*45.0;
            else
                Fare = 45.0;
        else
        Fare = (1/2)*45.0;
```

Flowchart for the negative logic solution is :

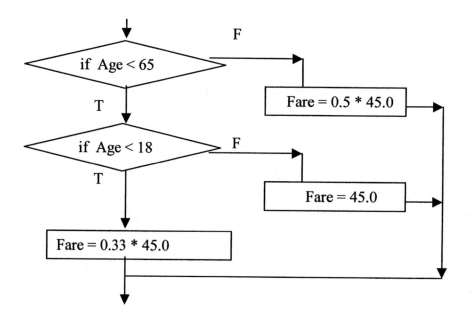

Logic Conversion

In order to improve on program readability or efficiency in terms of number of tests and instructions executed, it may sometimes be necessary to convert positive nested if instruction to a negative one and vice versa and the rules to guide in making such conversions are :

(1)   Write the opposite of each relational operator in every decision (recall operators <,<=, > ,>=, = =, != have respective opposites as >=, >, <=, <, !=, = =).

(2)   Interchange all the TRUE set of instructions with the corresponding *else* set of instructions.

Example 6.6: Calculate the number of bonus air miles earned given that bonus air miles earned by customers, is 100 if traveled miles exceed 5000 in a period of time, but 60 bonus air miles are earned if traveled miles only exceed 3000 while only 10 bonus air miles are earned otherwise by the customer. Write two positive "if" logic algorithmic solutions for the above problem by first defining the condition/action table. Then, write 2 negative logic solutions.

Condition	Action
air miles > 5000	bonus = 100
3000 < air miles ≤ 5000	bonus = 60
air miles ≤ 3000	bonus = 10

Solution 6.6.1 (Positive logic from top)

```
if      (airmiles > 5000 )
                bonus = 100;
    else    if    (airmiles >3000)
                bonus = 60;
          else
                bonus = 10;
```

Solution 6.6.2 (Negative logic equivalent of 6.6.1)

```
if      (airmiles <= 5000 )
        if      (airmiles  <= 3000);
                bonus = 10;
                else
                bonus = 60;
        else
        bonus = 100;
```

Solution 6.6.3 (Positive logic from bottom)

```
if      (airmiles <=  3000 )
        bonus = 10;
        else
        if      (airmiles <= 5000)
                bonus = 60;
                else
                bonus = 100;
```

Solution 6.6.4 (Negative logic equivalent of solution 6.6.3)
                :
        if   (airmiles > 3000)
                if   (airmiles > 5000)
                        bonus = 100;
                        else
                        bonus = 60;
                else
                bonus = 10;
                :

Note how indentation is used to improve the readability of the program/algorithm. In programming a problem, if you need to choose between decision logic, choose the one that is most efficient and most readable. Most efficient logic is usually characterized by fewer tests, and the logic easiest to understand for purposes of future maintenance of code.

6.2   The swith-case Instruction

The second decision logic instruction is the switch-case instruction. The switch-case instruction allows a decision to be made about which one execution path among many to choose. While the *if* instruction allows a decision to be made about which one execution path out of two and whether or not to execute the only defined path, the switch-case instruction chooses one out of many paths. The *if* instruction can implement any switch-case instruction by using nested *if* instructions. In particular, every positive logic nested *if* instruction has a switch-case logic instruction equivalent. switch-case instruction is made up of a number of sets of instructions only one of which will be selected if the switch expression evaluates to the case label attached to this set of instructions.

Example 6.7: Write an algorithm that finds which one of the five zones labeled A, C, K, L, Q in a city should have its count incremented by one. It reads the zone of a given house, increments appropriate zone count, and prints the number of houses in each zone.

106

Solution 6.7.1

```c
#include <stdio.h>
void main (void)
{

    char zone ;
    int  countA=0, countC=0, countK=0,countL=0, countQ=0;

    scanf ("%c", &zone);
    switch (zone) {
            case 'A':       countA++;
                            break;
            case 'C':       countC++;
                            break;
            case 'K':       countK++;
                            break;
            case 'L':       countL++;
                            break;
            case 'Q':       countQ++;
                            break;
            default:
                            printf("unknown zone\n");
    }
printf(" %d %d %d %d %d \n", countA, countC, countK, countL,
countQ);
}
```

General Structures of a switch-case Instruction

In Example 6.7.1 the case expression is a character variable, zone. If it has the value of 'A', then the action(s) after this label will be executed, otherwise if it has the value of 'C', the action on the 'C' label will be executed and so on. If it has a value other than the five listed values, the default part is executed. In C, it is important that the break statement ends each case so that only one alternative will be executed. The break statement is used to prevent the execution of another case's statements. The next instruction executed once a path has been chosen within the switch-case instruction is the instruction following end_of_case curly bracket }. The general form of a switch-case instruction is:

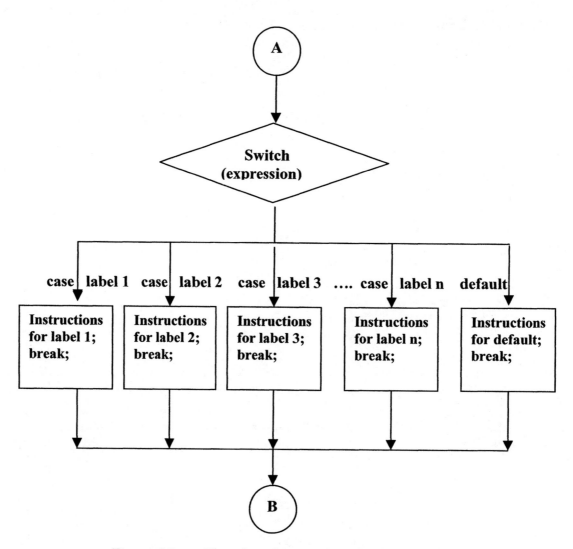

Figure 6.2:   Flowchart for switch-case Instruction

The switch-case instruction is written in a C program as follows:

```
switch (expression) {

        case label 1:    Instructions for case label 1;
                         break;
        case label 2:    Instructions for case label 2;
                         break;
            :
        case label n:    Instructions for case label n;
                         break;
        default: Instructions for default;
                         break;

}
```

Expressed using an *if* instruction, this switch-case general form means:

if   **(switch expression = = case label1)**
       instructions for case label1;
       else
       if   **(switch expression = = case label2)**
           Instructions for case label2;
           else
           if

           ⋮

           else
           if   **(switch expression = = case label*n*)**
              Instructions for case label*n*;
              else
              Instructions for case default;

Note that switch expression can be any expression of enumerative type (like int or char) that evaluates to data of the same type as the case labels. The default case in C is also optional. Thus, it is legal to have a switch-case instruction with no default case.

<u>Solution 6.7.2</u>

Give the nested *if* program segment to the problem in Example 6.7.

```
#include  <stdio.h>
void main(void)
{      char zone;
       int countA=0, countC=0, countK=0, countL=0, countQ=0;
       scanf( "%c", zone);

       if      (zone = = 'A')
               CountA++;
          else
               if      (Zone = = 'C')
                       CountC++;
                 else
                       if      (zone = = 'K')
                               CountK++;
                         else
                               if      (zone == 'L' )
                                       CountL++;
                                 else
                                       if      (zone = = 'Q')
                                               CountQ++
                                         else
                                               printf("unknown zone");

       printf( "%d %d %d %d %d \n", countA, countC, countK, countL, countQ);
}
```

<u>Example 6.7.2</u>

Give the flowchart solution for the problem in Example 6.7
   using switch-case Instruction.

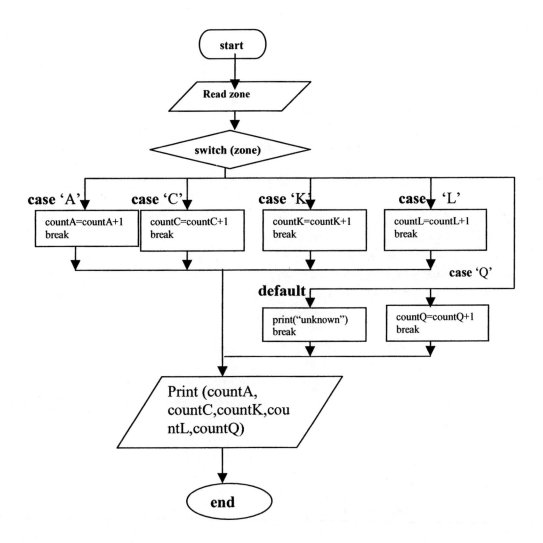

The switch-case instructions are also useful for developing menu-driven programs where a user is allowed to choose one out of many alternative options.

6.3 Exercises

1. A student in a computer class has four tests to write. To get an A in the course, the student must average at least 90% on the four tests. Given the student's scores on the 4 tests, write a C program to determine if the student should get an A or not.

2. Modify problem (1) above such that if a student averages 90 or more he gets an A, but an average of 80-89, gives him a B, an average of 70-79 gives him a C while an average of 60-69 gives him a D. Anything lower than 60 is a grade of F. Write a C program to determine a student's grade given his/her test scores.
   (a)   Give 4 different solutions using nested if instruction.
   (b)   Set up 4 flowcharts corresponding to (b).
   (c)   Give a solution using switch-case instruction.

3. A car rental shop has two plans. In the first plan, you can rent a car for $40 per day with unlimited mileage. In the second plan, you can rent a car for $30 per day with an extra charge of 15c per mile. Write a C program to determine which is the better plan for a customer to purchase given the number of days and total number of miles she plans to use the car.

4. Your friend got a new job where he/she can be paid according to one of 4 plans:

   plan A: A salary of $600 per month plus a commission of 3% of gross sales;
   plan B: A salary of $750 per month plus a commission of 2% of gross sales;
   plan C: A salary of $1000 per month plus a commission of 2% of gross sales over $9000;
   plan D: A salary of $1500.

   Given the average monthly gross sale, write a program to determine the best plan for your friend.

5. Write a program that finds and prints the smallest of 5 integers read as input.

6. Write a program that chooses which of the six languages English, French, Swahili, Japanese, Chinese and German to give services in, when a foreign service client types in a code of 1 to 6 corresponding to the 6 languages in the order given.

7. A palindrome is a number or text, which reads the same backwards as it does, when read forward. For example: 31213, 85958, 72427 and 59195 are palindromes. Write a program that reads in a five-digit integer and determines whether or not it is a palindrome. You can use integer division and modulus operators to obtain individual digits of the number.

8. Write a program that reads in the three sides of a triangle (as integers) and determines whether the triangle is an isosceles triangle (with two sides equal), an equilateral triangle

(with three sides equal), or a scalene triangle (with no sides equal). Also print a message if it is not a triangle.

Note: A triangle must have the sum of any of its two sides longer than the remaining side.

6.4 References

Kris Jamsa, "Jamsa's C Programmer's Bible – The Ultimate Guide to C Programming", first edition, Onword Press, Thomson Learning, 2002.

Elliott B. Koffman, "Turbo PASCAL" 5th ed., Addison Wesley, 1995.

Maureen Sprankle, "Problem Solving and Programming Concepts", 3rd ed., Prentice Hall, 1995.

Uckan Yuksel, "Problem Solving Using C – Structured Programming Technique", 2nd edition, WCB McGraw-Hill, 1999.

7. REPETITION LOGIC STRUCTURE

The third logic structure for programs and algorithms is the repetition logic structure. The repetition structure allows a sequence of instructions to be executed as long as a condition is satisfied. Problems involving counting and accumulating totals use repetition instruction. Three types of C program/algorithmic instructions that belong to repetition logic structure are <u>while,</u> <u>do-while</u> and <u>for</u> instructions.

Repetition instruction can either be counter control or event-control type. The number of times a repetition instruction executes a sequence of instructions is called the number of iterations it executes. If the number of iterations a repetition or loop instruction executes, is known before entering the loop the first time, then the termination of the loop can be controlled by counting the number of times it has executed and this type of loop instruction is called counter control loop instruction. On the other hand, if the number of times to execute a loop instruction is not known before hand but is determined by the effect of an instruction inside the loop, this loop is called an event-controlled loop. Loop instructions enable the same set of tasks to be done for different data sets, for example, computing the total score of each of the 300 students in a class given their assignment scores, quiz, test scores and the score evaluation formula.

7.1   while Instruction

The while instruction is one of the three instructions used to implement repetition. The while instruction tells the CPU to first test a condition(s) and as long as this condition(s) evaluates to true, to keep repeating all instructions between the "begin" bracket and "end" bracket of the while loop instruction. The general structure of the while instruction is:

```
Initialization Instructions;
     while (expression(s))
     {
             instruction 1;
             instruction 2;
             :
             instruction n;
             update instructions;
     }
```

The flowchart for while instruction is:

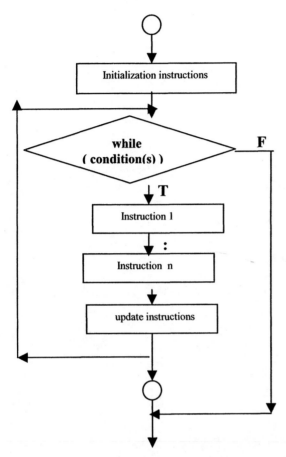

Figure 7.1:   *while Instruction Flowchart*

Example 7.1: Write an algorithm that counts the number of houses belonging to each of the five zones A, C, K, L, and Q in a city. A total of 300 houses are to be checked and the zone of each house is read in as input.

Solution 7.1

Since we are told there are 300 houses to check, we know up-front the number of times the loop needs to execute before termination and this is a counter_controlled loop.

```c
#include <stdio.h>

void main(void) {
        /*--- Declaration of local variables ---*/
        char zone;
        int countA=0, countC=0, countK=0, countL=0, countQ=0;
        int knt=1, Num_house=300;

        printf("Please enter the 300 zones for the houses: ");
        /*--- Read the 300 zones that houses are located in ---*/

        while (knt <= Num_house)
        {
                scanf("%c", &zone);
                /*--- Increment the corresponding zone ---*/
                switch( zone ) /*--- switch-case statement ---*/
                {
                        case 'A': countA++;
                                break;
                        case 'C': countC++;
                                break;
                        case 'K': countK++;
                                break;
                        case 'L': countL++;
                                break;
                        case 'Q': countQ++;
                                break;
                        case '\n': knt--;
                                break;

                        default: printf("Unknown zone\n");
                                break;
                } /*--- End of case statement ---*/

                knt++;
        } /*--- End of while loop ---*/

        /*--- Print the number of houses in each zone ---*/
        printf("\nZone A:%d\nZone C:%d\nZone K:%d\nZone L:%d\nZone
Q:%d\n", countA, countC, countK, countL, countQ);

}       /*--- End of Program ---*/
```

Note that the "case '\n': knt --; break;" instructions are used to subtract 1 added each time a newline character is read at the end of each input character. Usually, "while instruction" can be used for both event-controlled and counter-controlled loop. From the example and the general structure of a loop instruction, the following important parts of a loop instruction are identifiable.

1. Initialization of control variable and others.

   Control variable is the variable that its value determines when the loop should be terminated. The control variable needs to be set to an initial value before the test for termination and this initialization is done in the first part of the loop. In the example solution 7.1, the control variable is *knt* and it was initialized to 1 in the initialization part. Other variables initialized are those used to accumulate total or do some counting depending on the problem being solved.

2. Testing the control variables for termination.

   Since a loop instruction executes a set of instructions as long as a certain condition is true, the test to evaluate if this loop condition is satisfied, is performed with the control variable. In example solution 7.1, this test is done with the instruction while (knt <= 300).

2. Updating the control variable to proceed to next data item. If the control variable is not updated to advance to the next data item, the loop will execute infinitely because the test for loop continuation will then be true always, while the condition for loop termination is never reached. The condition for loop termination is reached when the test condition for loop condition is false. For example, if it is known that 300 houses are to be checked but initialization step sets knt=1 before entering the loop. Then, if this control variable is not incremented by 1 inside the loop body, the value of *knt* will always be 1 and the loop will execute infinitely. This is because the test "while (knt <= 300)" will always be true but a condition that evaluates to false is needed for the loop to be terminated in this case.

   This is an undesirable situation, which causes the CPU to do enormous work that is incorrect. Once there is an instruction inside the loop body, which changes the control variable appropriately, then at some point the test for termination will evaluate to true and in particular other data elements will be processed. In example solution 7.1, the statement that updates the control variable is knt =knt +1.

With the "while instruction", these three important components of a loop structure appear in the order listed above. Other instructions to solve the problem being addressed are included inside the loop.

Event-controlled Loops

From the example solution 7.1, it can be seen how a counter control loop is implemented using a while instruction, by counting and using the counter as the control variable. We can, on the other hand, be told that the number of houses to check their zone is unknown and the user is expected to keep typing in the zone of the houses as they arrive until there are no more houses to check indicated by entering '0', a special value used to mark the end of data, called Sentinel. This means that data lines look like the following:

```
A
A
A
C
Q
L
Q
Q
.
.
.
C
C
A
L
0  ◄──────────  sentinel value
```

One way to implement event controlled loop is with the use of a sentinel to mark the end of data values. A sentinel value is also called a dummy, a flag or signal value. It should be the same data type as the control variable used to test for termination.

Example 7.2: Write a program that counts the number of houses belonging to each of the five zones A, C, K, L, Q in a city. The zone of each house is entered for reading and a sentinel value of '0' is used to mark the end of data. Also record the total number of houses counted.

Solution 7.2

We do not know the number of houses to count but shall start counting as each house is processed and shall know that all houses have been processed once we read '0' (the sentinel value).

```c
#include <stdio.h>

void main(void) {
        /*--- Declaration of local variables ---*/
        char zone;
        int countA=0, countC=0, countK=0, countL=0, countQ=0;
        int knt=1, Num_house=0;


        printf("Please enter the zones for the houses: ");

        /*--- Read the zones that houses are located in ---*/
```

```
        scanf("%c", &zone);        /* for first zone initialization */
        while (zone != '0')
        {
                Numhouse++;
                /*--- Increment the corresponding zone ---*/
                switch( zone ) /*--- switch-case statement ---*/
                {
                        case 'A': countA++;
                                break;
                        case 'C': countC++;
                                break;
                        case 'K': countK++;
                                break;
                        case 'L': countL++;
                                break;
                        case 'Q': countQ++;
                                break;
                        case '\n': num_house --; /*removes newline read */
                                break;
                        default: printf("Unknown zone\n");
                                break;
                } /*--- End of case statement ---*/
                scanf("%c", &zone);        /* the update read operation */
        } /*--- End of while loop ---*/

        /*--- Print the number of houses in each zone ---*/
        printf("\nZone A:%d\nZone C:%d\nZone K:%d\nZone L:%d\nZone
Q:%d\n", countA, countC, countK, countL, countQ);
printf( "Number of houses counted: %d\n", num_house);

}       /*--- End of Program ---*/
```

Note that in this solution 7.2, the control variable is zone and the instruction for initialization is "scanf("%c", &zone);" which reads the first data element before the loop instruction. The instruction that does the updating is the second " scanf("%c", &zone);" inside the while loop instruction, which reads the next data element. The instruction that tests for termination is "while (zone != '0')", which wants the loop to be executed as long as zone is not equal to the sentinel value of '0'.

The End-of-File (EOF) marker

Another way to mark the end of data line being processed in a loop is by entering an end-of-file character to indicate that there is no more data. When EOF character, a system-dependent character, is used to mark the end of data, it serves as the sentinel. When input data is typed directly from the keyboard, on Unix system, the EOF character is

<return><ctrl/d>

In MSDOS, EOF character is

<ctrl/z>

In programs, eof variable is set to true when there is no more data. When a Read instruction finds a character other than the eof character, the eof variable is set to false. In many languages, eof variable is undefined initially and its value is set when a Read instruction is executed. For this reason, the first Read instruction executed before the "while test" for termination, serves to initialize the eof variable, which, in this case is the control variable. This means that the input data for the house zone problem on Unix now appears as follows:

```
        A
        A
        A
        C
        Q
        L
        Q
        Q
        .
        .
        .
        C
        A
        L
<return> <ctrl/d>
```

Example 7.3: Write an algorithm that counts the number of houses belonging to each of the 5 zones A, C, K, L, Q in a city. The zone of each house is entered for reading and the last data line marked with eof character. Also print the number of houses processed.

Solution 7.3

```c
#include <stdio.h>

void main(void) {
      /*--- Declaration of local variables ---*/
      char zone;
      int countA=0, countC=0, countK=0, countL=0, countQ=0;
      int knt=1, Num_house=1;


      printf("Please enter the zones for the houses: ");

      /*Both the initial and update read are done with the while test*/
      while ((scanf("%c", &zone)) != EOF)
      {
            /*--- Increment the corresponding zone ---*/
            switch( zone ) /*--- Case statement ---*/
            {
                  case 'A': countA++;
                        break;
                  case 'C': countC++;
                        break;
                  case 'K': countK++;
                        break;
                  case 'L': countL++;
                        break;
                  case 'Q': countQ++;
                        break;
                  case '\n': num_house --; /*removes newline read */
                        break;
                  default: printf("Unknown zone\n");
                        break;
            } /*--- End of case statement ---*/
            Num_house++;
      } /*--- End of while loop ---*/

      /*--- Print the number of houses in each zone ---*/
      printf("\nZone A:%d\nZone C:%d\nZone K:%d\nZone L:%d\nZone
Q:%d\n", countA, countC, countK, countL, countQ);
printf( "Number of houses counted: %d\n", Num_house-1);

}       /*--- End of Program ---*/
```

In the example solution 7.3, the control variable is eof (special system variable), which can only be set with a Read instruction. To test whether this EOF variable has been set to true, the instruction " while ((scanf("%c", &zone)) != EOF) " is used. If the last executed scanf instruction reads an EOF character because there is no more data, the EOF variable is set to true causing the expression ((scanf("%c", &zone)) != EOF) to evaluate to false, Once the repetition expression is false, the loop is terminated. The update instruction is also a scanf("%c", &zone) instruction inside the loop. In this example, both the initialization and update instructions are combined with the *while* test instruction. Note that to count the number of houses processed, the variable num_house is initialized to 1.

When the first data line is read and processed inside the loop, num_house gets updated to 2 just before the next data line is read. If this next data line is eof, test for termination will succeed. This means that while only one data line was processed, if we print the num_house variable immediately after the loop, we shall be getting a value of 2 (an incorrect value). This is because of the initialization of this variable to 1. Therefore, in other to get the correct number of data lines processed when the control variable is initialized to 1, after the while loop, an instruction that subtracts 1 from num_house is included.

7.2   do-while Instructions

The do-while instruction is the second instruction used to implement repetition. This instruction tells the computer to repeat the set of instructions between the "do" and the "while" keywords until the do-while expression is FALSE. This means, first time, execute all instructions between the "do" and "while", then, evaluate the do-while expression. If this expression is TRUE, repeat the execution of the instructions in do-while block and keep repeating until the expression evaluates to FALSE, and next the instruction following the do-while instruction is executed. The differences between do-while and while instructions are that :

(i) the test for loop termination condition is done at the beginning with while loop but the test for loop termination is performed at the end of a do-while loop.

(ii) With the do-while loop, the loop instructions are processed at least once before the termination condition is tested but in the while loop, the loop instruction may be processed zero times if the termination condition evaluates to false the first time. Thus, for problems that may need zero iterations, do-while loops should not be used (e.g., no data line read).

The format of the do-while instruction is:

```
Initialization instructions;
do
      {
              instruction 1;
              instruction 2;
              .
              instruction n;
              update instructions;
      } while (expression);
```

The flowchart for the do-while instruction is:

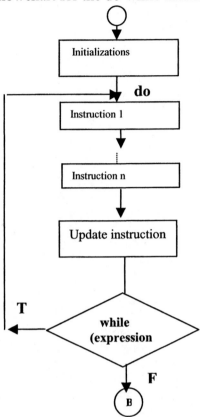

Example 7.4: A computer class took a quiz. The scores (integer in the range 0 to 100) for this quiz are available to you although the number of students who took the quiz is not known. Determine the class average on the quiz. You can use a sentinel value of -1 to mark the end of the data. Assume that at least one student wrote the quiz.

Solution 7.4

```c
#include <stdio.h>

main() {
    /*--- Declaration and initialization of local variables ---*/
    int score=0, Num_stn=0, sum=0;
    float average;

    /*--- Read quiz scores until '-1' is read ---*/
```

```
    printf("To exit type '-1'\n");
    printf("Please enter the student's quiz score: ");
    scanf("%d", &score);      /* initialization read */
    do {

            /*--- Increment the student counter ---*/
            Num_stn++;

            /*--- Add the scores read ---*/
            sum += score;
            printf("Please enter the student's quiz score: ");
            scanf("%d", &score);      /*update read */

    }      while( score != -1 ); /*--- End of do/while ---*/

    /*--- Calculate the average ---*/
    average = (float) sum/(Num_stn);

    /*--- Print the average ---*/
    printf("The class average is %.2f\n", average);

} /*--- End of Program ---*/
```

A do-while instruction can be used to implement both counter-control and event-control
loops. Any problem implemented with a while instruction can be converted to a do-while
instruction and vice versa. The while test condition and a do-while test condition are the
same. For example, in solution 7.4 , the do-while test condition is (score != -1) and it is
the same test condition for a while instruction, except that the while test condition is
placed at the beginning, where the "do" keyword is placed in the do-while instruction. If
well structured, the other loop components can work the same way with both "while" and
"do-while" instructions. When converting a "while loop" implementation of a problem,
to a "do-while loop" implementation, an "if instruction" can precede the "do" instruction
for the purpose of testing the first instance and this will enable it avoid executing the loop
body when there is no data. For example, the "while loop" segment below can be
converted to the following "do-while" segment.

```
:
scanf("%d", &score);
while (score != -1)
      {
            :
            scanf("%d", &score);
      }
```

_____

124

```
scanf("%d", &score);
If (score != -1)
    {
        do {
                :
            scanf("%d", &score);
        } while (score != 1);
    } /* this is end of if then */
```

7.3   for Loop Instruction (automatic loop control)

The third instruction for implementing repetition is the "*for* instruction". The *for* instruction can only be used to implement counter-control loops where the number of iterations is known at the beginning of the loop. With the "*for* instruction", the initialization, termination value, testing and update of the control variable all occur in the one *for* instruction. The *for* instruction increments or decrements the control variable automatically each time the loop is repeated. The general format of a *for* instruction is:

```
for (counter = begin value; counter  (relational_operator)  end value;
                counter=counter (+|-) step)
    {
            instruction 1;
            instruction 2;
            .
            .
            .
            instruction n;
    }
```

In the above format for the "*for* instruction", there are three parameters specified in the header instruction of the "*for*". The first parameter specifies the "begin" value of the counter variable. The second parameter specifies the loop continuation value for the counter. A loop continuation condition, *counter* $<=$ *end* is used when the update parameter (the third parameter in the instruction) is updating the counter at a positive step (that is, incrementing). This condition says to keep executing this loop for all values of the counter that are less than or equal to the specified end value. An alternative loop continuation condition *counter* $>=$ *end* is generally used when the update parameter is updating the counter at a negative step (that is, decrementing). When this condition is used, it says to keep executing the loop for all values of the counter that are greater than or equal to the specified end value. Other variations of these two forms of the second "for" parameters like counter $<$ end, counter $>$ end, can also be used with appropriate third parameter. The third parameter of the "for instruction" updates the control variable (counter) at a positive or negative step as specified.

125

In flowchart form, the for Instruction is :

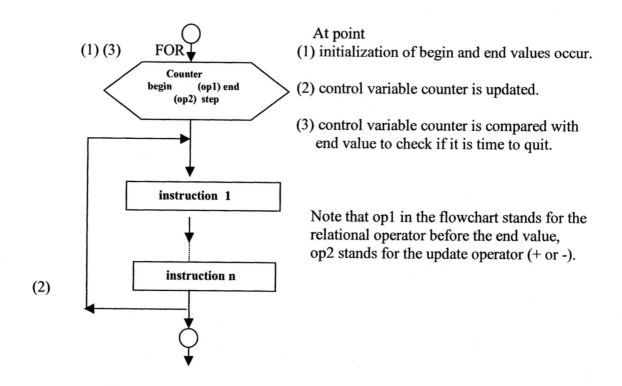

(1) (3)   FOR

At point
(1) initialization of begin and end values occur.

(2) control variable counter is updated.

(3) control variable counter is compared with
    end value to check if it is time to quit.

Note that op1 in the flowchart stands for the
relational operator before the end value,
op2 stands for the update operator (+ or -).

If the *step* leads to a positive increment of the counter, the "for" instruction starts by first initializing (setting) the control variable "counter" to "begin" value. Then, it compares the control variable with the *end* value to see if it should quit the loop or not. If counter <= end, it executes the loop instruction, otherwise, it quits the loop to go to the next instruction following the *for* instruction. At the end of each iteration, it updates the control variable by adding the value *step* to it. Thus, in this case, it becomes counter = counter + *step* before it goes back to the beginning of the loop to test for termination. Also, note that if *step* has a negative value (e.g., -1), then updating the control variable will constitute decrementing it and not incrementing it. In this case the "begin" value should be higher than the "end" value for the loop to execute at least once. Note that it is possible for a *for* instruction to execute zero times. This means that the test for termination evaluates to true the first time. This will happen, when *step* is positive, and the "begin" value is bigger than the "end" value, (e.g., for (knt = 5; knt <= 2; knt++)) or when *step* is negative, and the "begin" value is smaller than the "end" value (e.g., for (knt = 2; knt >=5; knt--).

Example 7.5: A computer class of 15 students took a quiz. The scores (integers in the range of 0 to 100) for this quiz are available to you. Determine the class average on the quiz.

Solution 7.5

```c
#include <stdio.h>

/*--- Control Module 0000 ---*/
void main(void) {
        /*--- Declaration and initialization of local variables ---*/
        int score=0, Num_stn=15, sum=0, knt=0;
        float average;

        printf("Enter 15 student's scores\n");
        /*--- Read quiz scores for 15 students ---*/
        for (knt = 1 ; knt <= Num_stn ; knt++) {
                printf("Please enter the quiz score: ");
                scanf( "%d", &score );

                /*--- Add the scores read ---*/
                sum += score;
        }       /*--- End for loop ---*/

        /*--- Calculate the average ---*/
        average = (float) sum/Num_stn;

        /*--- Print the average ---*/
        printf("The class average is %.2f\n", average);

} /*--- End of Program ---*/
```

7.4   Other Branching Instructions – goto, break, continue

goto Instruction

As in most programming languages, C provides a goto statement, which causes execution control to branch to a specific instruction with a specified label. The format of a goto instruction is:

```
        goto label;
        ....
        ....
label:
```

For example, the following program sequence uses the goto instruction to compute the sum of ten numbers read:

```c
#include <stdio.h>

void main (void)
{
 int Num, Sum = 0, knt = 0;
 label1:
        scanf ("%d", &Num);
        Sum += Num;
        knt++;
        if (knt < 10) goto label1;
        printf ("%d is the sum\n", Sum);
}
```

break Instruction

A C's break instruction in a loop causes the loop's execution to terminate immediately. The next instruction to execute after the break instruction, in this case, is the instruction following the loop instruction. The format of the break instruction is:

```
break;
```

For example, we can use the break instruction to prevent a loop that is summing ten numbers from getting up to ten iterations if we tell it to break as soon as 5 numbers are added, in the following way:

```c
….
….
for (knt = 0; knt < 10; knt++)
{
 scanf ("%d", &Num);
 Sum += Num;
 if (knt == 5) break;
}
….
```

continue Instruction

While C's break instruction in a loop terminates the execution of the loop, the C's continue instruction ends only the execution of the current iteration, increments the loop counter and continues to execute the next normal loop iteration. In other words, the continue instruction simply skips the current iteration but continues with the execution of the loop. The format of the continue instruction is:

```
continue;
```

For example, assume we want to add only the even numbers among the ten numbers read, the following segment allows us do that:

....

....

```
Sum = 0;
for (knt = 0; knt < 10; knt++)
{
 scanf ("%d", &Num);
 if (Num % 2)    /*it is odd*/
        continue;
 Sum += Num;
}
```

....

....

These instructions goto, break, continue generally make programs hard to read and maintain. Their use in clear, structured programming is discouraged. There are very few occasions when they are necessary, e.g., the break instruction in the switch-case instruction is necessary.

7.5   Nested Loops

A nested loop is a loop instruction inside an outer loop instruction. There may be several levels of nesting. The loop instructions involved in the nesting do not need to be the same types of loop instructions. This means that a "for" instruction can be nested inside a "while" instruction and vice versa.   Some problems like printing tables of values or matrices require two loops, an outer loop for changing the row to print, and an inner loop for changing the column to print.

Example 7.6: Write an algorithm which utilizes nested looping to produce the following table of values.   Print the heading first.

A	A+2	A+4	A+6
3	5	7	9
6	8	10	12
9	11	13	15
12	14	16	18
15	17	19	21

Solution 7.6

It is easy to observe from the table, a regular pattern which can be described using program instructions. The pattern is : " if we know the value at position row "r", column "c", then, to obtain the value at position row "r", column "c+1"(that is, the same row), we need to add 2 to the value at row "r", column "c". Also, if we want to obtain the element in the next row "r+1", but the same column "c", we need to add 3 to the element at row "r", column "c". Note that A is the first value 3 at position row 1, column 1.

```
#include <stdio.h>
void main(void) {
        /*--- Declaration of local variables ---*/
        int A, num_row, num_col, row, col;

        /*--- Read the number of rows and columns ---*/
        printf("Enter a value for A, number of rows and number of columns
        (Eg. 3 5 4): ");
        scanf("%d%d%d", &A, &num_row, &num_col);

        /*--- Print header ---*/
        printf("  A  A+2 A+4 A+6\n");

        /*--- Prints values based on the number of rows and columns ---*/
        for (row = A ; row <= A+((num_row-1)*3) ; row+=3) {
                for (col = row ; col <= row+((num_col-1)*2) ; col+=2) {
                        printf("%3d ", col);
                } /*--- End of second for loop ---*/
                printf("\n"); /*--- Skips to the next line ---*/
        }       /*--- End of first for loop ---*/

}       /*--- End of Program ---*/
```

A simpler version of the above solution, which is not as general is:

```
#include <stdio.h>
void main(void) {
        /*--- Declaration of local variables ---*/
        int num_row, num_col, row, col;


        /*--- Print header ---*/
        printf("  A  A+2 A+4 A+6\n");

        /*--- Prints values based on the number of rows and columns ---*/
        for (row = 3 ; row <= 15; row+=3) {
                for (col = row ; col <= (row+6) ; col+=2) {
                        printf("%3d ", col);
                } /*--- End of second for loop ---*/
                printf("\n"); /*--- Skips to the next line ---*/
        }       /*--- End of first for loop ---*/

}       /*--- End of Program ---*/
```

130

7.6   Recursion

Recursion is triggered by an instruction in either the main module or a sub-module of the solution which makes a call to a function (called a recursive function). When a call is made to a recursive function, recursion occurs because the original one function call to this function sets the recursive function calling itself a number of times in order to come up with a solution. Thus, recursion is a type of repetitive call made to a function by itself.

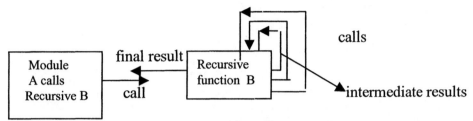

Figure 7.2:   Recursive Function B

Module A calls recursive B and this recursive function B calls itself 3 times. The result of the third and last call made to module B by itself must be returned before the result of its second call is obtained, result of function B's second call is used to complete the first call it made to itself and the result of this first call is used to obtain the result sent to module A, which made the initial function call to module B. The number of times a recursive function makes recursive calls to itself is determined by a base case. The base case is similar to the condition for loop termination and must be defined. If a base case is not included in the definition of the recursive function, it will loop indefinitely. The base case is the simplest form of the problem solved by this function and every value other than the base case needs the base case to be solved and so on.

For example, factorial problem,

$$1! = 1 \qquad \text{(this is the base case)}$$
$$2! = 2 * 1!$$
$$3! = 3 * 2!$$
$$4! = 4*3!$$

Thus, we can generalize with the formula

$$n! = n* (n-1)!$$

Once, we define a general behavior and a base case for termination, we can write a recursive function to compute n! given any positive n. Note that if n=1, it simply returns 1 because it is the base case. But if n = 2, it calls itself and finds it is still not the base case, then it reduces the problem to 2* 1! before making the second call to compute 1!. This second call discovers now that 1! = 1, returns this result of 1 to the first call so that it completes the computation 2*1! as 2*1 = 2 sent back to the calling function.

131

Example 7.7: Write a program to compute the factorial of any positive integer n using a recursive function.

Solution 7.7


```
#include <stdio.h>

/*--- Declaration of function prototypes ---*/
int factorial(int);

void main(void) {
        /*--- Declaration of local variables ---*/
        int n, nfact;

        /*--- Read value for N ---*/
        printf("Please enter a value for N: ");
        scanf("%d", &n);

        /*--- Calling the factorial function ---*/
        nfact = factorial(n);

        /*--- Print the factorial of N ---*/
        printf("N:%d Factorial of N:%d\n", n, nfact);

}       /*--- End of Program ---*/

/*--- Function definition for factorial ---*/
int factorial(int n) {

/*--- If n is 1 return 1 to the calling module else call factorial
            and send N-1, a recursive call ---*/
        if (n == 1 )
                return 1;
        else
                return (n*factorial( n-1 ));
}
```

Some problems are naturally recursive, e.g., the factorial problem. This means that defining a solution is easier when thought of as recursive. However, problems that can be solved recursively can also be solved iteratively. Since recursive call sets aside a temporary memory space for that instance of the function call, recursive approach carries more overhead in terms of memory space needed during execution and also takes more processor time. Another example of a naturally recursive problem is the problem of towers of Hanoi. The problem definition for the towers of Hanoi is: there are 3 pegs and 4 disks placed on the first peg. The task is to move the disks one at a time to peg 3 ensuring that at no time should a disk be placed on top of a smaller disk. The middle peg is an auxiliary peg which must be empty at the beginning and end of the game.

Starting
Position

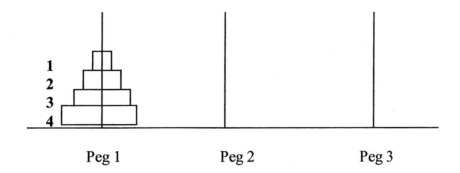

Peg 1   Peg 2   Peg 3

End
Position

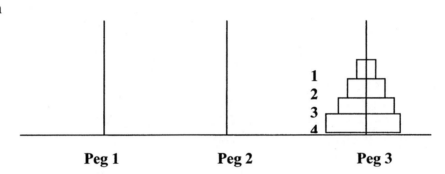

Peg 1   **Peg 2**   **Peg 3**

Solution to the Towers of Hanoi Problem

To solve this problem, the control module can execute the operation
(1) Transfer the 4 disks from Peg 1 to Peg 3.
This requires a function that is capable of transferring a disk or a number of disks from one peg to another. Constructing a function (Towers) to perform the transfer of N disks from Peg 1 to Peg 3 would require performing the following sequence of tasks:
(a) Get N-1 disks moved from Peg 1 to Peg 2
(b) Move the Nth disk from Peg 1 to Peg 3
(c) Move the N-1 disks now from Peg 2 to Peg 3.

The function, Towers implements tasks (a) to (c) through recursion and by accepting as its parameters, the number of disks to transfer, the begin peg to move them from, the end peg to move them to and the auxiliary peg for keeping intermediate results. When more than one disk is to be moved, it recursively stores temporarily all but the last biggest disk on the auxiliary peg before moving the biggest peg to the end peg. Then, the disks stored in the auxiliary peg are moved in a similar fashion to the end peg. The base condition that ensures termination of the recursive call is when there is no disk, it quits, otherwise it moves N-1 to auxiliary peg before moving the Nth disk to end peg. The implication is that when there is only one disk, it moves (1-1) or 0 disk to auxiliary peg before moving the 1 disk to the end peg. The solution to the problem is given below:

```c
#include <stdio.h>
/* Function prototypes */
void Towers(int, int, int, int);
void main (void)
{
        int  Ndisks, BeginPeg, AuxPeg, EndPeg;
        int Ndisks, BeginPeg, AuxPeg, EndPeg;

        /* body of the main module */
        scanf("Ndisks BeginPeg AuxPeg EndPeg are %d %d %d %d", &Ndisks,
        &BeginPeg,  &AuxPeg, &EndPeg);
        Towers(Ndisks,BeginPeg,AuxPeg,EndPeg);
 } /* of the control module   */


/*  Definition of the recursive function, Towers    */
void Towers (int Ndisks, int BeginPeg, int AuxPeg, int EndPeg)
{
        if  (Ndisks> 0)
                {
                        Towers(Ndisks-1, BeginPeg, EndPeg, AuxPeg);
                        printf ("Move disk %d from Peg %d to Peg %d\n",
                         Ndisks,BeginPeg, EndPeg);
                        Towers(Ndisks-1, AuxPeg, BeginPeg, EndPeg);
                }       /* of the if then        */
}       /* of function Towers              */
```

7.7   Exercises

1. Write a program to update your bank passbook in an account given the last printed balance, and all transactions since the last update with the following information (date of transaction, type of transaction and account). Your algorithm should print date of each transaction, type of each transaction and balance after each transaction. Possible transaction types are cash withdrawal (wd), cash deposit (dep), and bill payment (bpm). Read date as string.

    Sample input
    Last balance = 6,000.00

    Transactions

Date	type	amount
12 Mar , 1998	wd	500.00
25 Mar, 1998	dep	100.70
27 Mar, 1998	bpm	57.50

2.   (a).   What output is printed by the following loop? N is of type integer.

```
N = 0
while ( N <= 10 )
{
        N++;
        Printf("%d", N);
}
```

(b) How many times did the loop execute?
(c) What is printed if we change the first instruction to N = 1?
(d) How many iterations are executed this time?
(e) How should the algorithm be modified to have each number printed on a separate line?

3.   (a). What output is printed by this nested loop?

```
A = 5;
while  (A >= 1)
{
        B = 1;

    while  (B >= 1)
            {
```

```
                printf ("%d", B);
                        B--;
                }
                printf ("\n");
                A--;
        }
```

(b) Identify the statements that are updating the control variables.

(c) Re-write this program segment such that the two statements B-- and A-- are changed to B++ and A++ respectively. Modify any other instructions appropriately to produce the same results.

(d) Re-write this program segment using do-while instructions in place of while instructions.

(e) Re-write this program segment using a for instruction in place of a while instruction.

4. Write a program that computes the total weekly sales income of a small convenience store. Only 50 items are sold in this store and the code, unit price and number sold of each item are available to read for each week. However, it is not known ahead of time the number of weeks to be computed. The last data is marked with end_of_file marker. Print each week and the total weekly sales income for that week.

Sample input:

item code	unit price	number sold this week
01	$8.00	10
02	$0.50	200
.		
.		
50	$1.50	150

Sample output:

week	total sales income
1	$ _.00
2	$ _.00
.	
.	
.	

5. (a) Write a recursive function to compute the exponential notation or x^n (x raised to power n). Include a complete solution that calls this function. Show how 10^5 is computed using your solution.

(b) Solve the problem in 5(a) above using iterative approach.

(c) Which solution is more efficient ?

6. Write a program to compute the average test score obtained by each of the students whose 4 test scores for a course are given. Last data line is a sentinel value of –1 for only the first test score. Print the student name, test scores and average test score in the format shown in the sample output below.

Sample input

| 70 50 | 80 | 90 | John_James |
| 54 63 | 71 | 75 | Mary_Kate |

.

.

.

-1

sample output

student name	test scores	average test score
John James	70, 50, 80, 90	75.5

.

.

.

7. Modify the problem in 6 above to also print the student with the highest test average.

7.8   References

Nell Dale/ chip weems, "pascal", third edition, heath 1991.

Kris Jamsa, "Jamsa's C Programmer's Bible – The Ultimate Guide to C Programming", first edition, Onword Press, Thomson Learning, 2002.

Elliott B. Koffman, "Turbo PASCAL" 5th ed., Addison Wesley, 1995.

Reedy/Bittinges, Randolph, "Essential mathematics", 6th edition, Addison Wesley 1992.

Uckan Yuksel, "Problem Solving Using C – Structured Programming Technique", 2nd edition, WCB McGraw-Hill, 1999.

8.   ARRAYS DATA STRUCTURE

We have so far stored and manipulated variables of type integer (int), real (float), character (char), and Boolean (int). These types are primitive types provided by the programming language of use and hold only one data value each. Types integer, character and Boolean are also called ordinal types. An ordinal type value has a predecessor value and a successor value except the first element of the type, which has only a successor and no predecessor; and the last element of the type which has a predecessor and no successor. For example, character data type has characters coded in ASCII format 000 to 127 and character 065 (letter A) has a predecessor 064(character @) and a successor 066 (letter B). The ASCII code is listed in Appendix A.

The main point in this chapter is that sometimes it is easier for programs to handle data not as individual variables of primitive type but as a collection of data elements of the same type, which has elements identified through a subscript or index. An array is a data structure that can store multiple values of the same type under one variable name. For example, 100 seats in a classroom can be referred to as "seat" in a program. In this case, 100 memory cells are given for only one variable name "seat".

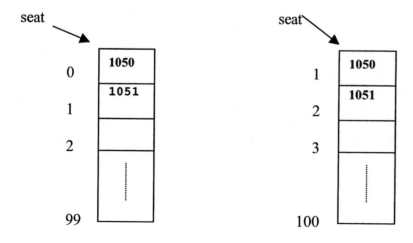

To store data or read data from the memory cell representing the second seat, we write seat [1] if the base is 0 or seat [2] if the base is 1. This type of tabular organization of a collection of data of the same type is called <u>Array</u> data type. C uses the base case of 0 for storing array data.

An array data structure allows us to use the same variable name for more than 1 data element of the same type. It allows more than one memory location to be reserved for a single variable. Each element of the array variable is referenced using its subscript. If we are not solving the classroom seat problem above with arrays, we shall need 100 variables of type string declared. Declaring too many variables makes both coding and reading the program more difficult as use of too many different variables makes the program more prone to error. Arrays are useful for many data values of the same type, e.g., integer scores of assignment 1 for 20 students, ages of all company workers and so on.

Array variables have to be declared at the beginning of the program in order to be used. The declaration of an array variable specifies both the size (number of elements in the array) and its dimension (number of subscripts needed to address each element of the array). A one-dimensional array has only one subscript while a multi-dimensional array has more than one subscript. An array is also called a table. If the size and the dimension of the array are not allowed to change within the program, it means the array is declared statically. On the other hand, if the number of array locations is a pointer variable which can be increased or reduced during program execution, then, it is dynamic array declaration.

8.1   One-dimensional Array

A one-dimensional array is a table with just one column. This means that only one subscript is needed to address any element of the table. To declare a one dimensional array variable for holding integer scores for assignment 1 of seven students, we write:

    int assn1 [7] ;

From this declaration, it is seen that the variable assn1 is a one dimensional array variable which has seven elements. There are two possible choices for base element (first element). Some programming languages make the first array element the 0th element and others make it the 1st element. If the base element is 0, with the above declaration, the 7th element has subscript 6. However, if the base element is 1, then the 7th element has subscript 7. In C, the base element is 0, meaning that the first array element begins at offset 0 and the last array element occurs one location before the array's size. The general format for declaring an array variable with name arrayname and data type, type with "size" number of elements is:

type arrayname[size];

Initial values can also be assigned to an array during declaration as for example:
int assn1[7] = {9, 8, 8, 7, 4, 6, 9};

This declaration initializes assn1[0] to 9, assn1[1] to 8, assn1[2] to 8 and so on, up to assn1[6] initialized to 9. The first element of an array can be referenced using the array name with a zero subscript, e.g., assn1[0] for the array assn1. The name of an array used without a subscript is a pointer to its first element. Thus, another way to reference the first element of an array is *arrayname, e.g., *assn1.

One-dimensional array is the simplest array structure. Like any other variable, an array variable can be read, printed, used in assignment instruction as the variable on the left-hand side or right hand side of the equality sign. An array variable can be used any where any simple variable can be used in other types of instructions (decision, repetition and function calls). In a function call, an array parameter is simply specified without including its dimension or size. However, if a function is receiving an array parameter through a function call, its function's parameter list in both the function prototype and the function definition, must indicate that an array is the expected argument. For example, the function header for a function to read data into a one-dimensional array is:

    void ReadData(int assn[], int size) ;
Its prototype is declared as:
    void ReadData(int [], int);

A valid function call to the function ReadData declared as given above is ReadData(assn1, 7). This function call is made in a calling module where the variable assn1 is already declared to be a one-dimensional array of integers with 7 elements. The size of this array is passed in this case since it is already allowed as a parameter in both the function prototype and function header. Note that in the function call, the actual parameter (assn1) used in the call does not have to be the same name as the formal parameter (assn) used in the function header. Passing the arrayname (e.g., assn1) as actual parameter in a function call is a call-by-reference call since the arrayname used alone is the address of the first element of the array. This means that a call-by-reference array formal parameter in a function header is declared using only the array type and its name and square brackets without the indirection operator (*) as in:
    void ReadData(int assn[], int size) ;   /* call-by-reference array with its size */
This function header allows the array assn[] to be modified inside the function since it is a call-by-reference parameter. To specify a call-by-value parameter using an array parameter, the formal array parameter should have its declaration in the function header preceded by the keyword "const". For example, to have a function to show the values of array assn1[7], we do not require this function to change the values of the array and thus, the appropriate function header is:
    void Showassn1(const int assn[], int); /*call-by-value array*/
The function prototype for the call-by-value array parameter with its size passed as well is:
    void Showassn1(const int [], int);

The function prototype does not require the array name, but requires the specification of its data type and dimension. The size of the array can also be passed as a parameter as is the case with the example above. However, in the function definition, the array name and size are used in instructions. Thus, passing the size of an array as another parameter is used to improve clarity of code, but is not a requirement. This enables the parameter "size" to be used in the function definition for controlling loop iterations. If the array size is not passed in as parameter, then, the number of elements in the array has to be entered inside the function. The size of the array may also be declared globally with a constant variable name in the variable declaration section or with the #define directive. When the size of the array is declared globally, it is not passed as a parameter during function call.

Example 8.1: Write a C program to read and print the marks for the 10 assignments obtained by student Maggie as well as her average assignment marks.

Solution 8.1

```
#include <stdio.h>

/*--- Control Module 0000 ---*/
void main() {
    /*--- Declaration and initialization of local variables ---*/
    int sum=0, assn[10], knt;
    float average;

    /*--- Read 10 assignment marks and store them in an array ---*/
    for (knt = 0 ; knt < 10 ; knt++) {
        printf("Please enter the mark for assignment %d: ", knt+1);
        scanf("%d", &assn[knt]);

        /*--- Total the scores read ---*/
        sum = sum + assn[knt];
    }
    /*--- Calculate the average --*/
    average = (float) sum/10;

    /*--- Print the average ---*/
    printf("Average: %.2f\n", average);

}       /*--- End of Program ---*/
```

The assignment marks for Maggie are:

assn cell	content
0	10
1	9
2	7
3	5
4	7
5	8
6	6
7	10
8	10
9	8

The problem in example 8.1 can actually be solved to obtain the same result without using an array since we are reading and printing, and thus, never needing to go back and look at the values of array elements after we go to the next element. However, if we are told to print all assignment marks less than the average assignment mark, then, it becomes absolutely necessary to store the data as an array since there is need to come back and compare each element after computing the average mark. In writing efficient codes, wise use of memory locations is encouraged.

Example 8.2: Write a program that computes the assignment average for assignments 1 and 2 in a small class of only seven students whose names and integer identifications are: Maggie (id 1050), John (id 1051), Ken (id 1052), Joy (id 1053), Pat (id 1054), Tim (id 1055), and Tom (id 1056). The program should read the student ids and compute the average mark obtained by each student. It should print the ids of the students, their averages as well as all student ids with an average higher than both assignment averages.

Solution 8.2

We can use one-dimensional arrays in form of parallel arrays (that is, two or more arrays in which values in the same elements relate to each other). The parallel arrays in this case are: student[7] for storing the seven student ids, assn1[7] for storing the corresponding assignment 1 mark for each of the seven students; and assn2[7] for storing the corresponding assignment 2 mark for the seven students.

```
#include <stdio.h>

/*--- Declaration of function prototypes ---*/

void ReadCalc(int [], int, int [], int [], float[], float *, float *);
void PrintResult(const int [], const float [], const int [], const int [], float, float);
void FindGoodstudent(const int [], const float [], float, float);
```

```c
/*--- Control Module 0000 ---*/
void main(void) {
      /*--- Declaration of variables ---*/
      int student[7];
      int assn1[7], assn2[7];
      float stn_ave[7], assn1_ave, assn2_ave;


      /*--- Function calls ---*/
      ReadCalc(student, 7, assn1, assn2, stn_ave, &assn1_ave,
               &assn2_ave); /*--- Call by reference ---*/
      PrintResult(student, stn_ave, assn1, assn2, assn1_ave,
               assn2_ave);
      FindGoodstudent(student, stn_ave, assn1_ave, assn2_ave);
}     /*--- End of Program ---*/


/*--- Function definition for ReadCalc---*/


void ReadCalc(int student[], int size, int assn1[], int assn2[], float
stn_ave [], float *assn1_ave, float *assn2_ave)
{
      /*--- Declaration of local variables ---*/
      int knt, assn1sum=0, assn2sum=0;

      /*--- Read assignment marks and names for 7 students ---*/
      for (knt = 0 ; knt < size ; knt++) {
           printf("\nPlease enter the student id:");
           scanf("%d", &student[knt]);
           printf("Please enter the mark of assignment 1:");
           scanf("%d", &assn1[knt] );
           printf("Please enter the mark of assignment 2:");
           scanf("%d", &assn2[knt]);

           /*--- Add the marks for assignment1 & assignment2 ---*/
           assn1sum += assn1[knt];
           assn2sum += assn2[knt];

           /*--- Calculate the average mark for the student ---*/
           stn_ave[knt] = (float) (assn1[knt]+assn2[knt])/2;
      }

/*--Calculate the class average for assignment1 and assignment2 ---*/
      *assn1_ave = (float) assn1sum / 7;
      *assn2_ave = (float) assn2sum / 7;

}                 /* end of function definition for ReadCalc      */
```

```
/******************/
/*--- Function definition for PrintResult ---*/
void PrintResult(const int student[], const float stn_ave[], const int
assn1[], const int assn2[], float assn1_ave, float assn2_ave)
{
      /*--- Declaration of local variables ---*/
      int knt;

      /*--- Print all 7 student's ids and averages ---*/
      printf("\n");
      printf("Student id     Assn1        Assn2        Average \n");
      for (knt = 0 ; knt < 7 ; knt++) {
            printf("%d       %d       %d        %.2f\n", student[knt],
                 assn1[knt], assn2[knt], stn_ave[knt]);
      }

      /*--- Print the class average for assignment1 & assignment2 --*/
      printf("\nAssn averages: %.2f %.2f\n", assn1_ave, assn2_ave);
}


/******************/
/* Funtion Definition for FindGoodstudent                      */
void FindGoodstudent(const int student[], const float stnave[], float
assn1ave, float assn2ave){
      int knt;
      for (knt = 0 ; knt < 7 ; knt++) {
            if ((stnave[knt] > assn1ave) && (stnave[knt] > assn2ave))
            printf ("student %d is a very good student\n",
            student[knt]);
            }    /* end of for loop */
}             /* end of function FindGoodstudent  */
```

The sample input data for solution 8.2 above is:

Student[7]	assn1[7]	assn2[7]
1050	10	9
1051	7	8
1052	8	8
1053	5	7
1054	10	4
1055	9	6
1056	6	9

The output data of solution 8.2 is given below:

1050	10	9	9.5
1051	7	8	7.5
1052	8	8	8.0
1053	5	7	6.0
1054	10	4	7.0
1055	9	6	7.5
1056	6	9	7.5

Assn averages: 7.89   7.33

student 1050 is a very good student
student 1052 is a very good student

8.2   Two – dimensional arrays

A two-dimensional array has two subscripts for addressing its elements, unlike a one-dimensional array, which has one subscript. The two subscripts of a two dimensional array are used to indicate in which row number and in which column number the element is located. A two-dimensional array is then a variable for a number of memory locations, conceptually laid out in a number of rows and a number of columns. For example, to store the marks for assignments 1 and 2 for the seven students discussed in the last section using separate arrays, we can use a more elegant approach to store all these 14 marks for assignments 1 and 2 for the 7 students in a two-dimensional array called assn[7][2]. The lay out of assn[7][2] is given below:

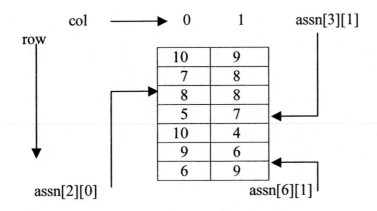

Generally, to declare a variable to be a 2-dimensional array of *type*, the following format is used:

type   variable[rowsize][columnsize];

For example, to declare this variable, assn as a two dimensional array variable with 7 rows and 20 columns, for use in the program, we include the following declaration:

int assn[7][2] ;

We can see there are 7 rows and 2 columns in this array which the declaration instruction indicates. Since there are more than 1 column, nested loop instructions are used to read from, or load data into this array. The elements of the array are indicated using their location in the table (which row, which column); e.g., assn[2][0] = 8, assn[3][1] = 7, assn[4][1] = 4 and assn[6][1] = 9, in the above array. Generally, data are read either rowise or columnwise. This means that we start from row 0 and read the element in row 0, column 0, and next the element in row 0, column 1 is read. Then, we move to the next row, which is row 1, where we read the two elements in columns 0 and 1 before proceeding to row 2 and so on. We can see that reading data rowise entails using an outer loop, which allows the row to be changing slower than an inner loop for changing the columns. In other words, we need a nested loop like the following to accomplish these types of rowise navigation.

```
for (r = 0; r < numrow; r++)
  {
  for (c = 0; c < numcol; c++)
      {
      ------------------
      ------------------
      }
  }
```

The instructions inside the double nested loop depends on what kind of tasks the program is performing. If the loops are used simply to read the two dimensional array variable, then the only instruction inside the innermost loop is scanf("%d", &variable[r][c]). Sometimes, some instructions are needed in the outer loop before or after the second *for* instruction

Example 8.3: Solve the problem of example 8.2, computing the assignment averages for assignments 1 and 2 as well as the average mark for each of the seven students using 2-dimensional array where necessary. Use the students' names here rather than their integer student ids.

Solution 8.3

```
#include <stdio.h>

/*--- Declaration of function prototypes ---*/

void ReadData(char [][10], int, int [][2], float [], float []);
void PrintResult(const char [][10], const int [][2], const float [],
const float []);
```

146

```c
void main(void) {
        /*--- Declaration of variables ---*/
        char student[7][10];
        int assn[7][2];
        float stn_ave[7], assn_ave[2];

        /*--- Function calls ---*/
        ReadData(student, 7, assn, stn_ave, assn_ave); /*--- Call by
reference ---*/
        PrintResult(student, assn, stn_ave, assn_ave);

}       /*--- End of Program ---*/

/*******************/
/*--- Function definition for ReadData ---*/
void ReadData(char names[][10], int size, int assn[][2],
            float stn_ave[], float assn_ave []) {
        /*--- Declaration of local variables ---*/
        int knt, c, assnsum[2]={0,0};

        /*--- Read the names for 7 students ---*/
        for (knt = 0 ; knt < size ; knt++) {
                printf("\nPlease enter the student name:");
                scanf("%s", names[knt]);

        /*--- Read 2 assignment marks for the student ---*/
                for (c = 0 ; c < 2 ; c++) {
                printf("Please enter the mark of assignment %d:", c+1);
                        scanf("%d", &assn[knt][c]);

                /*--- Add the marks for assignment1 & assignment2 ---*/
                        assnsum[c] = assnsum[c] + assn[knt][c];
                }

                /*--- Calculate the average mark for the student ---*/
                stn_ave[knt] = (float) (assn[knt][0]+assn[knt][1])/2;
        }
/*--- Calculate the class average for assignment1 & assignment2 ---*/
        for (c = 0 ; c < 2 ; c++) {
                assn_ave[c] = (float) assnsum[c]/7;
        }
}
/*******************/
/*--- Function definition for PrintResult ---*/
void PrintResult(cost char student[][10], const int assn[][2], const
float stn_ave[], const float assn_ave[])
{
        /*--- Declaration of local variables ---*/
        int knt, c;

        /*--- Print all 7 student's names and averages ---*/
        printf("\n");
        printf("Student Name      Assn1          Assn2          Average \n");
        for (knt = 0 ; knt < 7 ; knt++) {
                printf("%s", student[knt]);
                for (c = 0; c < 2; c++) {
                        printf("     %d ", assn[knt][c]); }
```

```
                    printf("%.2f\n", stn_ave[knt]); }
}         /* end of for knt  */


/*--- Print the class average for assignment1 & assignment2 --*/
printf("\nAssn averages: %.2f %.2f\n", assn_ave[0], assn_ave[1]);


/* Now, find students whose averages are higher than */
/* both assignment averages.                         */
for (knt = 0 ; knt < 7 ; knt++) {
      if ((stn_ave[knt] > assn_ave[0]) &&
            (stn_ave[knt] > assn_ave[1]))
      printf ("student %s is a very good student\n",
      student[knt]);
      }    /* end of for knt loop */
}          /* end of function PrintResult  */
```

In Solution 8.3, the function prototype for ReadData has a 2-dimensional array argument and thus the size of the array column is specified while that of the row is not. The variable assn[7][2] stores in the first column the assignment marks for assignment 1 and in the second column the assignment marks for assignment 2. The total assignment 1 mark is in assnsum[0] while that for assignment 2 is in assnsum[1]. The average student marks are in the array stn_ave[7]. Generally, actual parameters in function calls can be variables declared in the calling module, constant data values (e.g., 7) or expressions of the correct type (e.g., 7+4). Thus, the function call ReadData(student, 7, assn, stn_ave, assn_ave) made in the control module, passes the actual data value 7 as size (or number of students) to the function.

A 2-dimensional array with "a" rows and "b" columns is called an "a * b" (a by b) array. Thus, assn[7][2] is a "7*2" array.

Multi-dimensional Arrays

A multi_dimensional array is an array with n subscripts where n is bigger than 2. In other words, a multi-dimensional array has more than 2 subscripts or dimensions. An example of a multi-dimensional array is a 3-dimensional array which has 3 subscripts to indicate which row, which column and which depth is defining the location of a point (element) in a 3-D organization like that in a cuboid.

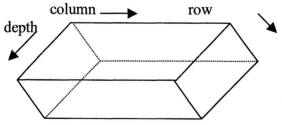

If the variable is cube[5][10][7] it means there are 5*10*7 = 350 data elements in this array variable cube. Any element among the 350 is referenced by cube[row][col][dep] where row, col and dep are assigned values between 0 and 4, 0 and 9, 0 and 6, respectively in the reference. Loading data into a 3 dimensional array like this, requires a triple nested loop instruction. In general, loading data into an n-dimensional array needs an n-time nested loop instruction.

8.3   Dynamic Variables and Dynamic Arrays

Static variables are created when they are declared in the program and are destroyed only when the function (block) they are declared in, terminates. For global variables, this means they are destroyed when the main program they are global to, terminates and for local variables, they are destroyed when the function they are local in, terminates. Static variables have static duration.

Dynamic variables can be created in a function when needed and destroyed when no longer needed before the function or program termination. Thus, dynamic variables have dynamic duration. To create a dynamic variable of type int, for example, we must first declare a pointer variable of type int (say, *markptr) and then we use the standard library function malloc (from header file <stdlib.h>) to assign an address of a dynamic memory space for int data to our pointer variable (markptr). The standard function malloc returns NULL if it is not able to allocate requested space. Creating a dynamic variable, pointed to by markptr, is done with the following declarations.

        int   *markptr; / *pointer variable to int data */
        markptr = malloc(sizeof(int)); /* assign address of dynamic space to markptr*/
The two declarations can also go in one initialized declaration as:
        int *markptr = malloc(sizeof(int));
With the above declared, we can now refer to the dynamic variable pointed to by markptr using the indirection operator (*) as in *markptr. We can assign a value to this dynamic variable using for example:
        *markptr = 10;
When we no longer want this variable, we can destroy it using the sequence of instructions:
        free (markptr) ;   /*memory is reclaimed but markptr still has the address*/
        markptr = NULL;   /*removes the address of the dynamic space(deallocates)*/

A dynamic array can also be created in a similar way by first declaring a pointer to the same type as the array and using malloc to reserve dynamic space. For example, to reserve dynamic space for the array mark[10] of int, we can use the following:
        int   *mark;
        mark = malloc(10 * sizeof(int));
This can also be declared in one line as:
        int *mark = malloc(10 * sizeof(int));
Note that the function calloc can also be used in place of malloc to accomplish the same thing and in addition, to initialize the dynamic array to 0 if it is numeric and NULL if it is character type. To destroy the dynamic array variable, use:
        free(mark);
        mark = NULL;

8.4   String Processing

String data type is implemented in C, as an array of char type. String data are non-numeric data that consist of a combination of ascii or textual characters. Examples of string data are "John Adams", "231 University Avenue W". In counting the length or number of characters in a string data, each blank space is also counted as a character. As already introduced in chapter 3, data of type string is declared in C as an array of characters using the general format:

char variable[number of characters];

Example declaration of string data is:
char studentname[20];

The declaration above specifies that the string variable, studentname can hold a string with up to 19 characters, that is, strings with 0 to 19 characters since the 20th character, the element studentname[19] is the null character '\0', which marks the end of every string. Thus, a string variable declared with size, n, actually can store a maximum of n-1 characters, plus the null character as the nth character of the string.

An Array of Strings

A student name like "John Adam" is declared as a one dimensional array of characters, char studentname[20]. If we want to declare a string variable to hold 10 such student names, this variable has to be declared as a 2-dimensional array of characters, studentname[10][20]. If these two array sizes are given constant names for clarity as numstudent=10, numchars=20 respectively, using these names, an array of 10 student names can be declared as :
char studentname[numstudents][numchars];

This array of 10 student names can also be initialized during declaration as:
char studentname[10][20] = {"John Smith", "John Adams", "Mary Goods",
        "Peter Kent", "Chu Lee", "Paul Best", "Okee Ndu", "Pat Madu",
        "Andrew New", "Mark Ogods"};

String Library Function and String Assignment Operations

In order to use any of the string builtin functions, the C library file, <string.h> has to be included in the program. These functions are used for assigning a string value to a string variable, assigning a substring of one string to a variable, concatenating two strings, returning the length of a string, etc. To assign a string value to a string variable, a simple assignment instruction (like newname="John Adams") does not accomplish this task in C as in other languages. The only place an assignment instruction is used to assign a value to a string variable is during declaration of the variable. A summary of available string builtin functions is provided in the table below.

function	description	example
strcat (s1, s2)	Appends string s2 to s1	strcat ("Hello ", "you") is "Hello you"
strchr (s1, c)	Returns the pointer address of first occurrence of character c in string s1 if found, otherwise null	strchr ("Hello", 'l') is &Hello + 2
strcmp (s1, s2)	Compares s1 to s2 and returns 0, <0, >0 if s1 equals, less or greater than s2	strcmp ("good", "good") = 0 strcmp ("good", "ok") = -1
strcpy (s1,s2)	Copies string s2 into string s2, which is returned	strcpy ("", "Passed") is "Passed"
strcspn (s1, s2)	Returns length of maximum initial segment of s1 with characters not in s2	strcspn ("Hello", "lo") is 2
strlen (s1)	Returns length of s1	strlen ("Important") is 9
strncat (s1, s2, n)	Appends leftmost n characters of s2 to the end of s1 that it returns	strncat ("Hello", "class", 2) returns "Hellocl"
strncmp (s1, s2, n)	Compares leftmost n characters of s1 to s2 and returns 0, >0, <0 if s1 equals, less or greater than s2	strncmp ("Hello", "class", 2) returns 1
strncpy (s1, s2, n)	Copies n leftmost characters of s2 into returned s1	strncpy ("Hello ", "your", 3) is "Hello you"
strpbrk (s1, s2)	Returns pointer address after first occurrence of any character in s2 found in s1, otherwise it returns null pointer	strpbrk ("Hello", "me") is &Hello +1
strrchr (s1, c)	Returns pointer address of last occurrence of c in s1 if found, otherwise returns null pointer	strrchr ("Hello", 'l') is &Hello + 3
strspn (s1, s2)	Returns the length of the maximum initial segment of s1 that contains s2	strspn ("Import", "port") is 4
strstr (s1, s2)	Returns the pointer address of the first occurrence of s2 in s1 if found, otherwise null pointer is returned	strstr ("Import", "port") is &Import + 2
strtok (s1, s2)	Breaks up s1 into its tokens delimited by any character in s2. While first call to strtok contains s1, subsequent calls for tokenizing the same s1 should have null as first argument.	strtok ("size_type", "_") has tokens "size", "type"

A summary of Important String Functions in C

In the body of the program, string values can only be assigned with the string copying functions like strcpy. The instruction, strcpy(s1, s2) will copy the string s2 into string s1. For example, strcpy(newname, "John") will copy the name "John" into the variable, newname. In using strcpy, the length of s2 should not be more than the declared length of s2 or there might be overflow of characters in memory into the next allocated location, which may cause a runtime error.

Other string copying functions for copying all or parts of one string to another are: strncpy(s1, s2, numchars) for copying the first numchars from string s2 into string s1, strcat(s1,s2) for concatenating the string s2 to string s1 keeping the result in s1, strncat(s1,s2,n) concatenates the first n characters of s2 to the end of s1. While the functions strcpy and strcat include the null character, '\0' at the end of the result string, the functions like strncpy and strncat which work with n characters of the source string, do not include the null character at the end of the result string unless this character happens to be one of the n characters. When strncpy or strncat are used, the null character, '\0' should be assigned at the end of the result string. For example, to copy the first 8 characters of the string, "Computer Science" into a variable, result, we use the following sequence of instructions:

strncpy(result, "Computer Science", 8);
result[8] = '\0';

This will have the effect of keeping the string, "Computer" in result. Note that result[0] to result[7] store the string "Computer", while the next element result[8] now has '\0' which is equivalent to NULL.

Other Functions for String Input/Output Operations–gets, fgets, puts, fputs, sscanf, fprintf

Recall that reading a string variable with scanf requires no address operator (&) since a string is an array and the name of the array is the pointer to, or address of, the first character in the string. The function gets (get string) is used to read an entire line of string data including embedded blank character. The format for the gets function call is:

gets (stringvariable);

E.g., gets(line);
The function, fgets is used to read a string of at most a specified length – 1 from a specified file pointer variable (fptr), into a string variable with the format:

fgets (stringvariable, length, filepointer);

The corresponding output functions for printing entire line of string to monitor and file are respectively, puts and fputs. Their formats are:

puts (stringvariable);

and

fputs(stringvariable, length, filepointer);

The sscanf is used to read data input of any type (like integer, string, float) into specified variables from a string specified as the first argument, using the given second argument format specifier. For example, sscanf ("June15 1960", "%s %d", &bdate, &byear) will read June15 into bdate and 1960 into byear. The format for sscanf is:

sscanf(string_to_readfrom, format specifiers, variablelist);

Similarly, sprintf is used to print the values of specified variables, not to the monitor, but into the first string argument with the format:

sprintf(string_to_readfrom, format specifiers, variablelist);

Other functions for string and character input/output exist in C and are available in the <stdio.h> library file. A summary of important one is provided in the following table.

152

function	description
fgetc(filpointer)	Reads next character from file as integer.
fgets(stringvariable,n,filepointer)	Reads up to n-1 characters from file into variable.
fprintf(filepointer, format specifiers, variablelist)	Prints values of variables in the list into file with specified file pointer using format specifiers.
fputc(charvariable, filepointer)	Prints character into file with filepointer.
fread(arraypointer, type size, numelements, filepointer)	Reads up to numelements of type with size bytes from file into elements of array in the first argument.
fscanf(filepointer, format specifers, variablelis)	Read into variable list data from file in first argument.
fwrite(arraypointer, type size, numelements, filepointer)	Prints into file up to numelements of type with size bytes from array in the first argument.
getc(filepointer)	Reads next character as integer from file.
getchar( )	Returns next character from the keyboard.
putc(charvariable, filepointer)	Similar to fputc. Writes character to file.
putchar(charvariable)	Writes character to standard output.
puts(charvariable)	Prints string to standard output.
sprintf(stringvariable, format specifiers, variablelist)	Prints variablelist into string variable instead of monitor.
sscanf(stringvariable, format specifiers, variablelist)	Reads data from string variable into variable list.

Some Other C string and character Handling Functions

8.5   Sequential Search

One important application of arrays is searching. Searching is the act of looking for a value in a table of values (an array) using a key value. Assume 100 test scores for students in a course are stored in an array score[100]. You want to find out if there is any 96% in the table of scores. In this case, your search key is 96 and the array to search is score[100]. There are two ways you can go about doing the searching, namely sequential or binary search techniques. With the sequential search approach, the test scores do not need to be sorted before the searching. The sequential searching entails comparing every element of the array with the search key until a match is found. If the first element of the array happens to be equal to the search key, a hit is made at just one comparison and searching ends, this is the best case scenario. On the other hand, if the last element (which is element 99) is the only 96 in the table of scores, then it means we can only find it after 100 comparisons and this is the worst case scenario. If the search key is not a member of values in the array, this is discovered only after 100 comparisons. Thus, on the average, the sequential search algorithm will compare the search key with half the number of elements in the array before finding or not finding a match.

Example 8.4: Given *n* test scores and a search key score, write a sequential search algorithm to return the position of the first element in the array equal to the key score.

153

Solution 8.4

```c
#include <stdio.h>

/*--- Declaration of global variables ---*/
int scores[99], key, position, size;

/*--- Control Module 0000 ---*/
void main(void) {
    /*--- Declaration of local variables ---*/
    int k, i;

    /*--- Read the size of the list ---*/
    printf( "Please enter the size of the score list: " );
    scanf( "%d", &size );

    /*--- Read the key to search for ---*/
    printf( "Please enter the search key: " );
    scanf( "%d", &key );

    /*--- Read the elements of the list ---*/
    for ( i = 1 ; i <= size ; i++ ) {
        printf( "Please enter the %d score: ", i );
        scanf( "%d", &scores[i] );
    }

/* Searching using k, keeping track of position searched */
    k=1;
    while (k <= size && key != scores[k]) {
        k++;
    } /*--- End while loop ---*/

    /*--- Print the result of the search ---*/
    if (k > size)
        printf("Element not found");
    else
        printf("Element %d is equal to %d\n", k, key);
}       /*--- End of Program ---*/
```

In solution 8.4, first the number of elements in the array to search and the search key are read. Then, the *n* elements in the array are read next before they are searched. The variable k is used to keep track of which array element is being searched next. Initially k is set to 0 because the first element is to be searched. The while instruction has a termination condition which says that as long as the search key is not equal to this element, and we have not searched the last element in the array, keep incrementing k to enable a search of the next element. However, if element k is equal to search key or k>n indicating the last element has been searched, the loop terminates. The "if instruction" following the "while loop" is used to find out which of the two conditions caused loop termination so that appropriate message is printed. Sequential search technique is simple and works well for small or unsorted arrays. It is however inefficient for large arrays because in the worst case, the algorithm will search through all n elements of the array before either finding the value or not finding it.

8.6   Binary Search Algorithm

Binary search is another technique for finding if a search key value is an element of an array. Binary search technique is faster than sequential search method if the array is sorted. Binary search works only if the array is sorted. For example, given a list of n test scores sorted in ascending order, binary search first compares the mid element with the search key. If the mid element is equal to the search key, then the key is matched after only one comparison. However, if the middle element is less than the search key, the left half of the list is discarded since all the elements on the left half of the list, are less than both the middle element and the search key. Then, we continue the searching process with only the right half of the list, which contains only elements bigger than the middle element. Again define the middle element of this new shortened list and compare it with the search key, if not equal, choose either the left half if middle element is greater than search key or choose the right half if middle element is less than search key. Continue this process until a match is made or the new lower bound becomes bigger than the size of the array (upper bound).

Example 8.5: Assume the following 10 test scores
      56   63   65   71   72   75   80   81   84   86
      are stored in an array test[10]. Find out if a score of
      84 is in this array using binary search.

Solution 8.5

```
#include <stdio.h>

/*--- Declaration of global variables ---*/
int test[10], key=84, number=10;
int UB, LB, found, mid, k;

/*--- Note that flag value equal 0 is false and 1 is ture ---*/

void main(void) {
        printf("Enter 10 test scores in ascending order\n");
        printf("A binary search will determine if 84 is in the list\n");

        /*--- Read 10 scores ---*/
        for (k = 0 ; k < 10 ; k++) {
             printf("Please enter test %d score: ", k);
             scanf("%d", &test[k]);
        }

/*First time the lower bound LB needs to be set to 1 */
/*- and the upper bound UB set to number.They are used to*/
/*--- define the middle element mid ---*/
        LB = 0;
        UB = number-1;
```

155

```
        /*--- We want to compare with middle element ---*/
        /*--- as long as a match is not found ---*/
        found = 0;

        while (!(found) && LB <= UB) {
/*- We check if the middle element is the same as the search key after
---*/
/*--- defining the middle element ---*/
                mid= (LB+UB)/2;
                if (test[mid] == key)
                        found= 1;
                else
                        if (test[mid] < key)
                                LB= mid + 1;
                        else
                                UB= mid - 1 ;
        } /*--- End while loop ---*/

/*--Find out if the last element of the array has been searched ---*/
/*--- This is the case when the new lower bound is bigger than the
upper bound ---*/
        /*--- Print the results of the search ---*/
        if ( LB > UB )
                printf("\nSearch key %d is not found", key);
        else
                printf("\nElement %d is equal to %d\n", mid + 1, key);
}       /*--- End of Program ---*/
```

Evaluation

With the list

56   63   65   71   72   75   80   81   84   86

1. number = 10, key = 84
    LB = 0,   UB = 9,   found = 0 = false

    1st iteration of while loop

        mid = (0+9)/2 = 4
        test[4] = 72 ≠ 84
        test[4] = 72 < 84

    ∴ LB = mid +1 = 5

    2nd iteration

       !(found) && (LB< UB)
    ≡ !(false) && (5< 9)
          T && T = T

156

mid = (5+9)/2 = 7
(test[7] =81) < (key = 84)

∴   LB = mid +1 = 7+1 =8

3rd iteration
    !(found) && (LB < UB)
≡   !(false) && (8< 9)
≡   T   &&   T = T

    mid = (8+9)/2 = 8
    (test[8] = 84) = (key = 84); found = true

4th iteration
    !(found) && (LB < UB)
≡   !(true) && (8 < 9)
≡   F   && T = F

Thus, 4th iteration is not executed.

The last "if" instruction checks if
    LB > UB
i.e. 8> 9   = F

∴ The printed message is:

Search key is element 8.

It can be seen that with binary search in this example, the search key is matched after 3 comparisons but with sequential search, it would be matched after 9 comparisons. In general, with n elements, binary search has time complexity of O(log n/log 2) meaning that highest number of comparisons is x where n ≈ 2^x. Thus, with 10 elements, $10 ≈ 2^4$, the highest number of comparisons using binary search is 4. With 1 million elements ($≈2^{20}$), only 20 comparisons are performed by this algorithm.

8.7   Sorting Techniques

Sorting of data is needed for binary search and in many other applications. Sorting is the process of arranging the data in either ascending or descending order using a key field. For example, we may want to sort a student record list for 300 students by grade and within each grade, have the list further sorted by student number. In this case, the primary sort key is the first key by which data in a file is sorted while secondary key is the second key by which data is sorted within the primary key order. Many organizations sort massive amounts of data, e.g., government office sorts list of names by area code. We, now discuss some sorting schemes called selection, bubble and quick sort techniques. The best sorting techniques are determined by number of comparisons and switches that take place before a list of n records are placed in a specific order.

8.7.1 The Selection Exchange Sort

The objective is to sort a list of *n* records in say, ascending order using selection exchange algorithm. The selection exchange algorithm starts by placing the *n* records in an unsorted part of the list U, while the sorted part of the list S is empty at initialization. The sub-list S is an adjoining list at the head of the sub-list U. Thus, initially, number of elements in S is zero while number of elements in U is *n*. Then, during each iteration where the number of elements in U is more than 1, the scheme finds the smallest element in U and makes it the first element of U, then this first element of U is made the last element of S instead, so that the number of elements in S increases by 1 while the number of elements in U decreases by 1.

Example 8.6: Given the following test scores:
```
    56    80    75    63    58    79
```
place the list in ascending order using selection exchange sort technique.

Solution 8.6

```c
#include <stdio.h>

/*--- Declaration of global variables ---*/
int scores[6]={56, 80, 75, 63, 58, 79};
int min, i, j, temp, num_score=6;

/*--- Control Module 0000 ---*/
void main(void) {
      for ( i = 0 ; i <= num_score-2 ; i++ ) {
            min = i;

/*-Checks if the element is larger than the next element */
            for ( j = i+1 ; j <= num_score-1 ; j++ ) {
                  if ( scores[min] > scores[j] )
                        min = j;
            }

/*If the element is larger, the two elements are switched */
            if ( min != i ) {
                  temp = scores[i];
                  scores[i] = scores[min];
                  scores[min] = temp;
            }
      }
```

158

```
/*--- Print the scores in ascending order ---*/
for ( i = 0 ; i <= num_score-1 ; i++ ) {
        printf( "%d ", scores[i] );
}
printf( "\n" );

}  /*--- End of Program ---*/
```

Evaluation

At Start S [ ]	Iteration 1 $\|U\|>1$, I=1, min=0, no swap	Iteration 2, $\|U\|>1$, I=2, min=4, swap	Iteration 3, $\|U\|>1$. I=3. ,min =3, swap	Iteration 4, $\|U\|>1$, I=4, min=3, no swap	Iteration 5, $\|U\|>1$, I=5, min=5, swap
56	S 56	S 56	S 56	S 56	S 56
80	80	58	58	58	58
U 75	U 75	U 75	63	63	63
63	63	63	75	75	75
58	58	80	U 80	U 80	79
79	79	79	79	79	U 80
$\|S\| = 0$	$\|S\| = 1$	$\|S\| = 2$	$\|S\| = 3$	$\|S\| = 4$	$\|S\| = 5$
$\|U\| = 6$	$\|U\| = 5$	$\|U\| = 4$	$\|U\| = 3$	$\|U\| = 2$	$\|U\| = 1$
					Since $\|U\| < 1$ now, it ends

The list is sorted after 5 (or num_score −1) iterations of the outer loop. This means that if there is a swap during each iteration, there are n swaps for a list of n elements.   The number of comparisons in the inner loop during each iteration is (n-i-1) for the ith iteration. Total number of comparisons for the (n-1) iterations is (n-1)*(n-i-1) = n^2-ni-n-1. The dominant term is n^2 and so the number of comparisons with this technique is n^2 while the number of swaps is n.

8.7.2   The Bubble Sort

To sort a list of n records in ascending order using bubble sort technique, the algorithm initially places an empty sub-list S for the sorted list at the bottom of the unsorted sub-list U. As long as the entire list is not sorted (list is sorted when no swap occurred in the previous iteration), it compares each element in U with the next element and switch if element is larger than next one.

Example 8.7: Given the following test scores
        56   80   75   63   58   79,   place   the   list   in
        ascending order using bubble sort technique.

159

Solution 8.7

```c
#include <stdio.h>

/*--- Declaration of global variables ---*/
int scores[]={56, 80, 75, 63, 58, 79};
int knt, temp, numleft, numscore=6, flag;

/*--- Control Module 0000 ---*/
void main(void) {
    /*--- List is initially unsorted ---*/
/*-Note that flag value equal 0 is false and 1 is true */
    flag = 0;

    /* Get number of elements to compare ---*/
    numleft = numscore - 2;

    while (flag != 1) {
/*--- Declare it sorted before checking if it is ---*/
        flag = 1;
        for (knt = 0 ; knt <= numleft ; knt++) {
            if (scores[knt] > scores[knt+1]) {
                temp = scores[knt];
                scores[knt] = scores[knt+1];
                scores[knt+1] = temp;
            /*--- Declare the list unsorted ---*/
                flag = 0;
            }
        } /*--- End for loop ---*/

/*--- Since each iteration leads to an element of ---*/
/*--- U list joining the S list at the bottom      ---*/
/*--- numleft needs to be adjusted ---*/

        numleft = numleft - 1;
    } /*--- End while loop ---*/


    /*--- Prints the list in ascending order ---*/
    for (knt = 0 ; knt <= 5 ; knt++) {
        printf("%d ", scores[knt]);
    }
    printf("\n");
}       /*--- End of Program ---*/
```

This technique is called bubble sort because the smallest elements slowly bubble their way to the top of the list. It is also referred to as sinking sort because the heavier elements gradually sink to the bottom of the list.

Evaluation

At Start S [ ]	Iteration 1 Sorted=f, numleft=5,	Iteration 2 Sorted=f, numleft=4,	Iteration 3 Sorted=f, numleft=3	Iteration 4 Sorted=f, numleft=2
56	56	56	56	56
80	75	63	58	58
U 75	U 63	U 58	U 63	63
63	58	75	75	75
58	79	S 79	S 79	S 79
79	S 80	80	80	80
|S| = 0	|S| = 1	|S| = 2	|S| = 3	|S| = 6
|U| = 6	|U| = 5	|U| = 4	|U| = 3	|U| = 0
Sorted = f	Sorted=f because there were swaps on intial list to produce list 1	Sorted=f because there were swaps on list 1 to produce list 2	Sorted=f because there were swaps on list 2 to produce list 3	Sorted=t because there were no swaps on list 3 to produce list 4

Number of swaps in each iteration of the outer loop is (n-1) in the worst case as in iteration 1, and zero in the best case as in iteration 4. Number of iterations of the outer loop is $n-1$ in the worst case, and 1 in the best case if input list is sorted. Therefore, total number of swaps in the worst case is (n-1)*(n-1) = n^2 (dominant factor). There are n-1 comparisons in each iteration of the outer loop and n-1 iterations of the outer loop leading to a total of n^2 comparisons.

With n as the number of elements in the list to be sorted and s the number of elements already in sorted order, a simpler version of the bubble sort, which always goes through the list ((n-1) * (n – s)) times, even if the whole list is already sorted is given below.

```
#include <stdio.h>
void main (void) {
  int  score[6]={56, 80, 75, 63, 58, 79}, numscore=6;
  int  temp, numleft, j ;
  for (numleft=numscore-2; numleft >= 0; numleft--)
  {
        for (j = 0;  j <= numleft;  j++)
    {
      if (score[j] > score[j+1])
         {    temp = score[j];
             score[j] = score[j+1];
             score[j+1] = temp;    }
             } /* end of for j */
    } /* end of for numleft  */
      for (j=0; j < 6; j++)
```

```
        printf("%d", score[j]);
}    /* end of main */
```


8.7.3 QuickSort

The quicksort technique yields better performance than both selection and bubble sort techniques. The quicksort algorithm works by partitioning the list using the first element of the unsorted list. Using the first element of U, it determines the final location for this element. This element is placed such that all elements to its left are less than it and all elements to its right are greater than or equal to it, recursively, partitioned until sorted.

For example, to sort

56   80   75   63   58   79

It finds the final location of the first element of the list (56) to obtain left and right sub-lists. The final location of an element is found by first comparing each element from the rightmost element with the element (56) and exchanging the position of this element with that of the first element found less than it. That is, comparison goes as $79 < 56$, $58 < 56$, $63 < 56$, and so on. Thus the position of 56 is still first after this initial operation. The second operation that finally determines the location of an element is to compare elements of the list starting from the second element on its left and switch positions with first element found greater than this element. With our current list no elements are on the left of 56. So, the final position for 56 is position 0. This means we now have a sorted sub-list S with only 56 and an unsorted part U with 80   75   63   58   79 and we must continue the process.

```
        56    80    75    63    58    79
        |__|  |_____|

         s              u
```


Next, find the final position for 80. Since $79 < 80$, we swap to obtain

56   79   75   63   58   80

Next, we try to find an element to the left of 80 which is greater than 80. Since there is none, our remaining unsorted list is now

```
|56|  |79    75    63    58|  |80|

 s             u             s
```


162

Find the final position of 79, since the first number on the unsorted list which is less than 79 is 58, it switches 79 with 58 to place it in position 3 of U. There are no elements to the left of 79 now in the list U which are greater than 79, its final position then becomes 3. The list now is :

⌊56⌋ ⌊58   75   63⌋ ⌊79   80⌋
 s   u   s

Next, 58 is at the head of U and we need to determine its proper position. Its position on U is determined as the 1st position meaning that it has no left sub-tree to sort further. Thus, it is a sorted partial list now. This leaves the remaining unsorted list with only 2 elements shown below.

⌊56   58⌋ ⌊75   63⌋ ⌊79   80⌋
    s   u   s

The position of 75 is determined as 2nd of U to get the list

56   58   63   75   79   80

which is the sorted list.

The steps in partitioning the list to be sorted into a left sublist and a right sublist is shown in a binary like form given below. Each of the left and right sublists is recursively partitioned, with the element whose right position is found last at the root of the binary partition can also be shown in a binary tree form given below.

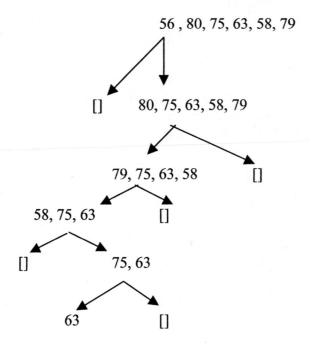

163

The sorted list is obtained by traversing this tree, visiting the left subtree first, followed by the root and then the right subtree.

A draft of the quicksort algorithm is given below:

```c
#include <stdio.h>
int n=6,  num[6]={56, 58, 75, 63, 79, 80}, firstelement=0, lastelement=5;

/* The function prototypes would now follow  */
void Quicksort(int [] , int, int);
int Partition(int [], int, int);
void swap(int *, int *:w);
void main(void)
{
    int  k ;
    Quicksort(num,firstelement,lastelement);
    for (k= 0; k < n;  k ++)
    {
        printf("%d\n", num[k]);
    }

} /* end of the main */
/* Quicksort is a recursive function which accepts three input parameters namely */
/* (1) the array to be sorted (2) the first position of the array and (3) the last position */
/* of the array. Local variable currentlocation is used to keep track of the current   */
/* position of the number on the unsorted list.                                         */

void Quicksort(int num[], int firstposition, int lastposition)
{
 int  currentlocation;
 if  (firstposition >= lastposition) return;    /* means this sublist is now sorted */
 currentlocation = Partition (num, firstposition, lastposition);
 Quicksort (num, firstposition, currentlocation-1) ;  /* sorts the left sub-tree  */
  Quicksort (num, currentlocation+1, lastposition) ;  /* sorts the right sub-tree  */
}

int Partition(int num[], int firstposition, int lastposition)
{
   int  forever = 1;
   int currentpos= firstposition;
  while (forever) {
        /* Look for an element on the right of list less than current element */
        while (currentpos != lastposition)
          {
```

```c
                if (num[currentpos] <= num[lastposition])
                        lastposition--;
                if (currentpos == lastposition) return position;
                if (num[currentpos] > num[lastposition])
                        {
                swap(&num[currentpos],&num[lastposition]);
                currentpos = lastposition;  }
        }       /* end of while check for element on the right this round */
    /* Now Look for an element on the left of list greater than current element */
        while (currentpos != firstposition)
            {
                if (num[currentpos] >= num[firstposition])
                        firstposition++;
                if (currentpos == lastposition) return position;
                if (num[currentpos] < num[firstposition])
                        {
                swap(&num[currentpos],&num[firstposition]);
                currentpos = firstposition;  }
        }       /* end of while check for element on the left this round */
    }       /* end of while forever */
}       /* end of the function Partition          */

void swap (int  *X, int   *Y)
{
        int   temp;
        {
        temp = *X;
        *X = *Y;
        *Y = temp;
        }
}
```

8.8   Exercises

1.   (a) What output will be produced by the following program segment?. Assuming array A[0] ...A[19] has the values 0, ... , 19 respectively.

```
for        (i =0; i <   20; i + +)
{
  if (A[i] % 2 = = 0)
                  printf ("%d \n",  A[i]);
     else   printf( "%d \n", A[i]/ 2);
}
```

(b)   Assume you have the following table of scores,

70	51	65	83
83	65	67	71
90	70	71	77
92	85	88	80

write a program using top-down design to read this table, print the average and minimum value of each row and column.

2.   (a) Write a program to print the number of times each score in the score table of question 1(b) re-occurs.

(b)   Write a program to print all scores from the score table of question 1(b) greater than or equal to 90%.

3.   You can spend $3.50 at the Laundromat washing your load of clothes 10 lbs or less; or you can have them do it for 50 cents per pound of clothes. Given a list of 20 Laundromat customers, the weight in pounds of clothes they wash weekly for 4 weeks, information regarding whether they washed their clothes themselves or not, write a program that computes the Laundromat's weekly revenue and their total monthly revenue.

Sample input

Week 1

Customerid	Weight of clothes	Self or full serve
C001	23	S
C002	45	F
.		
.		
.		
C020	19	S

Week 2

C001	--	--
.		
.		

week 3

.
.

week 4

4. In an organization, employees have status defined by annual salaries as follows:

Status	Annual Salary
1	70,000 – 100,000
2	50,000 – 69,999
3	30,000 – 49,999
4	15,000 – 29,999
5	< 15,000

Given the annual salaries of this company's employees, write a program that prints the number of employees in each status, the highest and the lowest salaries in each status. Keep reading salaries until end of file.

5. You have been asked to write a program to calculate the average test score, standard deviation and test scores falling in the ranges < 40, 40 – 49, 50-59, 60 – 69, 70 – 79, >=80, for your class of 300 students. Input data are the 300 integer test scores and the mathematical formulae for mean and standard deviation (S.D) are:

$$\text{Mean} = \left(\sum_{i=1}^{n} X_i\right) / n$$

$$\text{S.D} = \sqrt{\left[\frac{\left(\sum_{i=1}^{n} (x_i - \text{mean of } x)^2\right)}{(n-1)}\right]}$$

6. Write a program to read a list of names and print them in ascending order using bubble sort technique.

7. Given a sorted list of 10 test scores, write a program to find the position of a specific score using
    (a) Sequential search technique.
    (b) Binary search technique.

8. Write a C program that reads whole line of student records organized as follows:
    John Adams   Computer Science
    Mary Cooks   Mathematics
    Todd Black   English
    The program should print the first name, last name, and department of each student read.

9. Write a C program that reads about 100 records of the type in question 8 above and prints the number of students in each of the three departments as well as their names.

10. Write a C program that reads new names and new phone numbers of a retail store clients (about 20 such records) and uses this new list to update an existing list of 100 client records that may or not have these new records already.

11. Given a list of 5 names, write a C program to arrange these names in ascending order.

8.9   References

Nell Dale/ Chip Weems, "Pascal" , 3rd edition, Heath, 1991.

H. M. Deitel/ P. J. Deitel, " C How to Program", second edition, Prentice Hall, 1994.

Elliot B. Koffman, "Turbo Pascal", 5th edition, Addison Wesley, 1995.

Reedy/Bittinger/Rudolph, "Essential Mathematics", 6th edition, Addison Wesley 1992.

Maureen Sprankle, "Problem Solving & Programming Concepts", 3rd edition, Prentice Hall , 1995.

9. POINTERS, FILES, RECORDS & OTHERS

9.1 Pointers

The type of a variable is determined by the type of data it can store and the type of operations that can be performed on this variable. As introduced in chapter 4, a pointer is a variable that can store or hold only memory addresses as its value.

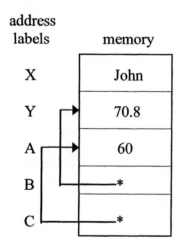

In the above memory cell set-up, the cells labeled X, Y and A hold ordinary data values of type string, real and integer respectively. However, the memory cell labeled B contains a memory address, which is the address of a real variable. Similarly, cell C holds a memory address of an integer value. Thus, B is a pointer variable of type real meaning that the address it points to, contains a real value while C is a pointer variable of type integer, indicating that it points to an integer value.

To declare a pointer variable to be of any data type we do:

type_of_data_it_points_to   *pointervariable;

E.g.,
float *B;   /* declares B a pointer to real data */
int *C;   /* declares B a pointer to integer data */

Operations on Pointer Variables

A pointer variable can only be initialized to 0 or null (which means that it points to nothing yet) or assigned an address value through the use of address operators (&) which returns the address of a memory variable already known by the program. For example, to assign the addresses of variables Y and A, already declared as in above, to pointer variables B and C respectively, we use:

    B = &Y;
    C = &A;

The indirection operator or dereferencing operator (*) is used to obtain the value of the memory location which has the address a pointer variable holds.

For example, Print(*B, *C) will print 70.8 and 60, while Print(B, C) will print integer memory addresses for variables Y and A. Assuming we want to modify the values (adding 10) in Y and A only through the pointer variables B and C.

    *B = *B + 10.0;
    *C = *C +10;

The effect of these two instructions is that the values of Y and A now become 80.8 and 70 respectively.

Arithmetic Operations on Pointers

Only a few arithmetic operations may be performed on a pointer variable. Since memory addresses are integers, a pointer may be incremented with an integer value. A pointer may also be subtracted from another pointer.

Assignment Operation

A pointer can be assigned to another pointer variable if both pointer variables are of the same type, e.g., if both variables are pointers to an integer variable, pointers to a string variable etc.

9.2   File Processing

In chapter 8, we discussed some sorting algorithms, which can be used to sort thousands or millions of records, for example, student records, employee records, or airline reservation records. So far, we have written algorithms and programs that read data from the standard input device, which is the keyboard. Thus, if we need to run a program to read and process a thousand student records, being read from the keyboard, it means that every time we re-run the program, we start all over to re-type the one thousand records.

This approach will not only make data processing with programs slow and unpleasant but also error-prone.

All data processed by a program through variable names are memory data, which are lost at the end of the program unless saved in a file. In order to re-use data read by a program for processing or data created by a program during processing, a disk file must be used to store the data. Then, we need to prepare the program to read from a disk file and not from the keyboard. Thus, if we want a program to read student records with the following fields: student id, name, major, gpa, we first create a disk file given a disk file name with data as follows:

Disk file called <u>stnrec.dat</u>

16582	John Muss	Math	8.5
51193	Jimmy Gray	Stats	10.0
63211	Grace Green	CS	11.5
70582	Tammy Toms	CS	9.5
....			
....			

Since programs only work with variables, a file pointer variable has to be declared at the beginning of the program/algorithm which is linked to this disk file and used to access each record or data item in the file.

A file structure consists of a number of records with each record representing a real life entity. A record is made up of a sequence of fields or attributes (e.g., student id, name, major, gpa). Each field of a record can be of any type. Records in a file could be accessed either sequentially or randomly. Records are usually identified uniquely using a primary key field (e.g., student id). Sequential access files may store records of a file in primary key order and access to the nth record is accomplished only after all the (n-1) records have been scanned. At the beginning of the program, the file pointer points to the first record in the file. Random access files allow one record out of many to be accessed without going through all of the records before it.

A group of related files about an organization makes up a database, for example, stnrec.dat file, course_rec.dat file, prof_rec.dat file etc. For a file to be used in a program/algorithm, the following steps should be taken:

(1) Declare a file pointer variable also called file logical variable name: This step is similar to defining a variable of type File, which tells the program compiler that records of data may be read, written, appended or updated in a disk file. The format for this declaration in C is:

```
FILE      *filepointer;
```

This declares filepointer as a pointer to data of type FILE

e.g.,

FILE   *stnptr; /* declares stnptr as a pointer to data of type FILE*/

(2) Open the file (with fopen in C): In this step, the file variable needs to be associated to a disk file, which has to be opened for either a read (r), write (w), update (r+) or append (a). The format for using the fopen command to form a connection with an already declared file pointer variable (like stnptr) declared in step 1 above is :

> **filepointer = fopen ("disk file name", "mode");**

e.g.,
stnprt = fopen ("stnrec.dat", " r");

This instruction prepares the program file pointer variable *stnptr* for use in referencing records of the disk file stnrec.dat which in this case can only be read and not altered in any way. In C, a file is opened with fopen instruction, which returns a pointer (file pointer) to a structure of type FILE. This returned file pointer is used by the program's input and output instructions. If fopen cannot open the specified disk file, it returns NULL. Programs should use an instruction like the following to test for successful opening of a disk file.

> **If ((filepointer = fopen("DISK FILENAME", "r") != NULL)**
> **{ /* means file opened successfully   */**
> **}**
> **else { /* means there was an error opening the file   */**
> **}**

(3) Read/Print records from/into the file: This is the actual instruction responsible for reading from or writing a record into the file. A record can be read from a file only if it had been previously opened for a read (r), or update (r+). A record can be written into a file only if it had been opened for a write(w), an update (r+) or an append (a). The format for writing this instruction is :

> **fscanf(filePointer, "format specifiers", variable list to be read);**
> **fprintf(filePointer, "format specifiers", variable list to be printed);**

e.g.,
fscanf (stnptr, "%s %s %s %f ", studentid, name, major, &gpa);
fprintf (stnptr, "%s %s %s %f \n", studentid, name, major, gpa);

The difference in the use of scanf/printf instruction when a file is involved, is that the file pointer is specified as the first argument of the instruction. The file version of the instructions fscanf/fprintf are also used. Several other instructions for reading data from a file or printing data into a file in C exist and a more detailed discussion of those can be obtained from a C reference book listed in the reference section.

(4) Close the file: Since the memory for a file had been reserved with an fopen instruction, there is need to relinquish this memory space by closing the file using the following instruction.

> **close (filePointer);**
>
> e.g.,
>
> close (stnptr);

File End-of-File marker with File Pointers

Data files contain file end of file (feof) markers. An feof marker indicates the end of data records in a file. If we need to keep reading records from a data file until there is no more data, we need to specify the disk file the feof marker check is applying to, using its file pointer variable. Thus, an argument is included after the feof to specify which file is being checked. The format for specifying a file whose feof marker should be checked is:

> **feof (file_pointer_variable)**

e.g.,

feof (stnptr)

To keep reading from stnptr file until there is no more data, use a segment like the following:

```
#include <stdio.h>
void main (void)
{       FILE *stnptr;
        char studentid[15], name[20], major [15];
        float gpa;
        int k;

        if (stnptr=fopen("stnrec.dat"," r") != NULL)
        {       k = 1;
                fscanf (stnptr, "%s", studentid);
                while (!feof(stnptr))
                {
                        fscanf (stnptr, "%s %s %f", name, major, &gpa);
                        k++;
                fscanf (stnptr, "%s", studentid);
                }       /* end of while */
        printf("Number of records in file is", k);
        }       /* end of if stnptr */
        else  printf("file not opened successfully");
}       /* end of program */
```

Note that the first argument of an fscanf instruction, when reading data from a disk file, is the file pointer variable set by the program to point to this disk file (to represent this disk file).

9.3   Record Data Structure

Although logically, a file is made up of a number of records, physically, many languages like C view each file simply as a sequential stream of bytes. The implication is that no structure is imposed except that defined by the programmer. With no structure imposed on this data in the file, it becomes difficult for the program to refer to the 82nd record for instance. However, if we define a record structure to suit the records in the file, then we can read the records from the file into an array of records by index using the appropriate subscript.

A record data structure allows us to refer to a number of memory locations corresponding to its fields of varying data types using only one variable name. While an array can be used for many locations of the same type (e.g., all integers, or records, or real), fields of a record may be of any type. A record data type is defined first and many variables can subsequently be declared of this type in the program. In defining a record structure, a name is given to this structure and all its fields with their data types are listed. The format for defining a record structure or type is:

```
        struct record_type
        {       type field1;
                type field2;
                .
                .
                .
                type fieldn;
        }       /*      of record type*/
```

Now to declare variable of this type, use:

```
struct record_type      record_variable;
```

For example, the record student in our stnrec.dat has studentid of type string, name of type string, major of type string and gpa of type real. The instructions for both declaring this type and initializing a variable of this type are:

```
struct  student_type {
        char studentid[15];
        char name[20];
        char major[15];
        float gpa;
    }   /* of student record type     */
```

struct student_type   student_var;

The record variable can also be declared with the struct type declaration if the variable immediately follows the ending curly bracket of the declaration. Initial values can also be assigned to struct variable declaration.

<u>Use of typedef declaration</u>

Developing programs that are readable and easy to modify in the future allows for less costly and quicker upgrades to existing software systems. Example of software system upgrades are MS Windows 3.1 upgraded to MS Windows 95, then upgraded to MS Windows 98, then, MS Windows 2000 and XP. Three techniques used in program design in C to develop easily readable and modifiable programs are:
1. Top-down program design with functions.
2. Use of named constants in programs.
3. Use of typedef declarations to define alias type names in programs.

The first two approaches have been discussed in earlier chapters and the use of typedef is discussed in this section.

In C, typedef declaration is used to define synonyms or other names (aliases) for data types. The format for the typedef declaration is:

tpedef   type   aliaslist;

For example, assume we have the following declaration in a program.
        float   regular_salary, overtime_salary;
We may choose to rename the data type (float) with an alias (salary) that better describes the float variables being declared. To rename float type with salary, we use the typedef declaration as:
        typedef float salary;
This says that there is a data type called salary, which is similar to float data type. Thus, variables can be declared to be of salary type using:
        salary regular_salary, overtime_salary;

In the same way, we can rename the student record structure we defined earlier on, in the struct declaration, to give it an easier name with no hyphen using:
        typedef   struct student_type studenttype;
Note that the keyword "struct" needs to be included with the record type name in the typedef declaration of a record type.

Operations on Record Variables

Once the program has declared a record variable, then, we can read and write each record by reading and writing its fields. If an entire record needs to be read, all of its fields in order are read. A field of a record variable is addressed by having the record variable name followed by a period, then the fieldname. For example, to print the name field of a student record above, the instruction is Printf("%s",student_var.name).

To read an entire student record, we use:

```
scanf ("%s %s %s %f", student_var.studentid,
          student_var.name, student_var.major,
          &student_var.gpa);
```

All other valid operations on program variables can be performed on these fields of the record (e.g., printf, assignment instructions etc.)

An array of student records to store more than one student record can also be defined as follows:

struct record_type   record_var[size] ;

e.g.,

student_type student_var[100];

This will reserve memory for 100 student records of the type above. If we want to print the 51st student record we simply use:

printf("%s %s %s %f", student_var[51].studentid, student_var[51].name, student_var[51].major, student_var[51].gpa);

```
Example 9.1: Read records from a disk file into an array of
    record data structure and print the number of records
    read.  Although there are not more than 100 records in
    the file, it is not known the exact number of records,
    thus, you can read till end of file.
```

Solution 9.1

```
#include <stdio.h>

/*--- Record type ---*/
struct Student_Type {
      char studentid[15];
      char name[15];
      char major[15];
```

```
        float gpa;
};

typedef      struct Student_Type student_type;

/*--- Control Module 0000 ---*/
void main(void) {
      /*--- Declaration of local variables ---*/
      FILE *inFptr;
      student_type students[100];
      int k;

      /*--- Let inFptr be a pointer to the file students.dat ---*/
      if ( (inFptr = fopen("students.dat", "r")) == NULL )
            printf( "File could not be opened\n" );
      else {
            /*--- Initialize the counter ---*/
            k= 1;

      /*- Read the contents of the file and increment the counter ---*/
            fscanf(inFptr,"%s%s%s%f", students[k].studentid,
            students[k].name, students[k].major, &students[k].gpa);
            while (!feof(inFptr)){
                  fscanf(inFptr,"%s%s%s%f", students[k].studentid,
                        students[k].name, students[k].major,
                              &students[k].gpa);
                  k++;
            }
      }

/*- Minus 1 from the counter to compensate for the EOF character being
read ---*/
      k= k-1;

      /*--- Close the file ---*/
      fclose( inFptr   );


      /*--- Print the number of records in the file ---*/
      printf("There are %d record(s) in the file.\n", k);
}     /*--- End of Program ---*/
```

Example 9.2: A small corner store has 200 items each described with its item code, name, location, unit price, and available quantity. Write a program that stores records of each item in a disk file, Sort the records by the item code and print all items that have less than 10 available quantity.

Solution 9.2

```c
#include <stdio.h>

/*--- Record type ---*/
struct Item_Type {
      char code[15];
      char name[15];
      char location[15];
      float price;
      int qty;
};

typedef     struct Item_Type item_type;

/*--- Declaration of function prototypes ---*/
void ReadData( FILE * );
void SortData( item_type *, int );
void CheckStock( item_type *, int, FILE * );
void PrintResult( FILE * );
item_type item_rec[10]; /* Only 10 records are used here */

/*--- Control Module 0000 ---*/
void main(void) {
      /*--- Declaration of local variables ---*/
      FILE *inFptr, *outFptr, *lessFptr;

      /*--- Let inFptr be a pointer to the file items_r.dat ---*/
      if ( (inFptr = fopen("items_r.dat", "r")) == NULL )
           printf( "File could not be opened\n" );

      /*--- Let outFptr be a pointer to the file items_w.dat ---*/
      if ( (outFptr = fopen("items_w.dat", "w")) == NULL )
           printf( "File could not be opened\n" );

      /*--- Let lessFptr be a pointer to the file items_less.dat ---*/
      if ( (lessFptr = fopen("items_less.dat", "w")) == NULL )
           printf( "File could not be opened\n" );
      else {
           /*--- Function calls ---*/
           ReadData( inFptr );
           SortData( item_rec, 10 );
           CheckStock( item_rec, 10, lessFptr );
           PrintResult( outFptr );
      }

      /*--- Close the files ---*/
      fclose( inFptr   );
      fclose( outFptr  );
      fclose( lessFptr );
}     /*--- End of Program ---*/

/*--- ReadData Module 1000 ---*/
/*--- Function definition for ReadData---*/
```

```c
void ReadData( FILE *inFptr ) {
      int i;

/*--Read the records from items_r.dat, save them in an array ---*/
      for ( i=0 ; i<10; i++ )
            fscanf( inFptr, "%s%s%s%f%d",
            item_rec[i].code,item_rec[i].name,
                  item_rec[i].location, &item_rec[i].price,
            &item_rec[i].qty );
}


/*--- SortData Module 2000 ---*/
/*--- Function definition for SortData---*/
void SortData( item_type *item_rec, int numitems ) {
      item_type temp;
      int i, j, min;

      for ( i = 0 ; i <= numitems - 2; i++ ) {
            min = i;
            for ( j = i+1 ; j <= numitems - 1  ; j++ ) {
                  /*--- Checks if the current code is greater than the
            next ---*/
                  if((strncmp(item_rec[min].code,item_rec[j].code)) > 0 )
                        min = j;
            }

            /*--- If the item code is greater than the next item code,
            switch them ---*/
            if ( min != i ) {
                  sscanf( item_rec[i].code,      "%s", temp.code );
                  sscanf( item_rec[i].name,      "%s", temp.name );
                  sscanf( item_rec[i].location, "%s", temp.location );
                  temp.price = item_rec[i].price;
                  temp.qty   = item_rec[i].qty;

                  sscanf( item_rec[min].code,      "%s",
                  item_rec[i].code );
                  sscanf( item_rec[min].name,      "%s",
                  item_rec[i].name );
                  sscanf( item_rec[min].location, "%s",
                  item_rec[i].location );
                  item_rec[i].price = item_rec[min].price;
                  item_rec[i].qty   = item_rec[min].qty;

                  sscanf( temp.code,     "%s", item_rec[min].code );
                  sscanf( temp.name,     "%s", item_rec[min].name );
                  sscanf( temp.location, "%s", item_rec[min].location);
                  item_rec[min].price = temp.price;
                  item_rec[min].qty   = temp.qty;
            } /*--- End of if ---*/
      } /*--- End of for loop ---*/
}

/*--- CheckStock Module 3000 ---*/
/*--- Function definition for CheckStock---*/
void CheckStock( item_type *item_rec, int numitems, FILE *lessFptr ) {
```

```
        /*--- Declaration of local variables ---*/
        int i;

        /*--- Output the records with less than 10 quantity to the file
        items_less.dat ---*/
        for ( i = 0 ; i < numitems ; i++ ) {
                if ( item_rec[i].qty < 10 )
                        fprintf( lessFptr, "%s %s %s %.2f %d\n",
                        item_rec[i].code, item_rec[i].name,
                        item_rec[i].location, item_rec[i].price,
                        item_rec[i].qty );
        } /*--- End of for loop ---*/
}


/*--- PrintResult Module 4000 ---*/
/*--- Function definition for PrintResult---*/
void PrintResult( FILE *outFptr ) {
        /*--- Declaration of local variables ---*/
        int i;

        /*--- Output the 10 sorted records to the file items_w.dat ---*/
        for ( i = 0 ; i < 10 ; i++ ) {
                fprintf( outFptr, "%s %s %s %.2f %d\n", item_rec[i].code,
                item_rec[i].name, item_rec[i].location, item_rec[i].price,
                        item_rec[i].qty );
        } /*--- End of for loop ---*/
}
```

Discussion

In example 9.2, the record structure for an item in the store is first defined and given the name item_type. This means, variables of this record type can now be declared. The first variable declared of this type is item_rec[10], which is also an array of 10 records that have the structure of item_type. One input file pointer variable (inFptr) is declared for read and two output file pointers (outFptr and lessFptr) are declared for writing processed records. While the output is used to print all 10 item records sorted by the item code, lessFptr is used to print all records which have available stock less than 10. Notice how pointer variables are passed as arguments to functions ReadData, CheckStock and PrintResult. In the solution, all files have these file pointer variables declared, then opened, read from or written into and finally closed. In sortData, the process of swapping any two records of the array entails copying each field of same record type called temp and later all copied fields are transferred to the fields of the second record.

9.4   Introduction to Other Structures

In this section, only a brief introduction to some other more advanced data structures is given.

9.4.1 Stacks

A stack is a variable, which refers to a sequence of memory locations. Associated with this stack variable is a size *n,* which is the maximum number of memory locations that belongs to this list. A stack is a list of values with n or fewer members where only the top of stack is available because all additions to the list and all deletions from the list occur through the top of stack. Thus, it is a last in, first out structure. The size of this structure grows and shrinks as instructions are being executed. The only operations defined on a stack are PUSH to add a value to the top of stack, and POP to delete a value from top of the stack. Stacks are useful in processing recursive function calls.

Example 9.3: Assume we have a stack variable for integers called S. With the following algorithm on structure S and current values of integer variables A, B, Y as 10, 2, 3 respectively, show the state of stack, A, B, and Y after executing this algorithm.

Instruction.

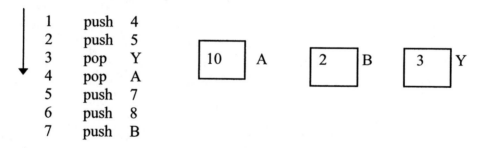

```
1    push   4
2    push   5
3    pop    Y
4    pop    A
5    push   7
6    push   8
7    push   B
```

10 A   2 B   3 Y

Solution 9.3

stack after execution

Top of stack pointer

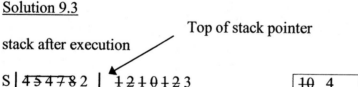

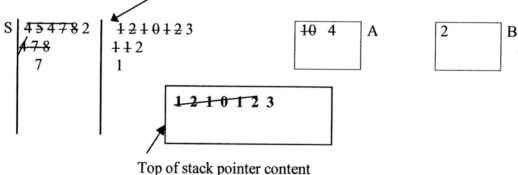

Top of stack pointer content

182

Instructions are executed sequentially from 1 to 8. The top of stack points to the topmost element of stack. After executing instruction 1, top of stack holds 4 while stack points to subscript 1. Executing instruction 2, causes 5 to be pushed on top of stack which is now pointing at element 2, while the previous element of top of stack which is 4 gets pushed down to stack element 1. Instruction 3 pops (removes) the top element of 5 and places it in variable Y while instruction 4 removes the next top element of 4 to place in variable A. Now stack S is empty at element 0. The three next subsequent pushes have the effect of placing 2 finally on top of stack pushing down 8 to element 2 while the element 7 is at the lowest stack position of 1.

9.4.2   Linked Lists

A linked list is a data type consisting of a sequence of records where each record points to its successor except for the last record which points to nothing. To remember its successor, each record has its last field holding the address of its successor (a pointer variable). The records in sequence do not need to be kept physically together. The figure 9.1 shows a linked list of person records.

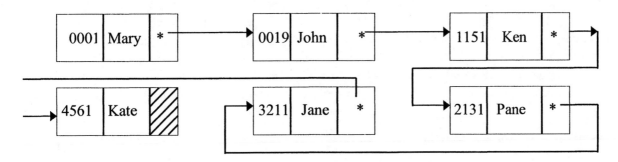

Figure 9.1.   Linked List of Records

To declare records of this type, we can do:

```
struct list_type
        {char id[15];
        char name[20];
        list_type      *listptr ;
        }
```

To declare variable of type linked list, we declare a variable that points to the head of the list as follows:

```
struct  list_type         *listptr ;
```

The link field of the first record points to the second record, that of the second record points to the 3rd and so on. It is easier to add or delete records from a linked list file than an array of records. Operations that can be defined on a linked list include function for inserting any record in the correct order or position in the list, deleting a record from the list, printing a record, printing the list.

Note that in the declaration of the list record type, the last field in the record is a pointer to a record of the same list type (a type of recursive type definition that uses its own type). Deleting a record from the list requires that the preceding record is found, so that link field is set to address of its new successor (no longer the record being deleted). First, the link field of the record being deleted is copied to a temporary variable to remember its successor's address before the link field of the record is set to null to disconnect it.

A linked list can also be implemented using an array of records where the link field holds the index of the records successor.

9.4.3   Binary Trees

While stacks and linked lists are linear data structures, a tree is a non-linear data structure with the following properties. A binary tree consists of a number of nodes. Each node is a record whose fields include two pointers, one points to the left sub-tree while the other points to the right sub-tree. Thus, every node has only a left and a right sub-tree. However, if both left and right sub-trees of a node are null (pointing to nothing), the node is a leaf node. The topmost node of the tree is called the root node. The sub-trees of a node are called its children while a node is the parent of its children (sub-trees). All children of a node are siblings. Figure 9.2 shows an example of a binary tree.

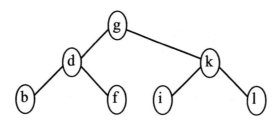

Figure 9.2. A binary tree

In the binary tree of Figure 9.2, g is the root node while b, f, i and l are leaf nodes. The nodes d and k are siblings and children of g. The node d is the parent of b and f.

A way to declare records of this type is :

184

```
struct  btree_type {

              char node_name[20];
              btree_type     *leftPtr;
              btree_type     *rightPtr;
       }
```

Declaring a variable to be a btree_type entails declaring a pointer variable to the root node as:

```
struct  btree_type    btree_ptr;
```

Operations on Binary trees

Functions can be defined for creating a btree, inserting nodes into a btree, deleting nodes, printing a sub-tree, cutting a sub-tree, printing the tree and finding a given node, its parents, children or siblings.

Binary Tree Traversal

Records stored as a binary tree have to be processed and printed in order and are better done using tree traversal techniques. The three tree traversal techniques used are:

(1) Preorder which requires that the tree recursively be traversed by first visiting (printing) the node (n) followed by visiting its left sub-tree (l) and finally its right sub-tree (r). Thus, preorder traversal requires the order of operation as "n l r".

(2) Inorder traversal which requires that the tree be recursively traversed by first visiting the left node (l) then the node itself (n) and finally the right node (r) to obtain the order "l n r".

(3) Postorder traversal: this technique recursively traverses the tree by first visiting the left node (l) then the right node (r) before finally visiting the node itself (n). In summary, the order is "l r n".

When b_tree of figure 9.2 is traversed the results are as follows:

(1) preorder: g d b f k i l
(2) inorder: b d f g i k l
(3) postorder: b f d i l k g

9.5   Exercises

1.   (a) What are pointers used for?
(b) Assume we have declared and initialized an integer variable A and a character variable B, write program instructions to declare C a pointer to A and D a pointer to B.
(c) Assume A has the value 20 and B has the value "N", write a program instruction to print the values of A and B using only their pointer variables in your instruction.
(d) Write a program to assign the values of the pointer variables C and D from 1(b) to pointer variables E and F respectively and print the values of all variables.
(e) Write a program to add 12 to the value in A and replace the value in B with "Y" using only the pointer variables C and D.

2.   An airline has flight information from departure to arrival time in a data file. This file needs to be updated frequently to keep track of the number of seats sold, number of seats remaining, departure time, arrival time, departure airport and destination airport. The file is updated whenever a reservation is made or cancelled, or when a flight begins or ends. The airline agents need to be able to inquire about a particular flight and about all flights to one particular airport. The company also needs a report on all completed flights. First design the input record and develop an algorithm and a program that solves this problem providing all the operations required by the airline.

3.   Fastloan, a financial company that grants loan to hardworking college students wants you to develop an algorithm and a program, which reads a data, file of applicant records and produces an output file containing only records of approved applicants. Loan is granted based on the policy that the total of student's annual living expenses excluding tuition minus the student yearly work income must not exceed the student's annual tuition. The input file has records on each student applicant specifying student id, name, rent cost, feeding cost, clothing cost, transportation costs, tuition, and annual work income.

4.   Write a program that reads a data file of graduating university students in a faculty. Each student has an id, name, major and GPA (between 0 and 13). Your program defines classes for students as follows:

GPA	Class
11-13	first class
8-10	second class
5-7	third class
2- 4	pass
0-1	fail

Print into an output file students in each performance category.

5. Assuming you are given the following list of integers 18, 5, 10, -2, 23.
   (a) show a diagram of how you can store these integers in order using a linked list.
   (b) show a declaration of a linked list data type to handle this list.
   (c) Discuss how another integer 7 can be inserted into this list.
   (d) Discuss how an integer can be deleted from this list.

6. (a) What is a stack ?
   (b) What are operations on a stack ?
   (c) Write the program instructions to first store the integer 18, 5, 10, -2, 23 in stack and then to store the element now on top of stack in variable C and element 10 in variable D.

7. (a) What is a binary tree ?
   (b) Draw a binary tree with integer nodes.
   (c) Write the result of preorder traversal of the tree .
   (d) Write the result of inorder traversal of the tree.
   (e) Write the result of postorder traversal of the tree.

9.6   References

H.M Deitel/P.J. Deitel, "C how to program", second edition, Prentice Hall, 1994

Maureen Sprankle, "Problem Solving & Programming Concepts", 3rd edition, Prentice Hall, 1995.

Uckan Yuksel, "Problem Solving Using C – Structured Programming Technique", 2nd edition, WCB McGraw-Hill, 1999.

10. RECAP OF PROGRAM STRUCTURE AND INSTRUCTIONS

10.1 C Program Structure – program, function prototype, function definition, return
10.2 Data Types and Formats for Variables – int, float, char, char variable[]
10.3 Input/Output Instructions – scanf, printf
10.4 C Operators and Assignment Instructions – all operator precedence order, cast
10.5 Decision Instructions – if/else, switch-case
10.6 Repetition Instructions – while, do-while, for, goto, break, continue
10.7 Arrays and String Functions
10.8 Files and Records
10.9 Files and Records

This chapter is provided to assist in revision and quick reference to materials discussed in the book chapters. It provides a recap (a quick re-visit) of formats for writing a C program and instructions. The summary in this chapter may also be allowed in examinations that are semi open book to encourage strengthening programming and problem solving skills nd dissuading unnecessary memorization of detailed syntax during examinations.

10.1 C Program Structure – program, function prototype, function definition, return

The general structure of a C program is given below:

```
#include  <stdio.h>

/* Optional global variable and function prototype declarations*/
[Input/Output variable declarations]
[Function prototype list: type and parameters]

void main (void)
{
 variable declarations;

 /*Now the sequence of executable instructions*/
 Instruction 1;
 Instruction 2;
 ….
 ….
 Instruction n;
}

/*Present the definition of each function*/
[Function definition 1]
[Function definition 2]
….
….
[Function definition n]
```

The general format for defining a function prototype in both an algorithm and a program is given as:

```
function_return_type    functionname (type for parameter1,
                          type for parameter2,  ......., type for parametern);
```

In both an algorithm and a program, the function definition is structured as follows:

```
function_return_type functionname ([type parameter1],
    [type parameter2], ..., [type parametern]);
        {
                [local variable declaration];
                instruction1;
                instruction2;
                .

                .

                instruction;
                [return (output variable or expression or 0)];
        }
```

The general format of a *return* instruction in C which sends back a value is:

```
return    expression;
```

A return instruction that sends back no value is used in the following format.

```
return;
```

10.2 Data Types and Formats for Variables - – int, float, char, char variable[]

The format for declaring variables in both an algorithm and a C program is:

```
datatype    variablename[,variablenames];
```

An equivalent expression for the format given above for declaring variables of type *datatype* is :

```
datatype    variablename1, variablename2, ......,variablenamen;
```

A string variable is declared with the format:

```
char   variablename[number_of_characters];
```

The format for declaring a pointer variable is:

```
data_type_pointed_to      *variablename;
```

The format for declaring constants in both an algorithm and a C program is:

```
const  datatype    variablename= value[,variablenames=values];
```

A constant name can also be defined with the #define directive using the format:

```
#define  constantname   value
```

The C Keyword List Not Used as Variable Names are provided below.

auto	break	case	char	const	continue	default	do	double	else	enum
extern	float	for	goto	if	int	long	register	return	short	signed
sizeof	static	struct	switch	typedef	union	unsigned	void	volatile	while	

Available simple data types and their data sets are provided below.

DATA TYPE	DATA SET	EXAMPLE DATA
Integer (int)	All whole numbers between -2^{31} to $(2^{31}-1)$	1999, -67
Real (float/double)	All real numbers (whole and decimal part)	1999.0, 2.58E5, 0.00581
Character (char)	All letters and special symbols	'A', 'B', 'b', '1', '8', '+'
String (char variable[ ])	Combination of more than one character	"Atlas", "956"
Boolean (int)	True , false	True (!0), false(0)

10.3 Input/Output Instructions – scanf, printf

The general format of C program scanf and printf instructions are:

scanf("**format specifiers**", **&variable1, &variable2, .. ,&variablen**);

printf("**format specifiers**", **variable1, variable2, .. ,variablen**);

10.4 C Operators and Assignment Instructions – all operator precedence order, cast

C Operator Precedence and Association Order (From Highest to Lowest) is provided as:

Operators	Names in Order	Association Order
(), [ ], ., ->	function call, array subscript, component selection, indirect component selection	left to right
++, --, +, -, *, &, !, ~, (type), sizeof	increment, decrement, unary plus and minus, indirection, address of, logical not, bitwise inverse, cast, sizeof	right to left
*, /, %	multiplication, division, modulus	left to right
+, -	addition, subtraction	left to right
<<, >>	right shift, left shift	left to right
<, <=, >, >=	less than, less or equal, greater than, greater or equal	right to lift
==, !=	equals to, not equal to	left to right
&	bitwise AND	left to right
^	bitwise Exclusive OR	left to right
|	bitwise OR	left to right
&&	logical AND	left to right
||	logical OR	left to right
?:	conditional operator	right to left
=, +=, -=, *=, /=, %=, &=, ^=, |=, <<=, >>=	simply equal, assign sum, assign minus, assign product, assign division, assign remainder, assign AND, assign Exclusive OR, assign OR, assign left shift, assign right shift	right to left

The format of C's Operator Assign Operations is given below.

> **variable operator= value;**

This above boxed instruction is equivalent to:

> variable = variable operator value;
>
> > For example,
> >
> > total += 40 is equivalent to total = total + 40

An assignment instruction in an algorithm or a C program has the form:

> *variable = expression;*

The form of the cast expression is:

> **(Type) Expression**

10.5 Decision Instructions – if/else, switch-case

Note that the general form of *if/else* instruction in C skips the "then" keyword that is included in many other programming languages.

> **if (decision Boolean expression is true)**
> > **{**
> > > **sequence of instructions**
> > > **to execute if expression is TRUE;**
> >
> > **}**
> > **else**
> > > **{**
> > > > **sequence of instructions to**
> > > > **execute if expression is FALSE;**
> >
> > **}**

The switch-case instruction is written in a C program as follows:

> **switch (expression) {**
>
> > **case label 1: Instructions for case label 1;**
> > > **break;**
> >
> > **case label 2: Instructions for case label 2;**
> > > **break;**
> >
> > > **:**
> >
> > **case label n: Instructions for case label n;**
> > > **break;**
> >
> > **default: Instructions for default;**
> > > **break;**
>
> **}**

10.6 Repetition Instructions –while, do-while, for, goto, break, continue

The general structure of the while instruction is:

```
Initialization Instructions;
    while (expression(s))
    {
            instruction 1;
            instruction 2;
            :
            instruction n;
            update instructions;
    }
```

The format of the do-while instruction is:

```
Initialization instructions;
do
    {
            instruction 1;
            instruction 2;
            .
            instruction n;
            update instructions;
    } while (expression);
```

The general format of a *for* instruction is:

```
for (counter = begin value; counter  (relational_operator)  end value;
                counter=counter (+|-) step)
    {
            instruction 1;
            instruction 2;
            .
            .
            instruction n;
    }
```

The format of a goto instruction is:

```
        goto label;
        ....
        ....
label:
```

The format of the break instruction is:

```
break;
```

The format of the continue instruction is:

| continue; |

10.7 Arrays and String Function

The general format for declaring a one dimensional array variable with name arrayname and data type, *type* with "size" number of elements is:

| type arrayname[size]; |

To declare a 2-dimensional array variable of *type*, the following format is used:

| type   variable[rowsize][columnsize]; |

10.8 Builtin Functions and String Functions

Available mathematical functions are summarized below.

Function	Description	Example
sqrt(x)	Square root of x	sqrt(25.0) is 5.0
exp(x)	exponential function e^x	exp(1.0) is 2.72
log(x)	natural logarithm of x (base e)	log(2.72) is 1.0
log10(x)	logarithm of x (base 10)	log10(1.0) is 0.0
fabs(x)	absolute value of x (for x real)	fabs(-15.3) is 15.3 fabs(5.0) is 5.0
Abs(x)	Absolute value of x (for x int)	Abs (-245) is 245
ceil(x)	rounds x to the smallest integer not less than x	ceil(7.1) is 8 ceil(-6.3) is -6
floor(x)	rounds x to the largest integer not greater than x	floor(7.1) is 7 floor(-6.3) is -7
pow(x,y)	x raised to the power of y (x^y)	pow(2,3) is 8 pow(16,.25) is 2
sin(x)	trigonometric sine of x (x in radians)	sin(0.0) is 0.0
cos(x)	trigonometric cosine of x (x in radians)	cos(0.0) is 1.0
tan(x)	trigonometric tangent of x (x in radians)	tan(0.0) is 0.0

Available mathematical functions are summarized below.

Function	Description	Example
sqrt(x)	Square root of x	sqrt(25.0) is 5.0
exp(x)	exponential function e^x	exp(1.0) is 2.72
log(x)	natural logarithm of x (base e)	log(2.72) is 1.0
log10(x)	logarithm of x (base 10)	log10(1.0) is 0.0
fabs(x)	absolute value of x (for x real)	fabs(-15.3) is 15.3 fabs(5.0) is 5.0
Abs(x)	Absolute value of x (for x int)	Abs (-245) is 245

ceil(x)	rounds x to the smallest integer not less than x	ceil(7.1) is 8 ceil(-6.3) is -6
floor(x)	rounds x to the largest integer not greater than x	floor(7.1) is 7 floor(-6.3) is -7
pow(x,y)	x raised to the power of y (x^y)	pow(2,3) is 8 pow(16,.25) is 2
sin(x)	trigonometric sine of x (x in radians)	sin(0.0) is 0.0
cos(x)	trigonometric cosine of x (x in radians)	cos(0.0) is 1.0
tan(x)	trigonometric tangent of x (x in radians)	tan(0.0) is 0.0

Some useful character handling functions from the C character handling library are:

Function	Description	Example
isdigit(c)	returns a true value (non zero) if c is a digit and 0 otherwise	isdigit('A') is 0
isalpha(c)	returns a true value (non zero) if c is a letter and 0 otherwise	isalpha('A') is 1
isalnum(c)	returns a true value (non zero) if c is a letter or digit and 0 otherwise	isalnum('+') is 0
islower(c)	returns a true value (non zero) if c is a lowercase letter and 0 otherwise	islower('c') is 1
isupper(c)	returns a true value (non zero) if c is an uppercase letter and 0 otherwise	isupper('a') is 0
isspace(c)	returns nonzero if c is whitespace char and 0 otherwise	isspace('a') is 0
ispunct(c)	returns nonzero if c is punctuation char and 0 otherwise	ispunct(';')is 1
tolower(c)	returns c as a lowercase letter	tolower('A')is 'a'
toupper(c)	returns c as an uppercase letter	toupper('b') is 'A'

In C some string conversion functions found in the <stdlib.h> header file are:

Functions	Description
atof (s1)	Converts s1 to double
atoi (s1)	Converts s1 to int
atol (s1)	Converts s1 to long int

Some general utilities found in the header file <stdlib.h> are:

Functions	Description
rand ()	Returns a random number between 0 and Rand_Max (a constant >= 32767)
srand (seed)	Uses seed as a seed for a new sequence of random numbers in subsequent calls to function rand

Other utility functions in the <time.h> header file are:

Functions	Description
clock_t ()	Returns the processor time used by the program. Called at the beginning

| | and end of program to determine CPU time in clocks. CPU time in seconds is obtained by dividing this time by constant CLOCKS_PER_SECOND. | |

A summary of important string builtin functions is provided in the table below.

function	description	example
strcat (s1, s2)	Appends string s2 to s1	strcat ("Hello ", "you") is "Hello you"
strchr (s1, c)	Returns the pointer address of first occurrence of character c in string s1 if found, otherwise null	strchr ("Hello", 'l') is &Hello + 2
strcmp (s1, s2)	Compares s1 to s2 and returns 0, <0, >0 if s1 equals, less or greater than s2	strcmp ("good", "good") = 0 strcmp ("good", "ok") = -1
strcpy (s1,s2)	Copies string s2 into string s2, which is returned	strcpy ("", "Passed") is "Passed"
strcspn (s1, s2)	Returns length of maximum initial segment of s1 with characters not in s2	strcspn ("Hello", "lo") is 2
strlen (s1)	Returns length of s1	strlen ("Important") is 9
strncat (s1, s2, n)	Appends leftmost n characters of s2 to the end of s1 that it returns	strncat ("Hello", "class", 2) returns "Hellocl"
strncmp (s1, s2, n)	Compares leftmost n characters of s1 to s2 and returns 0, >0, <0 if s1 equals, less or greater than s2	strncmp ("Hello", "class", 2) returns 1
strncpy (s1, s2, n)	Copies n leftmost characters of s2 into returned s1	strncpy ("Hello ", "your", 3) is "Hello you"
strpbrk (s1, s2)	Returns pointer address after first occurrence of any character in s2 found in s1, otherwise it returns null pointer	strpbrk ("Hello", "me") is &Hello +1
strrchr (s1, c)	Returns pointer address of last occurrence of c in s1 if found, otherwise returns null pointer	strrchr ("Hello", 'l') is &Hello + 3
strspn (s1, s2)	Returns the length of the maximum initial segment of s1 that contains s2	strspn ("Import", "port") is 4
strstr (s1, s2)	Returns the pointer address of the first occurrence of s2 in s1 if found, otherwise null pointer is returned	strstr ("Import", "port") is &Import + 2
strtok (s1, s2)	Breaks up s1 into its tokens delimited by any character in s2. While first call to strtok contains s1, subsequent calls for tokenizing the same s1 should have null as first argument.	strtok ("size_type", "_") has tokens "size", "type"

The format for the gets function call is:

gets (stringvariable);

The function, fgets is used to read a string of at most a specified length – 1 from a specified file pointer variable (fptr), into a string variable with the format:

fgets (stringvariable, length, filepointer);

The corresponding output functions for printing entire line of string to monitor and file are respectively, puts and fputs. Their formats are:

| puts (stringvariable); |

| fputs(stringvariable, length, filepointer); |

The sscanf is used to read data input of any type (like integer, string, float) into specified variables from a string specified as the first argument, using the given second argument format specifier. For example, sscanf ("June15 1960", "%s %d", &bdate, &byear) will read June15 into bdate and 1960 into byear. The format for sscanf is:

| sscanf(string_to_readfrom, format specifiers, variablelist); |

Similarly, sprintf is used to print the values of specified variables, not to the monitor, but into the first string argument with the format:

| sprintf(string_to_readfrom, format specifiers, variablelist); |

Other functions for string and character input/output exist in C and are available in the <stdio.h> library file. A summary of important one is provided in the following table.

function	description
fgetc(filpointer)	Reads next character from file as integer.
fgets(stringvariable,n,filepointer)	Reads up to n-1 characters from file into variable.
fprintf(filepointer, format specifiers, variablelist)	Prints values of variables in the list into file with specified file pointer using format specifiers.
fputc(charvariable, filepointer)	Prints character into file with filepointer.
fread(arraypointer, type size, numelements, filepointer)	Reads up to numelements of type with size bytes from file into elements of array in the first argument.
fscanf(filepointer, format specifers, variablelis)	Read into variable list data from file in first argument.
fwrite(arraypointer, type size, numelements, filepointer)	Prints into file up to numelements of type with size bytes from array in the first argument.
getc(filepointer)	Reads next character as integer from file.
getchar( )	Returns next character from the keyboard.
putc(charvariable, filepointer)	Similar to fputc. Writes character to file.
putchar(charvariable)	Writes character to standard output.
puts(charvariable)	Prints string to standard output.
sprintf(stringvariable, format specifiers, variablelist)	Prints variablelist into string variable instead of monitor.
sscanf(stringvariable, format specifiers, variablelist)	Reads data from string variable into variable list.

10.9 Files and Records

The format for declaring a file pointer variable in C is:

| **FILE   *filepointer;** |

The format for using the fopen command to form a connection with an already declared file pointer variable is :

196

```
filepointer = fopen ("disk file name", "mode");
```

The formats for reading from or printing into a file are:
```
fscanf( filePointer, "format specifiers", variable list to be read );
printf( filePointer, "format specifiers", variable list to be printed );
```

Format for closing a an input/output file is:
```
close (filePointer);
```

The format for specifying a file that its feof marker should be checked is:
```
feof (file_pointer_variable)
```

The format for defining a record structure or type is:
```
        struct record_type
        {       type field1;
                type field2;
                .
                .
                .
                type fieldn;
        }       /*      of record type*/
```

Now to declare variable of this type, use:
```
struct record_type      record_variable;
```

The format for the typedef declaration is:
```
tpedef   type   aliaslist;
```

An array of record type can also be defined as follows:
```
struct  record_type     record_var[size] ;
```

Format for declaring records of linked list type is:
```
struct list_type
        {char id[15];
        char name[20];
        list_type       *listptr ;
        }
```

To declare variable of type linked list, we declare a variable that points to the head of the list as follows:
```
struct  list_type       *listptr ;
```

197

11. SAMPLE TESTS, LAB EXERCISES AND ASSIGNMENTS

11.1 Statement on laboratory Exercises and Assignments
11.2 Sample Quiz 1
11.3 Sample Quiz 2
11.4 Sample Midterm
11.5 Sample final Examinations

11.1   Statement on Lab Exercises and Assignments

Laboratory exercises and the dates they are worked on are given next in this section. The weeks are numbered beginning with the first week of classes which begins at the middle of the week. Assignments indicating due dates are handed out in class during the term. Source programs, input data, output data and script files showing compilation and running of programs are handed in or shown to lab instructor and graduate assistant (GA) during each lab.

Working in groups of 2 or 3 students, is strongly recommended in the labs.

Lab. Exercises #1 (Lab date: Week 3 of classes)

Objectives are to:
1.   Learn basic Unix commands for preparing a source C program file, compiling a C program and executing a C program with input data from the keyboard. Also, learn how to use script file for handing in record of source program file, compilation and execution of programs.
2.   Practise on concepts taught in chapter 1 of text including how to present solutions to simple problems in the form of an algorithm (or program), how to identify the necessary input and output data of a problem. Also, practise on conversions of numeric values from one number base to another, and character data from character to ASCII code and vice versa.

Que. 1. Do question 11 of section 1.5 of text.
    Type, compile and run the C program equivalent of Algorithm 1.1 given as Figure 1.7 in the book. Hand in your source program file, the input data and the output of your run. Use the following set of input data:

5.1	4.3
4.2	4.5
5.3	5.2
5.7	6.0
4.1	4.3
5.0	5.3

5.2	5.3
5.6	5.5
4.8	4.8
4.9	4.9

Hints on how to solve

Materials needed to complete this exercise are: a Uwindsor computer account (ensure your computer account is already activated), a computer connected to either main sgi server or davinci server (if in a lab, the computer terminals are already connected to these two servers). Computer connected to, must have a text editor and a C compiler for typing, compiling and executing your programs.

Now follow these sequence of steps to complete the required task.

i. Connect to sgi or davinci server.

ii. Logon to the server using your computer user id and password.

iii. Open a terminal window with either an editor like nedit or pico.

iv. Type the program in Figure 1.7 of text book and save in a file called lab01.c

v. Open a new terminal window for compiling and running your program.

vi. In the new window, type:
ls   <return>
[This Unix command lists all files in the current directory. You will see the file lab01.c listed]

vii. Now compile this program by typing:
cc lab01.c   <return>
[If there are syntax errors, they will be listed on the terminal and you must go back to the program window, correct them, save the corrected program, and repeat the compilation of the corrected program. When there is no more compilation error, you are ready to move on to step viii.]

viii. Run (execute) the compiled program by typing:
a.out   <return>
[After successful compilation, the executable code is stored in a default file called a.out by C compilers so that typing the name of this file starts the process of running the program.]

ix. If the cursor is blinking at a blank line during execution of this program, it means that it is executing the scanf instruction, where the program tells the CPU to read a girl's height and a boy's height from the keyboard. Thus, the user (yourself) must type in two real numbers for these two variables separated by a blank space and a <return> after the typing the second height on each data line. Since the program instructs the CPU to pick 10 pairs of girl/boy heights, you need to type input data as follows:

5.1	4.3
4.2	4.5
5.3	5.2
5.7	6.0

4.1	4.3
5.0	5.3
5.2	5.3
5.6	5.5
4.8	4.8
4.9	4.9

x.   You can see the result of the program printed on the terminal window.

Que. 2. Compile and run the same program of Figure 1.7 of text and show the source code, compilation, execution, program input and output data in a script file.

Hints on how to solve

A record of all Unix commands executed during a logon session or part of a logon session can be saved in a script file by simply initiating the recording with the Unix script command and ending the recording when completed, with an exit command as follows.

i.   Open a Unix terminal window and type:
script lab01_scriptfile   <return>
[The general command is *script filename*, our script file here is lab01_scrptfile]

ii.   Now display your source program file with the Unix cat command as:
cat   lab01.c   <return>
[The command *cat filename* is used to display contents of filename on the screen]

iii.   Now compile the program by typing:
cc   lab01.c   <return>

iv.   Now Run the program by typing:
a.out   <return>

v.   Now, the CPU is waiting for you to type in the 10 pairs of heights as before:

5.1	4.3
4.2	4.5
5.3	5.2
5.7	6.0
4.1	4.3
5.0	5.3
5.2	5.3
5.6	5.5
4.8	4.8
4.9	4.9

vi.   After the result of the program has been displayed, you must exit script session by typing:
exit   <return>
[Failure to exit will prevent the script file from being saved and created.]

Que. 3. Practise with other Unix commands to list all the files in your directory, see the contents of your script file, send the script file to your GA, send your script file to your home computer so that you can print it.

Hints on how to solve

i.   To see all files in the current directory including the script file, type:
     ls   <return>

ii. To see contents of the script file, type:
     cat   lab01_scriptfile   <return>   or
     more lab01_scriptfile   <return>

iii. To send a file like your script file lab01_scriptfile (which is currently on the server.uwindsor.ca) to your home computer so that you can print it, you need to use ftp command to transfer files from one computer to another. To use ftp, follow the steps below:

   a. From your home computer, connect to internet, open your MSDOS prompt window. Then, in the MSDOS window, go to a directory on your home PC that you keep your 60-140 work (say c:\temp) by typing:
      cd   c:\temp   <return>
      [This is a dos command that takes you to temp directory on the hard disk of your home PC so that you can transfer the script file from server to this directory with ftp. Note that you should have temp directory already on your PC by the time you are going there or use any directory you already have].

   b. Now, run the ftp command to connect to server.uwindsor.ca as:
      ftp   server.uwindsor.ca   <return>

   c. Logon with your server user id and password when prompted.

   d. Now you are in ftp and can only use ftp commands for downloading files (get filename), for uploading files (put filename), for changing directory (cd), for listing files (ls) etc..
      To download the script file, lab01_scriptfile from server, do:
      get   lab01_scriptfile   <return>
      [This will place this file in your home PC in the directory C:\temp because this is the directory you ran the ftp from.]

   e. To exit ftp, type bye as:
      bye   <return>

   f. Now, you can use your Notepad or Wordpad to simply print the file lab01_scriptfile from directory C:\temp.

iv. Other Unix commands include telnet for connecting to a remote computer so that you can use the programs in the remote computer. For example, you can connect to server.uwindsor.ca from your home PC using telnet as follows:

   a. At your home PC, from the Run window of the Start menu bar (or from the MSDos prompt window), type telnet server.uwindsor.ca as:
      telnet   server.uwindsor.ca   <return>
      [This will establish a connection with the remote machine while you are on internet]

   b. Logon to server.uwindsor.ca with your user id and password when prompted.

home

201

c. You can now use any Unix commands on server for listing your files, compiling your C programs and running your C programs as well as editing your C programs (note though that only non-window based text editors like pico or vi can be used when you connect to the server remotely through a PC).

v. The secure shell client (ssh) and secure shell file transfer commands are not available on all operating systems, but can be downloaded. Only these secure versions of telnet and ftp programs for connecting to a server and transferring files to/from a server are allowed for remote access to davinci server.

vi. To create a new directory on Unix, use the mkdir command as:
mkdir   dirname   <return>

vii. To change to a different directory on Unix, use the cd as:
cd   dirname   <return>
[Note that dirname stands for the entire path of the directory from root (/)or home directory (~)]

viii. To move up one directory, for example to the parent directory, use:
cd   ..   <return>

ix. Whereever you are, to go to your home directory, use:
cd   ~   <return>

x. To make a copy of lab01.c file and keep in lab01cp.c, use:
cp lab01.c lab01cp.c   <return>

xi. To delete a file like delete lab01.c after making a copy, use:
rm   lab01.c   <return>

xii. To rename a file from lab01.c to lab02.c, use:
mv lab01.c lab02.c   <return>

Use the ASCII table in Appendix A of course text, for exercises involving ASCII conversion.

Que. 4. Here is a message coded in ASCII using eight bits per symbol. What does it say?

01000011 01101111 01101101 01110000 01110101 01110100
01100101 01110010 00100000 01010011 01100011 01101001
01100101 01101110 01100011 01100101

Que. 5. Show how the following instructions are represented in binary using ASCII by writing the codes for the instructions.
A = A + B;
++a;

Que. 6. Convert each of the following binary representations to its decimal form.
(a) 0101   (b) 10010   (c.) 10000

Que. 7. Convert each of the following decimal representations to its equivalent binary form.
(a) 18   (b) 27   (c.) 205

Que. 8. Name all the hardware components of the computer and identify the function of each component.

Que. 9. What is an algorithm? What is a program?, What is a problem?, What are input and output data?

Que. 10. For each of the conversions you did in problems (1) to (4) above identify the input, output and algorithm.

Lab. Exercises #2 (Lab date: Week 4 of classes)

Objectives are to:

1. Practise on solving problems and writing simple algorithmic and C program solutions for the problems by going through the problem solving steps as taught in chapter 2 of text book.
2. Practise on the use of arithmetic, logical, relational, bitwise, increment and decrement operators in C's expressions and assignment instructions as taught in chapter 3 of book.

Que. 1. Solve the problem of Section 2.3 of book, question 2 by going through the problem solving steps.

Given the lengths and widths of two rectangular yards in meters on a street as well as the lengths and widths of the houses located in the yards, and knowing that parts of the yards not holding the houses are covered with grass, write a an algorithmic solution and a C program to determine the area of each property that has grass. Show all five problem-solving steps.

Hints on how to solve

Follow the following steps in solving the problem:

i. Understand the problem by learning what is required to be done, what are available as input data to work with. You can draw a picture to make the requirements clear. For example, for this problem, I could understand with the following pictures of the yards:

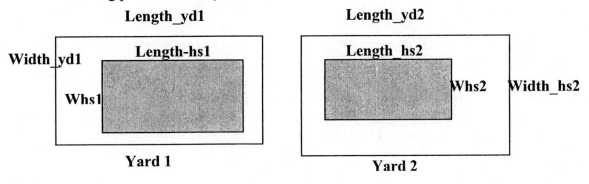

ii.   Identify all input, output data and their type as well as relationships between input and output data in equations:

Input data are:

Length_yd1   Length_yd2

Width_yd1   Width_yd2

Lhs_1   Lhs_2

Whs_1   Whs_2

Output data are:

grass_yard1   grass_yard2

Equations that link output data variables on the left hand side with input data variables on the right hand side in the correct logical order they will work are:

$$grass\_yard1 = (Length\_yard1 * Width\_yard1) - (Lhs\_1 * Whs\_1)$$

$$grass\_yard2 = (Length\_yard2 * Width\_yard2) - (Lhs\_2 * Whs\_1)$$

iii.   No need to break the problem solution into smaller modules now.

iv.   Write the algorithmic solution using the template for an algorithm similar to the formal algorithmic structure in Figure 3.1 of text book. Use the following template now.

       main module
       {
         Input data variables are:
         [fill in from step ii above]

         Output data variable are:
         [fill in from step ii above]

         /* Executable instructions consist of the equations that link output variables and input variables in the correct order. Write them next. Remember that input data have to be read first before being used to compute the output data. Finally, the output data have to be printed.   */

       }

v.   Now, translate the algorithm you have written in step iv above into a C program using the following template that is similar to the general structure of a C program presented in Figure 3.2 of text book.

```
#include   <stdio.h>
void main(void)
{
/* Now declare the input and output variables using int or float */
/* Remember to end every instruction with a semi-colon.*/


-----------------------------------------------------------------
-----------------------------------------------------------------


/* Next, translate each executable instruction in iv to a C instruction. */


-----------------------------------------------------------------
-----------------------------------------------------------------
-----------------------------------------------------------------
-----------------------------------------------------------------
}
```

   vi.   Now, type the program in v, compile and run with a set of test input data. You may use the following set of test data:

length_yd1= 80m, width_yd1= 55m,   length_hs1=50m, width_hs1= 40m
length_yd2= 100m, width_yd2= 60m, length_hs1=45m, width_hs2= 30m

       Show the results of your program in a script file.

Que. 2. Solve the problems of Exercise 2.3, questions 2 and 3 of course book by going through the problem solving steps.

Que. 3. Do questions 3, 4, 5, 7 and 8 from Section 3.3 of course book.

Que. 4. Discuss the problem solving steps.

Que. 5. Start to prepare for Quiz #1.

Lab. Exercises #3 (Lab date: Week 5 of classes)

Objectives are to:
1.   Practise on solving problems using top-down design approach by writing algorithms and programs with functions as taught in chapter 4 of text book.
2.   Feel comfortable with such concepts as: function prototypes, function call, function definition, call-by-value parameters, call-by-reference parameters, formal and actual parameters, local and global variables, structure and flowcharts, cohesion and coupling, variable scoping rules.

Continue to prepare for Quiz #1 if not yet written.

Que. 1. Do question 6 of Section 4.5 with examples.
Given the following program, show the values of the variables a, b, c, x, y, z in the main function after each function call to module2. Also, show the values of a, b, c in module2 immediately after executing each function call to module2.

```
#include <stdio.h>

/*  function prototype declaration for Module2   */
void module2(int, int, int *);
void main(void)
{
int a=3, b=4, c=5, x=7, y=8, z=10;

/*  body of main   */
  module2 (a, b, &c);   /* a first call to Module2   */
  printf("first call in main %d  %d  %d  %d  %d  %d \n", a, b, c, x, y, z);
  module2 (x, y, &z);   /* a second call to Module2   */
  printf("second call in main %d  %d  %d  %d  %d  %d \n", a, b, c, x, y, z);
}

/*  definition of module2   */
void module2 (int a, int b, int *c)
{
  a += 4;
  b += 4;
*c += 4;
  printf("in module2: %d  %d  %d %d \n", a, b, c, *c);
}
```

Hints on how to solve

i. First trace the above program with hand and write the values of the variables a, b, c, x, y, z in the main function after each function call to module2. Also, record the values of variables a, b, c in module2 immediately after executing each function call to module2.

In main	a	b	c	x	y	z
After 1st call to module2						
After 2nd call to module2						

In module2	a	b	c
After 1st call to module2			
After 2nd call to module2			

ii. Then, type in the program, compile and run to compare the results of your trace with that of your run.

If the two results do not match, talk to your lab instructor or GA for help

Que. 2. a) Question is: What is meant by the scope of a variable?
b) Give the variable scoping rules
c) Why is the use of parameters preferred over the use of global variables?

Que. 3. Do question 6 of Section 4.5.

Lab. Exercises #4 (Lab date: Week 6 of classes)

Objectives are to:
1. Keep practising on writing programs with functions as taught in chapter 4 of book. In particular, to feel comfortable with use of call-by-value and call-by-reference parameters.
2. Review all program logic structures as taught in chapter 5 of text book.

Que. 1. Do question 3 of section 4.5 of book.

Using top-down approach to problem-solving, write a C program that returns the fewest number of coins in change from a purchase of under five dollars, given a five dollar bill. The coins to be returned may include only toonies (two dollars), loonies (one dollar), quarters, dimes, nickels, and pennies. (Assume you can use a built-in function to convert a real n to an integer n.)

Example: purchase is 51 cents
change is $4.49
Coins: 2 toonies
1 quarter
2 dimes
4 cents

Hints on how to solve

i. Use the following structure chart.

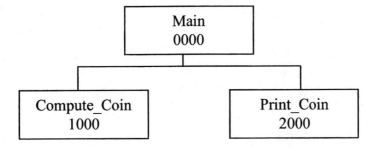

- Use the function Compute_Coin to calculate the number of toonies, loonies, etc. in the change.
- Use the Print_Coin function to print all the computed and requested output.

ii.   Use the integer division and modulus division to find the number of each category of coins left in the change. For example, if purchase is $0.51,

Change = 5.00 – 0.51 = $4.49 (recall there is input cash of $5.00).

To find the number of highest category of coin (toonies) in the change ($4.49), it is better to convert this real value to an integer value equivalent of (4.49 * 100 cents) = 449cents.

Now, to find the number of toonies (200cents) in 449 cents, we perform an integer divide of 449 by 200 and the remaining change will be the remainder (modulus) after this integer division. With the remaining change, we proceed to again find the number of next lower category of coin (loonie) by integer dividing the remainder by 100. We continue with the remainder in a similar fashion until the number of all category of coins are found.

The equations for performing the operations described above are as follows:

change = (int) ((cash – purchase) * 100)
rem_change = change   /* makes a copy of the original change */
toonies = rem_change / 200
rem_change = rem_change % 200
loonies = rem_change / 100
rem_change = rem_change % 100
quarter = rem_change / 25
rem_change = rem_change % 25
dime = rem_change / 10
rem_change = rem_change % 10
nickel = rem_change / 5
rem_change = rem_change %5
pennies = rem_change

iii.   Your job now is to understand the problem and use the two functions above and the main driver to write the program to solve the problem by making necessary function calls, passing the right parameters, placing the right instructions in the right function definition etc. You can complete the following program template in order to solve the problem.

```
#include  <stdio.h>

/* Now define the two function prototypes with their parameter types */

-------------------------------------------------
-------------------------------------------------

void main(void)
{

/* Now declare the input and output variables          */

-------------------------------------------------
-------------------------------------------------

/* Next, write the executable instructions including function calls*/

-------------------------------------------------
-------------------------------------------------
-------------------------------------------------
-------------------------------------------------

}        /* end of the main driver   */

/* Next, write the definitions of the two functions Compute_Coin and Print_Coin*/

write function header for Compute_Coin here
{
   /* write instructions in this function including any local variable declarations  */
   -------------------------------------------------
   -------------------------------------------------

      :
   -------------------------------------------------
   -------------------------------------------------

}        /* end of Compute_Coin function            */


write function header for Print_Coin here
{
   /* write instructions in this function including any local variable declarations  */
   -------------------------------------------------
   -------------------------------------------------

      :
```

```
--------------------------------------------------------
--------------------------------------------------------
```
}   /* end of Print_Coin function   */

Type, compile and run your program and show work in a script file.

Que 2. Define the two types of parameters. How do they differ? Under what circumstances would you use each type?

Que 3. Why are cohesion and coupling important to programmers?

Que 4. Name all the program logic structures, giving a simple example of each structure.

Que. 5. Name the major types of modules in a solution and explain their functions.

Lab. Exercises #5 (Lab date: Week 7 of classes)

Objectives are to:
1.   Practise on the use of decision instructions like *if* and *switch-case* instructions in problem solving as taught in chapter 6 of book.
2.   Begin to prepare for midterm test by revising how to write programs with valid C instructions, data types and functions discussed in chapters 1 to 6 of text book.

Que. 1. Do question 1 of Section 6.3 of book.
A student in a computer class has four tests to write. To get an A in the course, the student must average at least 90% on the four tests. Given the student's scores on the 4 tests, write a C program to determine if the student should get an A or not.

Hints on how to solve

i.   You can use the following program template for your solution.

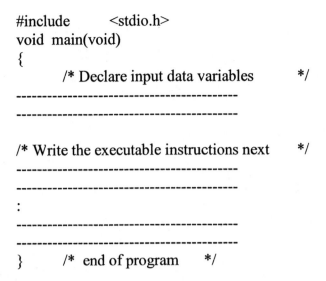

```
#include        <stdio.h>
void main(void)
{
        /* Declare input data variables        */
        ----------------------------------------
        ----------------------------------------

        /* Write the executable instructions next     */
        ----------------------------------------
        ----------------------------------------
        :
        ----------------------------------------
        ----------------------------------------
}        /* end of program     */
```

ii.   Compile and run your program with the following sample data and show your work in a script file.

| 70 | 85 | 90 | 78 |
| 90 | 95 | 89 | 99 |

Que. 2. Do question 2 of Section 6.3 of book.

Modify problem (1) above such that if a student averages 90 or more he gets an A, but an   average of 80-89, gives him a B, an average of 70-79 gives him a C while an average of 60-69 gives him a D. Anything lower then 60 is a grade of F. Write a C program to determine a student's grade given his/her test scores.

(a) Give 4 different solutions using nested if instruction.

(b) Set up 4 flowcharts corresponding to (a).

(c) Give a solution using swich-case instruction.

Hints on how to solve

i.   To solve a decision problem with multiple conditions like the above, set up a condition_action table like the following:

mark	grade
>= 90	A
80 to 89	B
70 to 79	C
60 to 69	D
< 60	F

The correct grade can be obtained using a nested *if instruction* that can be written in four different ways corresponding to:

a. Positive nested if logic starting from top to bottom of the table.

b. Positive nested if logic starting from bottom to top of the table.

c. Negative nested if logic starting from top to bottom of the table.

d. Negative nested if logic starting from bottom to top of the table.

ii. Now answer questions 2(a) of the lab #5 exercise by writing the 4 programs and testing with sample data (may use the sample below). Show the lab instructor/GA in a script file.

```
70  85   90  78
90  95   89  99
50  60   45  68
70  80   63  85
60  65   69  64
```

iii. Complete questions 2(b) and 2(c) of lab exercise #5.

Que. 3. Begin to prepare for midterm test.

Lab. Exercises #6 (Lab date: Week 8 of classes)

There is no formal lab this date, to allow time for test revisions. Lab instructors and GA's will be available to answer questions you may have.

Objectives are to:
1.   Allow students time to revise for midterm test, discover areas they are having difficulties by themselves and ask individual questions in those areas.

Lab. Exercises #7 (Lab date: Week 9 of classes)

Objectives are to:
1.   Practise on use of repetition (loop) instructions like *while, do-while* and *for instructions* in problem solving as taught in chapter 7 of text book.
2.   Begin to prepare for quiz #2.

Continue to prepare for midterm test if not yet written.

Que. 1.   Do question 6 of Section 7.7 of book.

Write a program to compute the average test score obtained by each of the students whose 4 test scores for a course are given. Last data line is a sentinel value of –1 for only the first test score. Print the student name, test scores and average test score in the format shown in the sample output below.

Sample input

70	50	80	90	John_James
54	63	71	75	Mary_Kate

.
.

.

-1

sample output

student name	test scores	average test score
John_James	70, 50, 80, 90	75.5

.
.
.

Hints on how to solve

i. You need an event-control loop instruction because you do not know the number of data lines ahead of time. You can only tell that there are no more data when the first test score read is a sentinel value of –1.

ii. To give a hand in solving the problem, you can type and execute the following program first, which is similar. This following program, reads only one test score until a sentinel value of –1 is met. Your job now is to modify the program such that it can read 4 test scores and to solve the problem in lab question 1.

```
#include        <stdio.h>
void main(void)
{
        float   test1;
        scanf("%f", &test1);
        while  (test1 != -1)
        {
                printf("%f \n", test1);
                scanf("%f", &test1);
        }       /*  end of while       */
}               /*  end of program     */  .
```

Compile and run your program with test data and show your work in a script file.

Que. 2. Do questions 2 and 3 of Section 7.7

Que. 3. (Optional) Define a problem of your own that involves loops and solve.

Que. 4. Start to prepare for Quiz #2

Lab. Exercises #8 (Lab date: Week 10 of classes)

Objectives are to:

1.   Practise on the use of nested looping with functions and arrays in problem solving as taught in chapters 7 and 8. Also, practise on the use of flowcharts.

2.   In particular, to learn how to specify array parameters in function prototypes, function calls and function definitions. Also, to learn how to specify array parameters as call-by-value and as call-by-reference parameters.

3.   Continue to practise for quiz #2 if not yet written.

Que. 1. Assume you have the following table of scores,

70	51	65	83	85
83	65	67	71	91
90	70	71	77	80
92	85	88	80	79

write a program using top-down design to read this table, print the average and minimum value of each row and column.

Hints on how to solve

i.   Solve using the following structure chart.

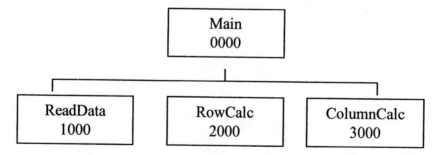

-     Use the ReadData function to read the two dimensional array table.
-     Use the RowCalc function to navigate the rows and obtain the minimum element, total and average of each row.
-     Use the ColCalc function to navigate the columns and obtain the minimum element, total and average of each column.

ii.   Parts of bigger programs like this can first be tested, made to work before completing the rest of the program. Thus, you can first complete the ReadData to ensure that data are being read well first. To learn that the function ReadData is working, you also need to include instructions for printing read data. The following program template provides the complete ReadData function and the instructions to print the data and you are expected to modify it to complete the solution.

```
#include        <stdio.h>
/* declare the function prototypes */
void  ReadData(int [][5], int, int);

void main(void)
{
        int  score [4][5], r, c;
        ReadData(score, 4, 5);

        /* Now print the table array */
for (r=0; r < 4; r++)
        {
                for (c =0; c < 5; c++)
                {
                        printf("%d ", score[r][c]);
                }
                printf("\n");
        }

}       /* end of the main driver */

/* Next, we present the function definition for ReadData */
void ReadData(int score[][5], int numrow, int numcol)
{
        int  r,c;
        for (r = 0; r < numrow; r++)
                for (c = 0; c < numcol; c++)
                        scanf("%d", &score[r][c]);
}                       /* end of function ReadData */
```

iii.   Now, complete the solution to the problem above by n including the function prototypes for the other two functions RowCalc and ColumnCalc. Then, make proper function calls to these functions in the main driver and provide the function definitions for the functions following the ReadData function definition.

Que. 2.   (Optional) Define a problem of your own that involves loops and solve the same way as in question 1.

Lab. Exercises #9 (Lab date: Week 11 of classes)

Objectives are to:
1.   Continue to practise on the use of arrays, repetition, decisions and functions in solving bigger problems.
2.   Also, continue to practise on use of flowcharts.

Que. 1.   For the following problem, give the structure chart, programs and flowcharts.

The class quiz consists of 40 True/False questions. There are 100 students who wrote the test. You are required to write a program to calculate the students' grades based on the highest score in the class given that:
Grade
A   will range from the highest score, to the highest score minus 3.
B   from the highest score minus 4, to the highest score minus 5.
C   from the highest score minus 6, to the highest score minus 7.
D   from the highest score minus 8, to the highest score minus 9.
F   will be anything below highest score minus 9.

Each student's ID and test answers will be entered. The output will be each student's ID, number correct, and grade, along with the single highest score for the class. Hint: You can use four one-dimensional ar

Hints on how to solve

i.   In understanding the problem, the following shows the sample input data and output data from the problem description.

ID[4][10]	Answer [4][40]					Numcrrt[4]	Grade[4]
20031	0	1	.....	0	0	35	A
20032	1	1	.....	0	1	14	F
20033	0	1	.....	0	1	25	F
20034	1	0	......	0	0	30	B

Anskey[40]					highestscore
0	1	......	0	0	35

Grade formula is:

highestsocore to (highestscore – 3)	: A	->	[35 to 32]
(highestsocore – 4) to (highestscore – 5)	: B	->	[31 to 30]
(highestsocore – 6) to (highestscore – 7)	: C	->	[29 to 28]
(highestsocore – 8) to (highestscore – 9)	: D	->	[27 to 26]
below (highestscore – 9	: B	->	[31 to 30]

ii. To be able to test the program, use smaller sized data. Use only 2 students and 5 test questions and test your program with the following sample data:

iii. You may use the following structure chart.

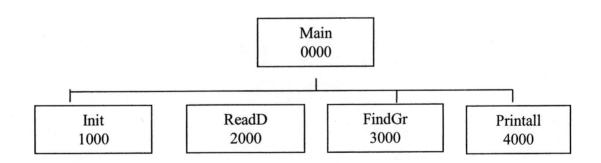

- Use the Init function to initialize Numcrrt array to 0.
- Use the ReadD function to read input data (ID, Answer, Anskey).
- Use the FindGr function to compute the grade for each student and the highest score.
- Use the function Printall to print all output.

iv.   Type in the following part of the solution, which only reads in the input data with the function ReadD and prints only the ID, Answers and Anskey read with the function PrintAll. Your job is to first type and run this program to ensure that you are reading your data well, then, complete the program by writing the function prototypes, calls and definitions for the functions Init, FindGr and Printall that will solve the given problem.

```c
/*To be able to test the program, I am substituting  2 for 100 students and 5
for 40 questions. Thus,  2 students write 5 True/False questions
Calculate grades based on the highest score in the class
 A: from the highest score to the highest score-3
 B: from the highest score-4 to the highest score-5
 C: from the highest score-6 to the highest score-7
 D: from the highest score-8 to the highest score-9
 F: below the highest score-9                                          */

#include <stdio.h>
/*declare function prototypes*/
void ReadD (char [][10], int [][5], int []);
void PrintAll (char [][10], int [][5], int []);

void main () {

  char ID[2][10];
  int answers[2][5], anskey[5];

  ReadD (ID, answers, anskey);
  PrintAll (ID, answers, anskey);
}

/* Here is function definition for ReadD              */
/*read data into arrays of studentID, answers, answer key */
void ReadD (char ID[][10], int answers[][5], int anskey[])
{
 int r, c;
 for (r=0; r<2; r++) {
    scanf ("%s", ID[r]);
   for (c=0; c<5; c++){
    scanf ("%d", &answers[r][c]);
}
  } /* end of outer for r  */
for (c=0; c<5; c++)
   scanf ("%d", &anskey[c]);

} /* end of function ReadD  */
```

```
/*The PrintAll function here is used to print only data read */
void PrintAll (char ID[][10], int answers[][5], int anskey[])
{
  int r, c;
  printf ("ID    Answers \n");
  for (r=0; r<2; r++){
   printf("%s", ID[r]);
    for (c=0; c<5; c++) {
                printf ("%d", answers[r][c]);}
        printf(" \n");    }        /* end of outer for r */
  printf("The answer key is: \n");
   for (c=0; c<5; c++) {
                printf ("%d", anskey[c]);} /* end of for c */
 }                      /* end of function Printall  */
```

iv. When you run the above sample program, you need to type in input data at the keyboard in the order you asked for them to be read in the function ReadD. You should type each ID on a separate line, followed by the 5 answers for this ID on the next line. At the end, you should type the 5 answers in the answer key. The input at the keyboard should look like the following:

```
20031
1  0 1 1 1
20032
0  0 0 1 1
1 0 1 1 0
```

Hand in your completed work to lab instructor and GA in a script file.

Que. 2. Solve any of the string processing questions in section 8.8 of book, questions 8, 9, 10, 11.

Lab. Exercises #10 (Lab date: Week 12 of classes)

Lab Examination

Objective:

1.   To test the students' ability to write, edit, compile and run programs for solving simple problems without using functions, but using only necessary read, print, assignment and decision instructions.

2.   To test students' ability to write, edit, compile and run programs for solving problems with functions, repetitions and arrays.

Instructions

a.   For each question, hand in a script file showing your source program file, compilation and running of the program as well as program input and output data.

b.   Use of email is not allowed during this lab exam.

Que. 1. Write a C program that determines the total bill (amount of money) to be paid by a convenience store customer, who bought 3 bottles of water, 4 bags of potato chips and 2 cartons of milk. The cost of each store item is given as input and your program should print the total cost of each item and the total bill for the customer.

                      ………………………….   [50 marks]

Sample Input data:

1.25	/* cost of each bottle of water */
0.90	/* cost of a bag of potato chips */
2.49	/* cost of 1 carton of milk */

Sample Output data:

Water 3 @ 1.25 each …	$3.75
Chips 4 @ 0.90 each …	$3.60
Milk 2 @ 2.49 each …	$4.98
Total	$11.33

Suggested Marking Scheme:

Correct program structure in a source file with correct input and output data declarations.	(20 marks)
Correct program structure in a source file with correct logic.	(20 marks)
Correct logic and correct input/output data assignments.	(10 marks)

Que. 2. Write a C program that uses at least an additional function called by main to calculate and print the sum and difference of corresponding elements of two integer arrays with 5 elements each. For example, if the sample input below is typed in, the output produced by the program is the sample output below.

                      …………………..   [50 marks]

Sample input data:		Sample output data:	
Array1	Array2	Sum_Array	Diff_Array
15	10	25	5
13	9	22	4
80	100	180	-20
5	6	11	-1
16	15	31	1

Suggested Marking Scheme:

Correct program structure in a source file with correct input and output data declarations. (10 marks)

Correct program structure in a source file with correct function prototypes. (10 marks)

Correct program structure in a source file with correct logic having function call(s) with correct actual parameters. (10 marks)

Correct program structure in a source file with correct logic having correct function definitions with correct formal parameters. (10 marks)

Correct logic and input/output data assignments. (10 marks)

Other Alternative Work this Lab:

Que.1. Revision for final examination may start.

Que 2. Fastloan, a financial company that grants loan to hardworking college students wants you to develop a program, which reads a data file of applicant records and produces an output file containing only records of approved applicants. Loan is granted based on the policy that the total of student's annual living expenses excluding tuition minus the student's yearly work income must not exceed the student's annual tuition. The input file has records on each student applicant specifying student id, name, rent cost, feeding cost, clothing cost, transportation costs, tuition, and annual work income.

Lab. Exercise #11 (Lab date: Week 13 of classes)

Revisions for final examinations during this lab. Bring your own questions.

11.2 Sample Quiz 1

UNIVERSITY OF WINDSOR
COMPUTER SCIENCE 60-140-01/04/05
QUIZ #1

Examiner: Dr. C.I. Ezeife   Given: Wed., Oct. 6, 1999 (modified)
                                    Student Name:
                                    Student Number:
                                    Lab. Section: 51,52,53,54,59/61,60/62,63,64,65,66
                                    (circle the correct one)

INSTRUCTIONS (Please Read Carefully)
No calculators allowed.
Examination Period is 1 hour.
Answer all questions. There are 40 multiple choice questions.
Use the Mark sense sheet. Use only a Pencil on mark sense sheet. Record and shade your name on the answer sheet (Surname first, then other names). Mark your answers carefully and clearly (fill in the appropriate circle completely). Select only one answer for each question. Turn in both examination paper and answer sheet. Also have your name on the examination paper.

---

40 Multiple choice questions:

1. A computer stores characters of information it processes
    a. as decimal digits   b. in character form
    c. as C language   d. as binary digits
    e. none of the above
2. An algorithm is
    a. exactly the same as a computer program   b. made up of just the input data
    c. is a sequence of steps for solving a problem
    d. an instruction   e. none of the above
3. A problem
    a. can be solved by the computer
    b. has input and output data as well as an algorithmic and program solutions
    c. has alternative solutions
    d. all of the above   e. none of the above
4. The CPU is the part of the computer that
    a. performs arithmetic and logical operations   b. processes instructions
    c. fetches and executes instructions   d. all of the above
    e. none of the above
5. Secondary memory is needed because
    a. primary memory is not fast enough   b. primary memory is too big
    c. primary memory is volatile   d. all of the above
    e. none of the above

6. Computer memory can be
   a. Read only memory
   b. Random access memory
   c. Secondary memory
   d. Only (a) and (b)
   e. all of (a), (b) and (c.)
7. What do you need to do to an algorithm to have it executed by the computer?
   a. Write it clearly and well
   b. Type it in WordPerfect
   c. Translate it into a program in a programming language
   d. write it in pseudocode
   e. none of the above

Assume the initial contents of memory addresses are as follows:

Address	Contents
00	61
01	15
02	18
03	27

If the computer executes the following sequence of instructions, answer questions 8 to 11 to report the effect of executing all these instructions in sequence.

Step 1: Put the sum of the contents of cells with addresses 00 and 03, into the cell at address 00.

Step 2: Put the content of cell 01 into the cell at address 03.

Step 3: Put the value stored at address 02 into the cell at address 01.

8. The new content of cell 00 is:
   a. 61
   b. 15
   c. 18
   d. 88
   e. none of the above
9. The new content of cell 01 is:
   a. 61
   b. 15
   c. 18
   d. 88
   e. none of the above
10. The new content of cell 02 is:
   a. . 61
   b. 15
   c. 18
   d. 88
   e. none of the above
11. The new content of cell 03 is:
   a. . 61
   b. 15
   c. 18
   d. 88
   e. none of the above
12. Fourth generation computers have high processing powers because:
   a. they are built on vacuum tube technology
   b. they are built on large scale integrated circuit technology
   c. they are built on single transistor technology
   d. (a) to (c)
   e. none of (a) to (c)
13. The advantage of writing computer programs in high level language is:
   a. High level language is easier for the programmer than strings of bits.
   b. High level language is faster to execute by the CPU.
   c. High level language is more portable than strings of bits.
   d. (a) and (b)
   e. (a) and (c.)
14. A program written in a high level language needs to be first converted into strings of bits before it can be executed by the CPU in the process called:

a. coding
b. compilation
c. problem solving
d. problem analysis   e. none of the above

15. A main memory with capacity 64 megabytes has
  a. 64 thousand cells
  b. 64 million cells
  c. 64 billion cells
  d. 64 cells   e. none of the above

16. An example of a high level language is:
  a. COBOL
  b. FORTRAN
  b. C
  d. PASCAL   e. all of the above

17. The appropriate sequence of steps for solving a problem is:
  a. Write an algorithm, code into a program, define its input and output data.
  b. Define input and output data, then define the algorithm and program.
  c. Define output data, define algorithmic solution, then define input data.
  d. none of the above
  e. all of (a) to (c.)

18. A computer software system can be:
  a. Operating systems
  b. Network application
  c. Compilers
  d. Productivity tools
  e. all of (a) to (c.)

19. Assume a variable NumDays is of integer type and has value 50. The number of whole weeks (of 7 days each) in NumDays is:
  a. 5
  b. 0
  c. 1
  d. 7   e. none of the above

20. How many days in NumDays of question 19, do not fall into a week?
  a. 5
  b. 0
  c. 1
  d. 7   e. none of the above

21. The data type of the following data "true" in C is:
  a. integer
  b. float
  c. char array[]
  d. int   e. logical

22. To find out if proposed solutions are correct, it is important to evaluate or test all expressions and equations. Given that X=3, Y=9 and Z=2, what is the value of the expression:
  6 \ X + Y % Z - 1
  a. 25
  b. 24
  c. 12
  d. 23   e. none of the above

23. What is the value of the following Boolean expression, if A=1, B=0 and C= 1.
  !(A) && ! (C) || A && B
  a. TRUE
  b. FALSE
  c. unknown
  d. all of the above   e. none of the above

24. The binary digit representation for the decimal number 91 stored in memory is:
  a. 1011001
  b. 1111001
  c. 111001
  d. 1011000   e. none of the above

25. Write a C language equation for the following mathematics equation
  $$q = \frac{kA (T_1 - T_2)}{L}$$
  a. q = kA (T_1 - T_2)/L
  b. q = k * A * (T_1 - T_2)/L
  c. q = kA (T1 - T2)/L
  d. q = (k * A * (T1 - T2))/L

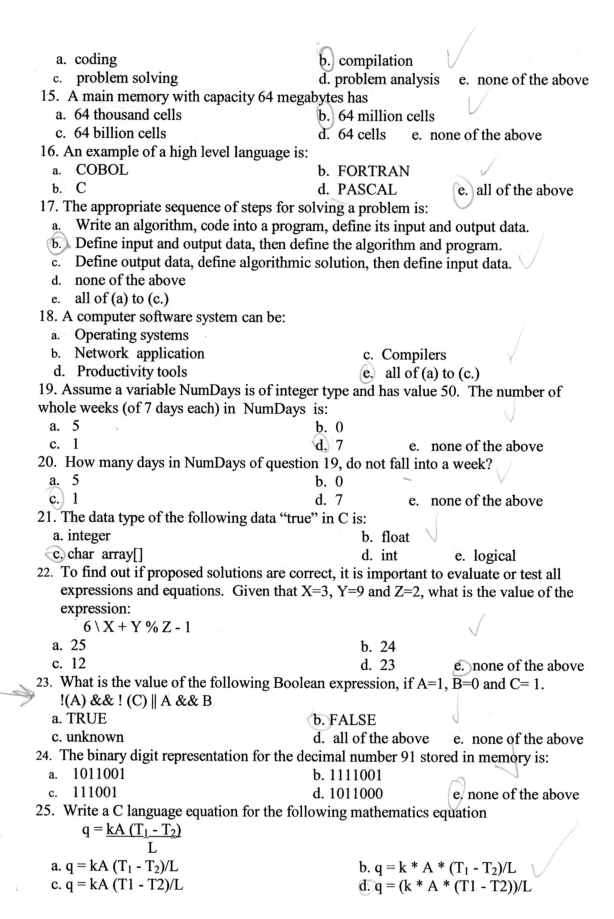

e. none of the above

26. A program is a
    a.   computer hardware   b. CD-ROM
    c.   version of an algorithm written in a programming language
    d. (a) and (b)   e. (b) and (c.)

27. The C increment and decrement operations k++ and k- - respectively mean:
    a.   k=a+1 and k=a-1
    b.   k=k+1 and k=k-1
    c.   k=k+sum and k=k-sum
    d.   k +=2 and k -= 2
    e.   none of the above

28. Most reasonable input variable names for two numbers to be averaged are:
    a. Num1, Num2   b. Read, write
    c. Add, Display   d. all of the above   e. none of the above

29. Most reasonable output variable name for two numbers to be averaged is:
    a. average   b. Sum
    c. Num1Num2   d. Num1   e. Num2

30. The simple program segment for getting the sum of two numbers is.
    a.   scanf("%d %d",Num1, Num2);   b. scanf("%d %d",&Num1, Num2);
        sum = Num1 + Num2;   sum = Num1 + Num2;
        printf("%d",sum);   printf("%d",sum);
    c. scanf("%d %d",&Num1, &Num2);   d. Read Num1, Num2;
       average = (Num1 + Num2)/2;   Sum = Num1 + Num2;
       printf("%d",sum);   Print Sum;
    e. none of the above

31. A computer system is made up of
    a. keyboard, printer and software   b. hardware and software components
    c. keyboard, printer and CD-ROM   d. programs in a high level language
    e.   none of the above

32. The first parameter of a scanf or printf instruction is a string literal with format specifiers for variables to be read or printed. The format specifier for a string variable is:
    a. %d   b. %c   c. %f   d. %ld   e. none of a to d

33. The C instruction: printf("%5d", 25) will display the line below:
        column   1 2 3 4 5
    a.   2 5
    b.   2 5
    c.   2 5
    d.   2 5
    e.   none of the above.

Given the following C program:
```
#include <stdio.h>
void main(void){
    const char blank[4]= "****", fill[2]="&&";
        char feeling[7]= "happy";
        printf("I am %s", blank); }
```
34. Running this program once produces the following output:
   a. I am blank   b. I am &&
   c. I am ****   d. I am happy   e. I am feeling

35. To print the statement "I am happy" with the above program, without changing our
   constant declaration, we need to
   a. change nothing   b. change statement 2 to print ("I am %s", feeling)
   c. assign "happy" to blank in the body of algorithm
   d. (b) and (c.)   e. none of the above

Given the following program:
```
#include <stdio.h>
void main(void){
    float salary, percent_deduct, Projected_salary;
    scanf ("%f %f", &salary, &percent_deduct);
    Projected_salary = salary * (1 - percent_deduct);
    printf("%f ", Projected_salary); }
```
36. Given that salary = $10000.00 and percent_deduct = 0.05, what is printed by this
   program?
   a. $10000.00   b. $10500.00
   c. $15000.00   d. $9500.00
   e. none of the above

37. What is printed by the above program if salary = 5000.00 and percent = 0.10?
   a. $5500.00   b. $5000.00
   c. $6000.00   d. $4500.00
   e. none of the above

What data type would you use to represent the following items in questions 38 to 40?
38. Number of students in the 60-140 class
   a. char   b. char variable[]
   c. int   d. float   e. int with values 0 or !0

39. Whether assignment 1 is handed in or not?
   b. char   b. char variable[]
   c. int   d. float   e. int with values 0 or !0

40. The letter initial for a student's name
   c. char   b. char variable[]
   c. int   d. float   e. int with values 0 or !0

11.3. Sample Quiz 2

Examiner: Dr. C.I. Ezeife   Given: Mon., Nov. 10, 1999 (modified)

Student Name:_____

Student Number:_____

Lab. Section: 51, 52, 53, 54, 59/61, 60/62, 63, 64, 65, 66
(circle one)

INSTRUCTIONS (Please Read Carefully)

No calculators allowed.

Examination Period is 1 hour.

Answer all questions. There are 40 multiple choice questions.

Use the Mark sense sheet. Use only a Pencil on mark sense sheet. Record and shade your name on the answer sheet (Surname first, then other names). Mark your answers carefully and clearly (fill in the appropriate circle completely). Select only one answer for each question. Turn in both examination paper and answer sheet. Also have your name on the examination paper.

---

40 Multiple choice questions:

1. The two important concepts that enable several programmers working on the same problem to work independently and yet be able to integrate their results effectively are

    a.   repetition and decision logic   b. compilation and linking
    c.   coupling and cohesion   d.   variables and constants
    e.   none of the above

2. Which of the following items describes how data is modified?
    a.   function definition   b.   parameter list
    c.   variable declaration   d.   local variables
    e.   none of the above

3. Values are passed through which one of the following?
    a.   function definition   b.   parameter list
    c.   variable declaration   d.   local variables
    e.   none of the above

4. Top-down design approach to problem solving requires that
    a. we solve the problem using nested if statements.
    b. we give one complete and long solution for the problem
    c. we break down the problem into sub problems and integrate solutions of the sub-problems

227

d. (a) and (b)
e. (b) and (c.)

5.   What would be printed by the following program?
```
#include <stdio.h>
void main(void){
        int X=20, Y=3;
        printf ("Yes  X = %d and Y= %d ",X, Y);
}
```

a.   Yes 20 3
b.   Yes   X=20 and Y=3
c.   Yes   X= 3 and Y=20
d.   Yes 3 20
e.   none of the above

6.   What would be printed by the following program segment?

```
if (!(20 > 16))
        printf ("never");
else
        printf ("always");
```

a.   never   b.   always
c.   never always   d.   20 > 16
e.   none of the above

The next four questions refer to the following program.
```
#include <stdio.h>
void main(void){
        int Z = 0,  G = 0,  S = 0,  I = 1, T;
while (I < 20) {
     scanf ("%d", &T);   /* T does not need to be known to do the questions  */
     S += T;
     if (T >= 0)
       G ++;
       else  Z ++;
     I ++;
   }
}
```

7.   How many times is the while statement executed?
a.   19 times   b.   20 times
c.   once   d.   never
e.   until a number 50 or larger is entered

228

8. The value stored in variable S at the end of the execution of the loop could best be described as the
    a. average of the numbers read   b. largest of all numbers read
    c. sum of all numbers read   d. number of numbers read
    e. sentinel value terminating the loop

9. The value stored in variable Z at the end of the execution of the loop could best be described as the
    a. number of positive items read   b. sum of all positive items read
    c. number of negative items read   d. sum of all negative items read
    e. sentinel value terminating the loop

10. The loop control variable, which must be updated inside the loop body for the loop to terminate, is
    a. T   b. S
    c. G   d. Z
    e. I

11. What does this program segment display?

```
        do
                printf ("A false example");
        while (!(1));
```

    a. A false Example displayed once   b. A false Example displayed twice
    c. Nothing displayed d. A false Example displayed infinite number of times
    e. Loop will never execute

12. What does this program segment do?

```
S = 0;
I = N;       /* assume N is even  */
do {
        S += I;
        I -= 2;
} while (I != 0);
```

    a. Add all numbers from 1 to N   b. Add all the numbers from 1 to N-1
    c. Add the even numbers from 1 to N   d. Add the odd numbers from 1 to N
    e. none of the above

13. What does this program segment do?

```
int S=0, X;
for (I = N; I >= 1; I--)
    {
        X = ((I % 2) == 0 );       /* X is a logical type */
        if (X)
                S += I;  }
```

a. Add all numbers from 1 to N   b. Add all the numbers from 1 to N-1
c. Add the even numbers from 1 to N   d. Add the odd numbers from 1 to N
e. none of the above

14. For what exact range of values of variables X does the following program segment print 'C'?

```
        if (X <= 200)
                if (X < 100)
                        if (X <= 0)
                                printf ("A");
                        else
                                printf ("B");
                else
                        printf ("C");
        else
                printf ("D");
```

a. $0 < X < 100$ b. $X <= 0$
c. $100 <= X <= 200$ d. $X > 200$
e. $100 < X <= 200$

15. Functions are good to use in problem solving because
a. they help to solve the problem faster   b. they allow usability of code and results
c. they encourage top-down design   d. all of the above
e. none of (a) to (c)

16. What is the value of A after the call F(6, 4, 3) given the following definition of function F ?

```
        void function F(int B, int C, int *A) {
        int I, J, K, L=0; /* these are variables declared inside this function */
                for (I = 1; I <= *A ; I ++) {
                        for (K = 3; K <= C; K++) {
                                L += K;
                        }                      /*end of inner for loop*/
                }                              /*end of outer for loop*/
                *A = L;
        }                                      /*end of F */
```

a.   28   b.   30
c.   21   d.   33
e.   none of the above

17. What is an example of a formal parameter list in the program in question 16 above ?
   a. (6,4,3) in F(6, 4, 3)   b. (B, C, *A)
   c. I, J, K, L   d. all of the above
   e. only (a) to (b)

18. The local variables in this algorithm in question 16 above are:
   a. A, B, C   b. I, K, L
   c. I, J, K, L   d. all of the above
   e. none of (a) to (c)

19. Functions in our program can communicate with each other using one of these techniques:
   a. parameter passing   b. global variable
   c. return of values through functions d. all of the above
   e. none of the above

Use the following program to answer the next four questions

```
#include <stdio.h>

/*   function prototype declaration for Module2   */
void module1(int, int, int *);
void main(void){
int a=3, b=4, c=5, x=7, y=8, z=10;
/*   body of main   */
        module1 (a, b, &c);    /* a first call to Module1   */
        module1 (x, y, &z);    /* a second call to Module1  */
}
/*   definition of module1   */
void module1 (int a, int b, int *c){
        a -= 2;
        b -= 2;
        *c -= 2;
}
```

20. The values of the variables a,b,c in main after the first function call to Module1 are:
   a. 3, 4, 5   b. 3, 4, 9
   c. 3, 4, 3   d. 7, 8, 8
   e. none of the above

21. The values of the variables a,b,c in Module1 after the first function call to Module1 are:
   a. 3, 4, 5   b. 3, 4, 9
   c. 3, 4,3   d. 1, 2, 3   e. none of the above

22. The values of the variables a,b,c in Module1 after the second function call to Module1 are:
   a. 7, 8, 10   b. 3, 4, 5
   c. 5, 6, 8   d. 7, 8, 8
   e. none of the above

23. The values of the variables x, y, z in main after the second function call to Module1 are:

a.   7, 8, 10   b.   3, 4, 3
c.   5, 6, 8   ·   d.   7, 8, 8
e.   none of the above

24. The effect of the following program segment can best be described as

```
if (X < Y)
    Z = X;
if (X=Y)
    Z = 0;
if (X > Y)
    Z = Y;
```

a. The smaller of X and Y is stored in Z.
b. The larger of X and Y is stored in Z.
c. The larger of X and Y is stored in Z, unless X and Y are equal, in which case Z is assigned zero.
d. The larger of X and Y is stored in Z, unless X and Y are not equal, in which case Z is assigned zero.
e. none of the above.

25. A list of complete test data set for X in the algorithm segment in question 24 above, assuming Y is 20 is:

a.   20, 100   b.   12, 20, 100
c.   -20, 20, 25   d.   (a) and (b)
e.   (b) and (c.)

Answer the next 5 questions with the program below.

This program finds all element of an array of 10 integers that are less than their (minimum value + 10).

```
#include <stdio.h>
int getmini(int []);
void main(void) {
int num[10] = {34, 15, 7, 30, 11, 16, 90, 55, 10, 8}, mini, r;
mini = getmini(num);
for (r=0; r<10; r++) {
if (num[r] < (mini + 10))
    printf("%d\n", num[r]); } }    /* end of main    */
/* definition of function getmini    */
int getmini(int  num[]) {
int r, smallnum;
    smallnum = num[0];
    for (r = 1; r < 10; r++) {
        if (num[r] < smallnum)
            smallnum = num[r];    }
return (smallnum);        }
```

232

26. The program's function prototype is:
    a. mini = getmini(num);
    b. int getmini(int []);
    c. int getmini(int num[]);
    d. void main(void)
    e. none of the above

27. The actual parameter in the function call to getmini is:
    a. mini   b.   r
    c. scanf   d.   array num
    e. none of the above

28. In main function, the call to the function getmini is an assignment instruction because:
    a. the actual parameter is an array
    b. main is void type
    c. getmini is int type and must return an int value
    d. getmini is void type and must return a value
    e. none of the above

29. In the function getmini, the instruction smallnum = num[0] does the following:
    a. stores the first element of array as smallnum
    b. stores zero as smallnum
    c. stores last element of array as smallnum
    d. stores address of array num as smallnum
    e. none of the above

30. Computed results are passed back to the calling main function through:
    a. call-by-value array parameter for smallnum
    b. call-by-reference array parameter for smallnum
    c. return instruction for sending computed integer value smallnum
    d. (a) and (b)
    e. (a) and (c)

This part contains 10 True or False questions. Use the same mark sense sheet for these questions as well.

For the next 5 questions, consider the following program skeleton:

```
int X1, Y4 ;
void Proc2(int);  /* function prototypes*/
void Proc1(int, int);
void Proc3(int) ;

void main(void) {
        int X, Y, Z;

        Proc1(X,Y);  /* function calss */
        Proc3(X);
}

void Proc1 (int X1, int Y1) {
        int Z1 ;
        Proc2(Z1); }

void Proc2 (int Y2)  {
        int Z2 ;
        ............
}

void procedure  Proc3(X3 int)  {
        int Z3 ;
        ......
}
```

31.   Z1 is local to Proc1 and global to Proc2.
        a.   True   b.   False

32.   Z3 can be accessed by all parts of the program.
        a.   True   b.   False

33.   Z is a global variable that is visible to, and can be accessed by, all parts of the
        program.
        a.   True   b.   False

34.   The statement Z1 = Z2 would be legal if it appeared in the body of Proc1.
        a.   True   b.   False

35.   Proc2 could be called in Proc1 with the parameter Y1.
        a.   True   b.   False

36.   The body of a loop instruction might not get executed at all.
        a.   True   b.   False

234

37.   Event-controlled loops do not know upfront the number of iterations to execute.
       a. True   b.   False

38.   A non-builtin function called in a program must be defined in the same program.
       a. True   b.   False

39.   Formal parameters are specified in the calling instruction.
       a. True   b.   False

40.   Actual parameters are specified in the calling instruction.
       a. True   b.   False

11.4   Sample Midterm Test

UNIVERSITY OF WINDSOR
COMPUTER SCIENCE 60-140-01/02
MIDTERM   TEST

Examiner: Dr. C.I. Ezeife   Given: Wed., Oct. 23, 2001 (modified)

Student Name:_____

Student Number:_____

Lab. Section(circle one): 51, 52, 53, 54, 55, 56, 57, 58, 67/68

INSTRUCTIONS (Please Read Carefully)

Examination Period is 1 hour 20 minutes. DO NOT WRITE WITH PENCIL.
Answer all questions. Write your answers in the spaces provided in the question paper.
Total Marks = 100.   Total number of questions = 3. Total number of pages = 7.

For Marking Purposes Only (this part not to be filled by students)

Question	Mark
1 (35 marks)	
2 (15 marks)	
3a (20 marks)	
3b (10 marks)	
3c (20 marks)	
Total Mark (100 marks)	

Use problem 1 described below to answer questions 1 and 2.

Problem 1:

Kevin, Pat and Mary went to a restaurant for lunch where they paid a total of a given amount (in dollars). They have agreed that Kevin should contribute 50% of the total lunch bill (amount), Pat should contribute 27%, while Mary should contribute 23%. Write a program to calculate and print the name and amount paid by each person using top-down design approach.

For example,
If the input total amount is $85.00,
Output will be:
Kevin $42.50
Pat $22.95
Mary $19.55
****
Use the following structure chart to write your program for problem 1 above.

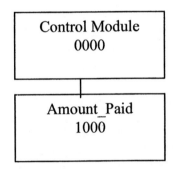

| Control Module |
| 0000 |

| Amount_Paid |
| 1000 |

1. Write a program for Problem 1 above using only parameter calls (give only the program solution).   (35 marks)

```
#include <stdio.h>
    float Amount_Paid (float, float);

{   void main (void)
    float Kevpd, Patpd, Marypd;

    char  Kev[10]="Kevin",  Pat[10]="Pat",  Mary[10]="Mary";
    const float Kev pc = 0.50, Pat pc = 0.27, Mary pc = 0.23;
    float bill;
    scanf ("%f", &bill);

    Kevpd= Amount_paid (bill, Kevpc);
    Patpd= Amount_Paid (bill, Patpc);
    Marypd= Amount_Paid (bill, Marypc);
    printf ("%s %of", Kev, Kevpd);
    printf ("%s %of", Pat, Patpd);
    printf ("%s %f", Mary, Marypd);
```

237

3

```
float Amount_Paid (float, float)
{
    return    bill * perc;
}
```

2. Test and verify that your program to Problem 1 above is correct using the given sample data of $85.00. Show the tracing of your entire solution for full marks.

(15 marks)

Control module:

First the following variables are declared:
Keupd, Mary pd, Pat pd (float)

Given the following program for a problem, answer questions 3a to 3c using this solution. Each of the 10 answers in questions 3a to 3c is worth 5 marks.

(50 marks total)

```
#include <stdio.h>
const float  pi=3.141;  /* global variables */
/* Now the function prototypes are declared */
void Circle_area (float, float);
void main(void) {
        float ice_radius=0.0, st_radius=0.0;
        float  ice_area=0.0, st_area=0.0, bench_area=0.0 ;
/* I now write the body of the main module */
        scanf ("%f %f", &ice_radius, &st_radius);
        printf ("%f %f \n", ice_radius, st_radius);
        Circle_area(ice_radius, ice_area);
        printf ("%f %f \n", ice_radius, ice_area);
        Circle_area(st_radius, st_area);
        printf ("%f %f \n", st_radius, st_area);
        bench_area = st_area - ice_area;
        printf ("%f %f %f\n", ice_area, st_area, bench_area);
}


/* The function definitions are presented next */
void Circle_area (float radius, float area) /*Note that both are call-by-value */
{
        area = pi * radius * radius;  /* note that there is no return instruction */
}
```

3a.) With a sample test data as follows: the values 10 and 15 are typed at the keyboard for ice_radius and st_radius respectively, write the values printed by the 4 printf instructions in the main function in the table below. Show your work to get full marks.

After printf instruction at Position..	Values Printed by CPU in correct order are
Instruction 2	10, 15
Instruction 4	10, 314.1
Instruction 6	15, 706.725
Instruction 8	314.1, 706.725, 392.625

3b.) List all global and local variables of each module/function in the table below:

function	Global variables	Local variables
main	pi	ice_radius, st_radius, ice_area, st_area, bench_area
Circle_area	pi	radius, area

3c.) Fill in the correct description of listed parts of the program solution of question 3 in the table below: (Place your answer to each question in the column on its right).

A function call in the main is ..	Circle_area(ice_radius, ice_area)
A list of formal parameters in the solution is..	void Circle_area(float, float)
A list of actual parameters in the solution is ..	void Circle_area(float, float)
A function prototype in solution 3 is ..	void Circle_area(float, float)

UNIVERSITY OF WINDSOR
COMPUTER SCIENCE 60-140
FINAL EXAMINATION SOLUTION

Examiners:Dr.C.I.Ezeife, Dr. B. Boufama, Mr. Pratap Sathi
Given: Wed., Dec. 12, 2001   (modified)
Student Name:_____

Student Number: _____

Lecture sections 01/02/31, Lab Section (circle one of):
                              51, 52, 53, 54, 55, 56, 57, 58, 67, 68
Lecture sections 03, Lab Section (circle one of): 59, 60, 61, 62
Lecture sections 30, Lab Section (circle one of): 63, 64, 65, 66

INSTRUCTIONS (Please Read Carefully)

Examination Period is 3 hours. Section A is worth 49% and Section B is 51%.
Answer all questions. Write your answers in the spaces provided in the question paper.
Total Marks = 100.   Total number of questions in section A is 7 and in section B is 2. A
total of 11 pages.

For marking purposes only (This part not to be filled by students)

Question	Mark
Section A (7 marks each)	
Question 1	
2	
3	
4	
5	
6	
7	
Section B	
Question 1 (31 marks)	
Question 2a (10 marks)	
Question 2b (10 marks)	
Total	

Section A (49 marks)

This section has 7 short answer questions. Each question in this section is worth 7 marks.

1. Write a program segment to swap the two elements of a one dimensional array of integers such that element Num[j] is stored as Num[k], while element Num[k] now gets stored as Num[j].

```
J = Num[j];
Num[j] = Num[k];
Num[k] = J;
```

2. Given the following array test with 10 elements as given below. Show the position (index/subscript) of the first element (LB) and that of the last element (UB) and the middle element (mid) in each iteration of the loop in algorithm Binary Search till it finds the search key value 80.

| 10 | 20 | 30 | 40 | 50 | 60 | 70 | 80 | 90 | 100 |

Fill in your answers in the following boxes and stop when is given.

Position of First element of list (LB)	Position of Last element of list (UB)	Position of Middle element of list (mid)
0	9	4
5	9	7

3. Write a program that reads the age of a person, then, follows the flowchart given below to decide what to print. The program should also read the working status (e.g., working senior or retired senior) of the person when his/her age is above 59.

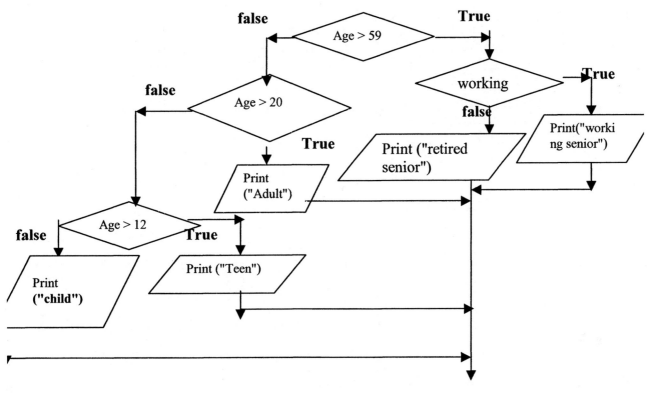

```
#include <stdio.h>
Void main (void)
{
    int Age;
    char work[1];
    printf ("Enter Age \n");
    scanf ("%d", &Age);
If Age > 59
    {
        printf (" Is this person still working (Y for Yes))";
        scanf ("%c", &Work[1]);
        IF (Work(1)=='Y')
        {
            printf ("Working Senior");
        Else {
```

{

4. The program below should read a list of ages and compute the maximum age. The integer number 0 is a sentinel. There are some logic errors (three of them), which cause the algorithm to work incorrectly. Correct these errors.

```c
Include <stdio.h>
void main(void) {
float Age, Maxi;

    scanf ("%f", &Age);
    Maxi = Age;
        while (Age = 0)    (Age != 0)
            {
            if (Age > Maxi)
                Age = Maxi;
                    → scanf ("%f", & Age)
            }
        printf ("Maximum age is: %f", Maxi);

}
```

5. Write a short program to read a list of numbers from a disk data file until end of file (and not from a key board) and find the minimum of all values read.

```c
# include <stdio.h>
void main (void)
{
int Num, mini;

FILE* fp;
fp = fopen ("diskfile", "r");

fscanf (fp, "%d", &Num);
mini = Num;
while (!feof (fp))
    {
    if (Num < mini)
        mini = Num;
    fscanf (fp, "%d", &Num);
    }
printf ("%d", mini);
fclose (fp);
}
```

6. There are currently 2000 people in a town. The population of this town increases by 3 percent every year. Write a program segment to determine how many years it will take for the population of this town to exceed 3000.

```
cpop = 2000;
years = 0;
while (cpop <= 3000)
{
        years = years + 1;
        cpop = (cpop * 0.03) + cpop;
}
printf ("%.f", cpop);
```

7. Declare a record structure of type *student* which contains fields (attributes) *name* (string), *stuno* (integer) and *gpa* (real). Create an array variable *studentrecords*, which can hold records of *student* type, then, write a program segment to read 100 records from the keyboard into this array.

```
struct student
{
        char name [20];
        int stuno;
        float gpa;
}
int K;
struct student studentrecords [100];
```

Section B (51 marks)

This section has 2 full programming questions.

1. The class quiz has 10 questions and the number of students who wrote the quiz is not known. The input data has rows of 10 integers (1 means that student's answer for this question is correct, while 0 means student's answer for question is incorrect). Each row of data is for one student. Thus, the last data line is marked with a sentinel value of -1 for question 1 (first column). The class has no more than 150 students registered who could have written the test.

You are required to write a program using arrays to compute and print the average quiz mark for the whole class. Also, compute and print for each question, the number of correct answers (that is, number of 1's).

Use only top-down design approach to solve the problem and solve using the structure chart given below. No global variables are allowed and make only parameter calls and process using array data structure for both your input and some output data. Read data from the keyboard. Note that headings and all need to be well printed for full marks.

If a Sample input for the student answers to the 10 questions is:

0	1	1	1	1	1	1	1	1	1
0	0	1	1	1	1	1	1	1	1
0	0	1	0	1	1	1	1	1	1
-1									

Then, sample output looks like:

Questions :	1	2	3	4	5	6	7	8	9	10
Total correct:	0	1	3	2	3	3	3	3	3	3

The average quiz mark is 8.0

Use the following structure chart to provide only a complete program solution.

Hint: RowCalc should be used to compute the class average, while ColCalc is used to compute the number of correct answers for each question.

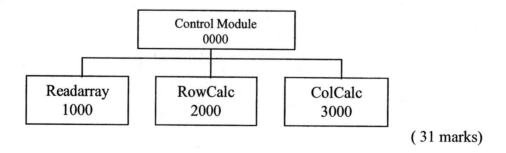

(31 marks)

```c
#include <stdio.h>
    void Readarray (int [][10], int *, int );
     void RowCalc (int [][10], int, int, float *);
      void colCalc (int [][10], int, int );

    void main (void)

{
        int answers [150][10];
        int   float average }
        int     numrow, num col;

        numcol = 10;

        Readarray (answers, & numrow, numcol));
        RowCalc ( answers, numrow, numcol, &average);
        ColCalc ( answers, numrow, numcol );
        printf (" %.f ", average);
    }

    void Readarray (int answers[][10], int *numrow, int numcol);
    {
        int r, c;
    while (answers [r][c] !=-1)
        {for ( c=1; c < 10 ; c++)
            {
                scanf ("%d", &answers [r][c]);
            }
            r++;
            c = 0;
            scanf ("%d", &answers [r][c]);
        }  *numrow = r;
```
249

```
void  RowCalc (int answers[][20], int numrow, int numcols[float
                                                        4ave.194]
{
   int r, c,  row cald [10] , allsum = 0;
   for (row = 0; row < numrow; r++)
      {
         row sum [row] = 0;
      }
   for (row = 0; r < numrow; r++)
      {
         if
```

2.   a) Write a program to calculate new salary for an employee in a company after an increase. The algorithm accepts two input values: salary (in dollars) and a performance level (a character). There are four performance levels: U for unsatisfactory, S for satisfactory, G for good and V for very good. The salary increase scheme is as follows. With the exception of employees with unsatisfactory performance, there is a 2.5% across-the-board increase for all employees. In addition, increases of 1%, 2% and 3% are granted to employees with satisfactory, good and very good performance levels, respectively. Note in particular, that employees with unsatisfactory performance will get no increase.
Your program should print the new salary after the increase. (Hint: Efficient solution gets highest mark here and you do not need to use a function or top-down design approach).

(10 marks)

b) Write a flowchart solution for the same reward amount problem given above in 2a.   (10 marks)

APPENDIX A

<u>ASCII   Character   Set</u>

Character	Code in Decimal	Character	Code in Decimal
nul	00	%	37
soh	01	&	38
stx	02	"	39
etx	03	(	40
eot	04	)	41
enq	05	*	42
ack	06	+	43
bel	07	,	44
bs	08	—	45
ht	09	.	46
nl	10	/	47
vt	11	0	48
ff	12	1	49
cr	13	2	50
so	14	3	51
si	15	4	52
dle	16	5	53
dcl	17	6	54
dc2	18	7	55
dc3	19	8	56
dc4	20	9	57
nak	21	:	58
syn	22	;	59
etb	23	<	60
can	24	=	61
em	25	>	62
sub	26	?	63
esc	27	@	64
fs	28	A	65
gs	29	B	66
rs	30	C	67
us	31	D	68
sp	32	E	69
!	33	F	70
"	34	G	71
#	35	H	72
$	36	I	73

J	74	e	101
K	75	f	102
L	76	g	103
M	77	h	104
N	78	i	105
O	79	j	106
P	80	k	107
Q	81	l	108
R	82	m	109
S	83	n	110
T	84	o	111
U	85	p	112
V	86	q	113
W	87	r	114
X	88	s	115
Y	89	t	116
Z	90	u	117
[	91	v	118
\	92	w	119
]	93	x	120
^	94	y	121
_	95	z	122
`	96	{	123
a	97	|	124
b	98	}	125
c	99	~	126
d	100	del	127

60-140 LECTURE SLIDES

60-140
Problem Solving and Programs with C

- FALL 2003
  INSTRUCTOR: DR. C.I. EZEIFE

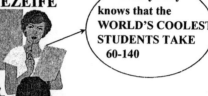

Everybody knows that the WORLD'S COOLEST STUDENTS TAKE 60-140

SCHOOL OF COMPUTER SCIENCE,
UNIVERSITY OF WINDSOR

60-140 Dr. C.I. Ezeife © 2003   Slide   1

---

1. Overview of Computer Systems

- Computers are classified based on their generation and type.
- The architecture of different generations of computers differ with advancement in technology.
- Changes in computer equipment have gone through four generations namely:
  - First Generation Computers (1945-1955): Bulky, expensive, consumed a lot of energy because main electronic component was vacuum tube. Programming was in machine language and wiring up plug boards.

60-140 Dr. C.I. Ezeife © 2003   Slide   2

Overview of Computer Systems

- Second Generation Computers (1955-1965): Basic electronic components became transistors. Programming in High level language with punched cards.
- Third Generation Computers (1965-1980): Basic technology became integrated circuit (I Cs) allowing many transistors on a silicon chip. Faster, cheaper and smaller in size, e.g., IBM system 360.
- Fourth Generation (1980-1990): Personal Computers came to use. Technology in use is large scale integration(LSI). Support for network and GUI.
- Higher Generations: Use of VLSI technology.

60-140 Dr. C.I. Ezeife © 2003   Slide   3

Types of Computers

- Computers belong to one of these types based on their size, processing power, number of concurrent users supported and their cost.
  - Microcomputers - support only a single user, very compact in size. Processing power is increasing but still limited when shared by many programs and users, e.g., IBM PC, laptops.
  - Mini Computers - More processing power can be shared among multiple users, e.g., SGI and SUN workstations. Generally, more expensive than micros

60-140 Dr. C.I. Ezeife © 2003   Slide   4

Types of Computers

- Mainframe Computers - Generally bigger than mini computers, and support hundreds of users at a time, e.g., IBM 370.
- Super Computers - Used for high performance number-crunching applications like processing satellite data from space, e.g., CRAY I.

- Every computer system is made up of hardware and software components.

Hardware Components

- The computer hardware consists of physical electronic components for performing the following functions:

Function	Component
Data Storage	Primary memory (RAM)
	Secondary memory - disks & CD-ROMs, tapes
Data Processing	Central Processing Unit (CPU)
Input of Data	Input devices, e.g, KB, mouse
Output of Data	Output devices, e.g., printer

Data Storage in Main Memory

- Computers represent information (programs and data) as patterns of binary digits (bits)
- A bit is one of the digits 0 and 1.
- Thus, to represent a bit, the hardware needs a device capable of being in one of two states (e.g., a switch of "on" for bit 1 and "off" for bit 0)
- Data and programs are represented as a string of binary digits
- E.g., 9 + 6 are represented as 00001001 and 00000110, then passed to an add circuit to produce binary result.

60-140 Dr. C.I. Ezeife © 2003   Slide   7

Data Storage

- Bits of data are stored in memory and bit collections of size 8 make 1 byte.
- A memory cell is made up of 1 to 4 bytes (ie. 8 bits to 32 bits) depending on the word length of the system.
- 1 kilobyte memory has 1024 bytes (10^3 or 2^{10})
- 1 Megabyte memory has 10^6 or 2^{20} bytes.
- 1 Gigabyte memory has 10^9 or 2^{30} bytes.
- Individual cells in a machine's main memory are identified with unique names called addresses
- The addresses of 1M memory are 0 through 1048575 if a memory cell is just 1 byte.

60-140 Dr. C.I. Ezeife © 2003   Slide   8

Data Storage in Memory

- Each cell of memory can be read or written (modified) individually.
- RAM is volatile because information stored is lost on power off
- Thus, secondary memories are used to store data for future use (disks, CD-ROMs and tapes).
- At the user and program level, physical storage addresses are commonly referenced using logical names or addresses like file names for block of data on disk, and variable names for memory cells.

60-140 Dr. C.I. Ezeife © 2003   Slide   9

Data Storage

- While numeric data are represented in binary, characters are represented using standard codes
- One code is ASCII (American standard code for Information Interchange) which uses seven bits to represent a character.

- Disks are a common storage device for storing information for future use. Storage space is generally more available on disk which are cheaper per unit of storage space than main memory.

60-140 Dr. C.I. Ezeife © 2003   Slide   10

The Central Processing Unit (CPU)

- CPU is the part of the computer responsible for fetching instructions and data from memory and executing them.
- Central Processing Unit (CPU): Processes information, arithmetic and logical (+, -, *, /, % and logical operations).
- It receives instructions and data from input devices which it stores in main memory.
- Later, it fetches these instructions and data from main memory and executes them to produce output (results)

The Input/Output Devices

- Input device accepts input from the user and thus has mechanisms for converting characters into bits, e.g., keyboard or mouse.

- Output device displays output or result of processing to the user, e.g., printer or monitor.

Software Components

- The software system drives the physical hardware components through a sequence of instructions called programs.
- There are many software systems in a computer
  - (1) Operating Systems for managing computer resources , e.g., UNIX, MSDOS, Windows 95.
  - (2) Compilers for translating high level language programs to machine language (bits), e.g., C, PASCAL compilers.

Software Systems

- (3) Network Software for allowing more than one computer to be connected together and to share information (e.g., telnet, ftp).
- (4) Productivity Tools for allowing users to perform daily business and office operations in a more productive fashion called productivity tools (e.g., word processors, database and spreadsheet programs)
- (5) Others, e.g., utility applications like virus checkers.

Overview of Algorithms & Programming Languages

- Computer Science as a field is involved with issues related to
  - algorithm definition, coding, refinement, analysis and discovery
  - as well as issues related to simulation of human intelligence.
- An algorithm is a sequence of steps that determines how a task is performed.
- Examples of real-life algorithms are
  - operating a laundry machine, playing a video game, baking a cake

Overview of Algorithms & Programming Languages

- Algorithms?
- Algorithms are executed by human beings or computers
- When executed by people, an algorithm needs to be presented at their level of understanding and in a language they understand
- When executed by machine (computer), an algorithm also needs to be presented at its level of understanding and in a language it understands.

Overview of Algorithms & Programming Languages

- Example of an algorithm: Example 1.1
- Find the largest common divisor of 2 positive integers. (The Euclidean algorithm)
  - Input: 2 positive integers, large and small
  - Output: their largest common divisor (LCD)
  - Procedure:
    - Step 1: Input large and small
    - Step 2: Compute Remainder (R) = large % small
    - Step 3: If R != 0

Overview of Algorithms & Programming Languages

  - then
    - Step 3.11: large = small
    - Step 3.12: small = R
    - Step 3.13: Go Back to Step 2
  - else
    - Step 3.21: LCD = small
- Step 4: Output the LCD of large and small
- Step 5: End

Overview of Algorithms & Programming Languages

- E.g., Find the largest common divisor of 16 and 40.

Algorithms & Programming Languages

- Focus of the course (60-140) is on how to discover programs for solving a task (problem solving)
- To do this, we may need to first define the precise sequence of steps for solving this problem represented as an algorithm in pseudocode.
- The computer does not understand pseudocode but a program written in a computer language.
- Thus, for the computer to execute our algorithm, it eventually needs to be translated into a program in a computer language.

Algorithms & Programming Languages

- Computer languages are machine language, assembly language and high level languages.
- High level programming languages are easier to use by humans since they are closest to English and Math.
- Current programming languages fall into one of the following four programming paradigms:

Algorithms & Programming Languages

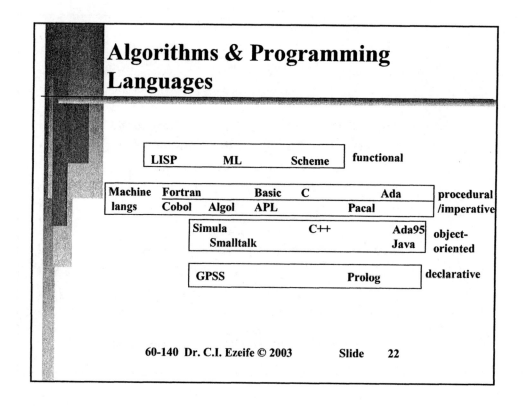

	LISP	ML		Scheme		functional
Machine langs	Fortran		Basic	C	Ada	procedural /imperative
	Cobol	Algol	APL		Pacal	
	Simula			C++	Ada95	object- oriented
		Smalltalk			Java	
	GPSS				Prolog	declarative

266

Algorithms & Programming Languages

- Before a program written in a high level language is executed by the CPU, it needs to be translated, linked and loaded into memory in a process called compilation and linking.
- Program preparation process is:
  - Step 1. Type Source program in high level language
  - Step 2. Compile to get object program in machine language.
  - Step 3. Link to get load module
  - Step 4. Load into memory to execute

Introduction to C Programming Language

- A C source program file must be given a name with .c extension, e.g., test.c and this file must be prepared with a text editor like Unix vi editor, nedit, pico or PC's notepagd or Turbo C++ Lite editor.
- A C compiler is used to compile a C program. To compile on Unix, use: cc filename.c
- Program instructions that violate the syntax of grammar rules of C will cause syntax errors and must be corrected before a successful compilation is achieved

Introduction to C Programming Language

- After compilation, the program is run to obtain the desired result. On Unix run with the command: a.out
- General structure of a simple C program is:

```
#include <stdio.h>
void main(void)
{
  /* Variables declared here */
   program instructions;
}
```

2. Problem Solving Steps

- Objectives
  - Understand what a problem is
  - Discuss Five problem solving steps
- Types of Problems
- 1. Problems with Algorithmic Solutions
  - Have a clearly defined sequence of steps that would give the desired solution
    - E.g. baking a cake, adding two numbers

Problem Solving Steps

- the sequence of steps or recipe for arriving at the solution is called the algorithm
- 2. Problems with Heuristic Solutions
  - Solutions emerge largely from the process of trial and error based on knowledge and experience
  - E.g. winning a tennis game or a chess game, making a speech at a ceremony
- Many problems will require a combination of the two kinds of solution

Problem Solving Steps

- In this course, we are mostly concerned with algorithmic problems.
  - computers are good at solving such problems
- Heuristic problem solving (getting computers to speak English or recognize patterns) is the focus of Artificial Intelligence
- What is a Problem?
  - It has some input and some desired output, and
  - we want to define a sequence of steps (algorithm and program) for transforming input data to desired output data.

Problem Solving Steps

- What is a problem's algorithmic solution?
  - the sequence of steps needed to reach the desired output or the best output data expressed in pseudocode.
- What is a Program?
  - the sequence of steps (algorithms) expressed(coded) in a computer language like C.

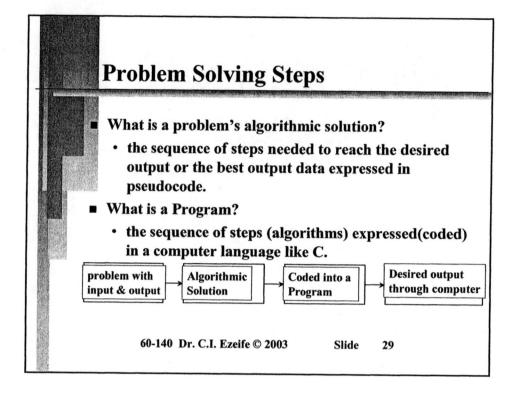

| problem with input & output | → | Algorithmic Solution | → | Coded into a Program | → | Desired output through computer |

Problem Solving Steps

- Example 2.1: Management wants to see the patterns in absenteeism across its two departments, dept1 and dept2 for one week. It is interested in knowing the total absenteeism in each department in the one week it collected data. You are required to identify the input and output data of this problem and attempt to define an algorithm and a program.

Problem Solving Steps

Problem Solving Steps

- **1. Defining the Problem Requirements**
  - may need knowledge or familiarity with a real life environment to understand the needs of a problem
- **2. Identifying Problem Components**
  - identify the problem inputs, outputs, constraints and relationships between inputs and outputs.
- **3. Possibly break problem solution into small modules**
  - This step uses top-down design to solve a big problem using structure chart. This step may be skipped for small problems.

Steps in Problem Solving

- **4. Design the Algorithm to solve the problem**
  - **Best among many alternative ways for solving the problem is chosen.**
  - **Define algorithmic solution for all modules in structure chart.**
  - **E.g., solution that is most cost efficient, space efficient or fastest.**
- **5. Implementation and Coding**
  - **Translate the algorithmic solution from step 4 to C programming language to obtain a program.**

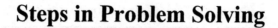

Steps in Problem Solving

- **Programs have to obey the grammar rules (syntax) of C and any violation results in a syntax error (called bug).**
- **A bug needs to be corrected during debugging before the program is accepted by the compiler.**
- **Other types of error that might need to be corrected during coding for correct results to be obtained are logic and runtime errors.**
- **The C implementation of Example 2.1 is:**
- **6. Evaluate the solution to ensure it produces desired results**
  - **A set of complete test data is used to test the correctness of the program**

Difficulties With Problem Solving

- Failing to outline details of the solution (algorithm and program) completely
- Failing to define the problem correctly
- Failing to generate a sufficient list of alternatives
- Failing to use a logical sequence of steps in the solution
- Poor evaluation of the solution (algorithm and program)
- Always remember that computer does not see and needs to be given all details about what to do.

3. Types of Algorithmic and Program Instructions

- Objectives
- 1. Introduce programming language concepts of variables, constants and their data types
- 2. Introduce types of algorithmic and program instructions
- 3. Discuss Read(scanf)/Print(printf) and Assignment instructions.
- Variables and Constants
- Variables and Constants are names for storage locations (memory cells) holding data values processed by the computer

273

Problem Solving Concepts (Variables and Constants)

- Programmers define data relevant to a problem as constants or variables
- Variables and constants form building blocks for equations and expressions used in problem solving.
- Both variables and constants have specific data types. E.g., alphabetic or numerical value
- Differences Between Variables & Constants
  - The value of a variable may change during processing of a problem in a program, but the value of a constant cannot change

Problem Solving Concepts (Variables and Constants)

- The format for declaring variables in both an algorithm and a C program is:

  datatype   variablename[,variablenames];

- The format for declaring constants in both an algorithm and a C program is:

const datatype
  variablename=value[,variablenames=values];

A constant can also be defined using preprocessor directive:
  #define   constantname   value

Problem Solving Concepts (Variables and Constants)

■ **Example 3.1 :** A class of ten students took a quiz. The grades (integers in the range 0 to 100) for quiz are available to you. Determine the class average on the quiz.

  • Identify the constants and variables you need to solve this problem

60-140 Dr. C.I. Ezeife © 2003   Slide   39

Variables and Constants

■ **Example 3.2:** An elementary school is organizing a summer camp for kids and would like to know what activities to provide. They have surveyed 200 kids asking them to select only three out of the following activities: skipping, swimming, jogging, roller blading, mountain climbing, tennis, drawing, basketball and walking. The question is: what variable or constant names do you need to solve this problem?

60-140 Dr. C.I. Ezeife © 2003   Slide   40

Variables and Constants

- Show the variables and constants needed to solve these problems.
- Example 3.3: You are required to count the number of 60-140 students who have completed assignment #1. The class has 250 students

- Example 3.4: Find the sum and product of 2 numbers.

Issues concerning Variables/Constants

- Rules for naming variables/constants differ from language to language. C allows unlimited number of alphanumeric characters.
- It is good problem solving practice to use variable names close to the meaning of its data values
- Multiple word variable names should be separated with underscore to make it more readable. E.g., Ass1_140
- Use variable names with less than 15 characters to avoid ambiguities.
- Check Table 3.1 of text for keyword names not to be used as variable names in programs.

Data Types

■ Input Data are facts (values) used by the computer to process algorithmic solutions and programs to a problem while output data are the results (values) produced by the computer after running the program.

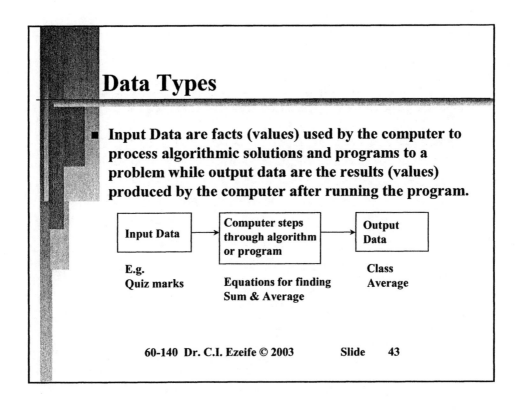

Data Types

■ Data are of many different types:

■ 1. Integer Data Type(called int or long int in C): Integers (whole numbers, e.g., 1577, -18). Arithmetic operations can be performed on this data type. Example declarations are: int age, score;
                    long int bignumber;

■ 2. Real Data Type(in C are float or double): numeric value with whole number and decimal parts, e.g., 23.75, 230000 or 2.3E5 in Scientific notation. Arithmetic operations are performed on this data type. E.g.,
        float salary;
        double bigrealnumber;

Data Types

- 3. Character Data Type(called char in C): all letters, numbers and special symbols (surrounded by quotation signs), e.g., "A", "a", "1", "+". E.g.,
    char grade, location='A';
- 4. String Data Type(implemented as char variablename[ ] in C)
  - Combination of more than one character (surrounded by quotation signs), e.g., "Randy", "85611", "519-111-2345". Eg declarations:
      char lastname[15], address[30];

Data Types

- 4. Boolean or LOGICAL Data Type (implemented with int in C)
  - TRUE or FALSE are the only data values.
  - In C, this an int variable with a value of 0 can be treated as logical type FALSE, while a value of not equal to 0 (like 1) is TRUE. E.g.,
      int flag=0; /* declares flag as false */
- Each data type has a data set, the set of values from which any datum of that data type is specified.

Data Types

Data Type	Data Set	Example Data
Integer(int)	All whole numbers, e.g., -2^{31} to $(2^{31}-1)$	1999, -67
Real (float/ double)	All real numbers (whole + decimal)	1999.0, 258923.61 0.00581
Character (char)	All letters, numbers, and special symbols.	"A","b","K", "1","8","+"
String(char variable[ ])	Combination of >1 chars.	"Atlas","956"
Logical (int with 0 or !0)	TRUE FALSE	TRUE FALSE

Operations on Character/String Data

- **1. Character/String data can be compared and arranged in alphabetical order (using their ASCII codes)**
  - **A comparison between characters 'A' and 'B' gives 'A' < 'B' since 65 < 66** (see Appendix A of text)
  - **The character string "Money" is greater than "Make" because "o"=111 > "a"=97 but > is not used for string comparison in C. String functions and processing are discussed in chs. 4 and 8.**
- **2. Other character and string operations including a lot of builtin functions are available in C and more details are in sections 4.3 and 8.5 of text.**

Uses for Different Data Types

■ 1. Numerical Data (integer(int/long int) and real(float/double))
  • used in business, government & academic applications for values such as salary, price, scores
  • used for numbers that will require some computations on them
  • E.g., number of employees, assignment marks, salary.
■ 2. Character Data (char)
  • used for initials, grades or things needing only one character. No mathematical calculation allowed.

Uses for Different Data Types

■ 3. String (char variablename[ ])
  • used for names, labels and things needing more than one character and not needing any mathematical calculation
  • e.g., student number, phone number & account number.
■ 4. Boolean (int with value 0 or !0)
  • used in making yes-or-no decisions
  • e.g., is a student's grade 'A' ?

Rules for Data Types

- 1. Data types are not usually mixed. E.g., character data cannot be placed in a variable memory location designated as numerical. C allows use of cast operator for type conversion when necessary.
- 2. Data defining the value of a variable or a constant will be one or four data types: numerical, character, string and boolean.
- 3. The use of any data outside the data set of the data type results in an error
- 4. Only valid operations on a data type are allowed. E.g., numbers designated as string type cannot be used in calculations.

Algorithmic Structure

- [Global Input/Output Variables]

[Function Prototype list : type and parameters]
Mainalgorithm
{
Input: Variables/ Constants lists and their types
Output: Variables lists and their types
Others: Variables/Constants lists and their types
/* Now the body of Main Driver or Control Module is defined*/
　Instruction 1;
　Instruction 2;
　　　:
　Instruction n;
}
[function definition 1] ...
[function definition 2]

C Program Structure

- #include <stdio.h>
[Optional Global Variable declarations]
[Function Prototype list : type and parameters]
void main(void)
{
variable declarations;
/* Now the body of Main Driver or Control Module is defined*/
  Instruction 1;

  Instruction 2;

    :

  Instruction n;
}
[function definition 1] ...
[function definition 2]

Types of Algorithmic Instructions

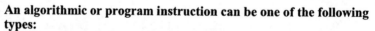

- An algorithmic or program instruction can be one of the following types:

  - 1. Read (scanf in C) or Print (printf in C) instruction - Read instruction is used to read data from the key board while a Write instruction prints output to the monitor.E.g.,
    Algorithm: Read (Num1);
            Print (Num1);
    C Program: scanf("%d", &Num1);
            printf("%d", Num1);

  - 2. Assignment instruction - used to copy a computed value on the right hand side of an equation to the memory cell labeled the left hand side of the equation. E.g., both algorithm and program: sum = Num1 + Num2;

Types of Algorithmic Instructions

- 3. A function call - used to delegate some portion of the task to a small independent program segment. Eg. In both algorithm and program: Compute_Product(Num1, Num2,&product);

- 4. A Decision instruction - used to decide between which one of a number of alternative instructions to execute. E.g., if (large % small ==0) lcd = small;

- 5. A Repetition instruction - used to cause a sequence of instructions to be executed repetitively a number of times or until some event occurs. E.g, while, do-while and for instructions.

60-140 Dr. C.I. Ezeife © 2003   Slide   55

Read(scanf) and Print(printf) Instructions

- Read (scanf) instructions get input data typed by the user from the key board, while print (printf) instructions display the value of a variable or an expression on the screen.

- The general forms of these two instructions are:
  In an Algorithm:
  Read(variable1, variable2,..., variable$n$);
  Print(variable1, variable2, ..., variable$n$);

- The format of C program scanf and printf instructions are:

- scanf("format specifiers", &variable1, &variable2, .. ,&variablen);

- printf("format specifiers", variable1, variable2, .. ,variablen);

60-140 Dr. C.I. Ezeife © 2003   Slide   56

Read(scanf) and Print(printf) Instructions

- Both scanf and printf accept a number of parameters (arguments).
- A parameter could be a variable name, an expression or a string literal.
- Both scanf and printf have the first parameter as a string literal for format specifiers (specifying the data type of the variables or data in the following parameters).
- Format specifiers for int is %d and %ld for long int, %f for both float and double, %c for char and %s for string.

Read(scanf) and Print(printf) Instructions

- Example 3.5: Find the sum of two numbers
  Algorithm: Read (num1, num2);
  Print ("The sum of", num1, "and", num2, "is", sum);
- C Program:
  scanf("%d %d", &num1, &num2);
  printf("The sum of %d and %d is %d", num1, num2, sum);
- Note that if the variable type for scanf is string, then, the address operator, &, does not precede the variable.

Output Formatting with printf

- Use the format specifier %E or %e to display a floating point number in exponential form, %o to display in octal, %x or %X to display in hexadecimal. E.g.,
  printf ("%e\n", pi*10); will print 3.14159e01.
- Specify the number of columns, "c", used to print an integer value with specifier %cd, e.g., %3d, %4d. E.g.
  printf ("%3d\n", 25);
  printf ("%4d\n", 25);
- The number of columns,"c", and number of digits,"d", to the right of decimal point for a floating point value is specified with %c.df, e.g., %8.1f.
  printf ("%8.1f\n", 3.14159);

Assignment Instructions

- An assignment instruction is used to read a value from a memory cell (any variable on its right hand side) and to assign a value to a memory cell (the only variable on its left hand side).
- The general form of an assignment instruction (in both algorithm and C program) is:
  variable = expression;
- Example 3.6: Copy the contents of variable assn1 to assn2.
- Solution: assn2 = assn1;
- Example 3.7: Copy the total of assn1 and assn2 to assn3
- Solution: assn3 = assn1 + assn2;

Expressions

- What is an expression?
- An expression is a variable, a constant or a literal or a combination of these connected by appropriate operators. There are of 3 basic types namely:
  - Arithmetic expressions : variables are numerical and connected by arithmetic operators (+,-,/,%,*)
  - Relational expressions : variables are any type (but same type on both sides of operator) connected by relational operators (<,><=,>=,==,!=). Result is boolean
  - Logical expression: apply to logical values using logical operators NOT (!), AND (&&), OR (||).

Operators

- Operators tell the computer how to process data
- They are used to connect data (operands) in expressions and equations to produce a result.
- Types of Operators
  - 1. Mathematical: addition, subtraction, multiplication, division, integer division, modulo division.
  - E.g. if Jane has worked 17 days during the month in a 5-day work week, how many weeks has she worked?

Operators

- 2. Relational Operators: <, >, <=, >=, == and !=
- Used to program decisions and need data operands of any type except the two operands must be same type.
- E.g., 31 > 15   is TRUE
- "Alpha" < "Beta" is wrong operation in C because string comparison is done with function (strcmp).
- 'C' < 'A' is FALSE
- Results of these operators are either TRUE (!0) or FALSE (0)

Operators

- 3. Logical Operators: Used to connect relational expressions (decision-making expressions)
- Logical operators are NOT (!), AND (&&), OR (||)
- E.g., Refuse registration into 60-141 if mark in 60-140 is less than 60% and student is a CS major.
- if (m60140 < 60) && (strcmp(major,"CS")==0)
    printf ("Error, Need a 60 in 60-140")
  else
          printf("Registration in 60-141 successful");
- Operands and results are logical type (TRUE or FALSE)

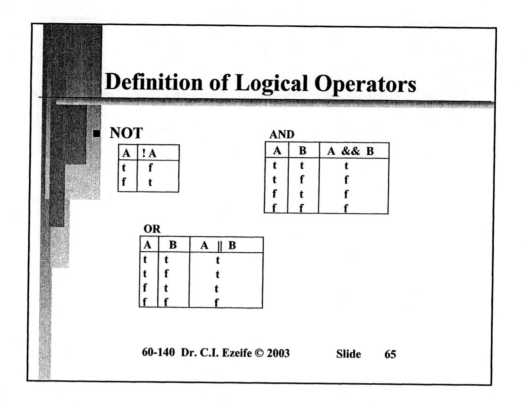

Definition of Logical Operators

- **NOT**

A	!A
t	f
f	t

AND

A	B	A && B
t	t	t
t	f	f
f	t	f
f	f	f

OR

A	B	A || B
t	t	t
t	f	t
f	t	t
f	f	f

60-140 Dr. C.I. Ezeife © 2003   Slide   65

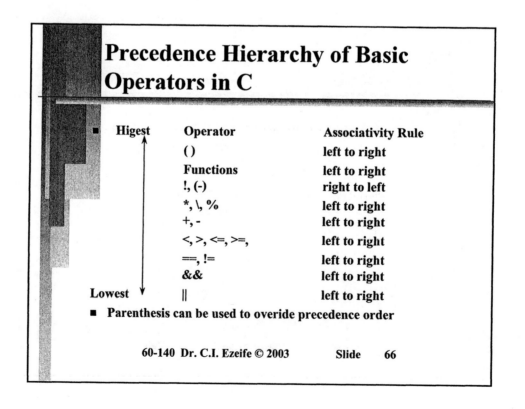

Precedence Hierarchy of Basic Operators in C

Higest	Operator	Associativity Rule
	( )	left to right
	Functions	left to right
	!, (-)	right to left
	*, \, %	left to right
	+, -	left to right
	<, >, <=, >=,	left to right
	==, !=	left to right
	&&	left to right
Lowest	||	left to right

- Parenthesis can be used to overide precedence order

60-140 Dr. C.I. Ezeife © 2003   Slide   66

Setting up Numerical Expression

- 1. Set up the following mathematical expression for use in a C program.
- a. $X(3Y + 4) - \dfrac{4Y}{X + 6}$
- Ans:
- b. Set up the following math equation as a C equation.
- $Y + 3 = X (Z + 5)$
- Ans:

Setting Up Relational Expression

- 1. Given the expression X is less than Y + 5, set it up for use in a C program.
- Ans:
- 2. In order to cash a check, a customer must have a driver's license (A) or a check-cashing card (B) on file at the store, set up this transaction for a C program.
- Ans:

Evaluating a Mathematical Expression

- Evaluating a math expression means assigning values to all variables and testing the result to determine if it is correct.
- Evaluate
- $5 * (X + Y) - 4 * Y / (Z + 6)$
  with X = 2, Y=3, and Z=6

Evaluating Relational/Logical Expressions

- Evaluate the Relational Expression
  A - 2 > B
  where A=6, B= 8

-

- Evaluate the logical Expression
  A && B || C && A
  with A=TRUE, B=FALSE, C= TRUE

Evaluating a Relational/Logical Expressions/assignment instructions

■

- Evaluate the following assignment instruction
  F = !(A < B) && (C || D)
  where A=4, B=2, C=TRUE and D=FALSE

60-140 Dr. C.I. Ezeife © 2003   Slide   71

Other C Operators

- 1. C's Increment Operator (++) for adding 1 to a variable.
  E.g., Num=Num + 1; is same as :
  Num++; (postfix form that adds 1 after using Num)
   and
  ++Num; (prefix form that adds 1 before using Num)
- 2. C's Decrement Operator (--) for subtracting 1 from a variable.
  E.g., Num = Num – 1; is same as:
  Num--;
   and   --Num;

60-140 Dr. C.I. Ezeife © 2003   Slide   72

291

Other C Operators

- **3. Bit Operations in C**
  - **A) Bitwise OR (|)** for ORing two bit values.E.g., 1 | 0 is 1, 1 | 1 is 1 and 0 | 0 is 0
  - **B) Bitwise AND (&)** for ANDing two bit values. E.g., 001111 & 010111 is 000111
  - **C) Bitwise Exclusive OR (^)** that returns 1 only when one of the two input bits is 1. E.g., 1 ^ 1 = 0, 0 ^ 0 = 0 and 1 ^ 0 = 1, 0 ^ 1 = 1.
  - **D) Bitwise Inverse operation (~)**, which flips the value of an input bit. E.g., ~ 1 is 0 and ~0 is 1.

Other C Operators

- **E) Bitwise left Shift operation (<<)** for shifting the input value a number of bits to the left. E.g., 00010101 << 2 is 01010100
- **F) Bitwise Right shift operation (>>)** for shifting the input value a number of bits to the right. E.g., 00010101 >> 2 is 00000101
- **4. C's sizeof operator**, which returns the number of bytes a variable of type requires. E.g., sizeof(int) is 4.
- **5. C's cast operator**, which accepts an expression as its operand and converts the type of the operand to the type specified by the cast operator. Used as:
  (Type) Expression

Other C Operators

- 6. C's Operator Assign Operations: Used for writing short forms of various forms of assignment instructions. These instructions have an arithmetic (+, -, *, /, %) or bitwise (<<, >>, ^, ~, |, &) operator preceding an assignment operator. General form is:
- Variable operator= value;
  E.g., total += 40 means total = total + 40;
  total -= 10 means total = total – 10;
  total /= 4 means total = total / 4;
- Figure 3.4 of text shows the comprehensive operator precedence and association order in C.

4. Problem Solving Tools (Top-Down Design)

- Objective: 1. Discuss structure chart
  - 2. Discuss functions and algorithms with parameters, local and global variables
  - 3. Discuss Built-in Functions and flowcharts.
- Top-down design approach to problem solving is based on the principle of "divide and conquer".
- It breaks down the problem to be solved into smaller sub-problems using the problem solving tool of structure chart

The Structure Chart

- Example 4.1: Write a solution that inputs three different integers from the keyboard and then prints the sum, average and product of these numbers. Use top-down design approach.

- Top-down design approach uses a structure chart with the main problem as the control module and the subtasks located below it.

- A module processes only those tasks directly below and connected to it.

The Structure Chart

- Modules are given unique number labels based on their level with the top labeled 0000

```
                        Control
                         0000
     ┌──────────┬──────────┼──────────┬──────────┐
  ReadData    FindSum    FindProd    FindAve    PrintResult
  1000        2000       3000        4000       5000
```

Types of Modules in a Problem

- 1. Control Module or the Main Driver: shows the overall flow of the problem and calls other modules
- 2. Init Module - for initializing data; e.g., Sum=0, knt=1
- 3. Read and Data Validation Module
- 4. Calculation Modules: for arithmetic calculation, string manipulations like sorting
- 5. File Maintenance Modules
- 6. Print Modules: Prints outputs
- 7. Wrap-Up Module: E.g. closing files.

Cohesion and Coupling

- In separating a problem into parts, it is desirable to
  - 1. Create modules that perform independent functions with one entrance and one exit -- cohesion
    - Cohesion allows modules to perform independent tasks
  - 2. But modules need to work together towards solving the bigger problem --- Coupling
    - Coupling allows connecting modules through an interface where data can be transferred from one module to another (communication b/w modules)

Coupling Techniques

- That is, how can data be communicated between modules? (3 approaches)
  - 1. Use of Parameters in functions, e.g., FINDSUM(X,Y,&Z)
  - 2. Use of function return values for sending output to a calling module.
  - 3. Use of Data that all modules can access (global variables)
- Top-Down design is achieved through cohesion (separating a large problem into independent modules) and coupling (modules working together towards one goal).

Advantages of Top-Down Design

- 1. Many programmers can work on a large problem producing faster results
- 2. It is much easier to write and test many small modules than a single one
- 3. It is much easier to modify small modules.
- 4. Reusability: a defined module can be used several times by any module.

Functions

- A function is a set of instructions that performs specific tasks and can return only one value although it can modify others through parameters (call-by-reference).
- Functions contribute towards the solution of a problem
- They mostly make the solution of a big problem more efficient because they can be reused, more elegant because it is structured and easier to read
- Many languages provide a variety of built-in functions.
- However, modules of the structure chart are defined as functions in the problem solution by the problem solver.

Functions

- A function needs to be provided for each module in the structure chart.
- In the solution, we first provide each function prototype used to tell the compiler functions to expect, the type of result they return and their parameter types
- Secondly, we provide the full algorithmic/program definition of each function
- Format for specifying a function prototype is
  functiontype functionname (type for par1, type for par2, ..., type for parn);

float   FindSum   Float

Functions Definition Structure

- Functiontype Functionname ([par1 type], ..[par*n* type]);
  {
      [local variable declaration];
      instruction1;
      instruction2;
      :
      instruction*n;*
      [return (output variable or expression or 0)];
  }

Function Parameters

- Parameters are data needed by the functions to return results
- E.g., in SQRT(N), N is the parameter, and in SUM(X,Y,&Z), X,Y,Z are the parameters.
- Parameters are surrounded by parenthesis
- rand( ) generates a random number
- A function can have 0 or more parameters
- A parameter can be a constant, variable or an expression

Parameters

- Parameters are data passed from one module (function) to another
- They enable us avoid using global variables so that we can improve on data protection
- Parameters are enclosed in brackets in the definition of the module (these are called formal parameters)
- Any other module can request the services of this module by specifying the actual value for each parameter in the exact order they appear in the definition and with same data type

Parameters

- Parameters used in the calling statements are called actual parameters
- The formal list and the actual list do not need to have the same name so long as they are in the correct order with the right data type.
- Parameters can be passed in two ways
  - 1. Call-by-Value: Here, only the value of the variable specified in the actual parameter list is passed to the module called (not its address)
  - means value it had in the calling module is not overwritten.

Parameters

- 2. Call-by-reference: The address of the memory location for the actual parameter is passed to the called module
- So, the value it has in the calling module before the call can be changed or replaced.

Address Operator (&), Pointer Variable and Indirection Operator (*)

- A pointer variable stores only memory addresses
- A pointer variable has to be declared before use in a program with the format:

datatype_pointed_to *variablename;

E.g., if in main, Num1 is an integer variable with value 35 and Sum is another int variable with value 200.

- We might want to call a function to find the sum of Num1 and Sum with the call FindSum(Num, &Sum).
- The actual parameter &Sum is the address of the variable Sum. This means that in the definition of

Address Operator (&), Pointer Variable and Indirection Operator (*)

- the function FindSum, the second formal parameter has to be declared as a pointer variable that points to an integer value. Thus, the Function header is:
- Void FindSum(int Num1, int *Sumf);
- Here, the formal parameter Sumf, is a pointer variable.
- Note that in the function call, FindSum(Num1, &Sum), the address operator (&) is used to obtain the address of the variable Sum in main.
- The indirection operator (*) is used to obtain the value pointed to by the pointer variable using the pointer variable name. E.g., to add and print the sum in main using the Sumf in the function FindSum, we use:
- *Sumf += Num1;
  printf ("%d", *Sumf);

60-140 Dr. C.I. Ezeife © 2003   Slide   91

Parameter Example (Example 4.2)

- Given the following algorithmic solution, show the values of the variables a, b, c, x, y, z in the control module (module 1) after each function call to module 2.

```
/*    function prototype declaration for Module2    */
void module2(int, int, int *);
void main(void) {
int a=3, b=4, c=5, x=7, y=8, z=10;
/*    body of main    */
module2 (a, b, &c); /* a first call to Module2    */
Module2 (x, y, &z);  /* a second call to Module2 */
}
void module2 (int a, int b, int *c)
{    a += 4;
    b += 4;
    *c += 4;        }
```

60-140 Dr. C.I. Ezeife © 2003   Slide   92

301

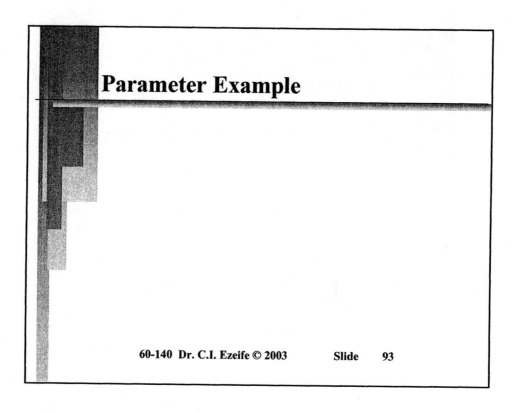

Parameter Example

The Algorithms/Programs

- Algorithms are mostly written in Pseudocode (a cross between English language and high level programming language)
- Each instruction in an algorithm should directly convert to a programming language statement during coding.
- Each module in the structure chart has a separate set of instructions in the algorithm defined as a function.

Algorithm Example (Example 4.3)

- Provide the algorithm and program to Example 4.1 using the structure chart already defined and parameters. Also provide the flowchart solution.

Flowchart

- The solution to a problem can be organized in a number of ways and each algorithmic solution corresponds to a flowchart.
- A flowchart is a graphical representation of an algorithm. It shows the sequence of execution of the instructions
- Flowchart and algorithm represent the same execution flow in different forms.
- A flowchart always starts at the top of the page with straight and neat connecting flow lines.

Flowchart

- Flowchart symbols are given below:

  ⬭   **Start, End, Exit**   ⬡ (count s (op)e i)   **Automatic counter for (count=s;count op e; count= count + i)**

  ▭   **Module**

  ◇   **Decision**   ◯   **On-Page Connectors**

  ▱   **Read, Print**

                                          ⬠   **Off-Page Connectors**

  ▭   **Processing**   →   ←   ↓ ↑   **Flow lines**

  ↳   **Indicating function parameters**

Local and Global Variables

- Cohesion and Coupling are realized through the concept of local and global variables
- In a module, the difference between local and global variables is in their scope (where, in which modules their values are allowed to be used)
- Local variables can be used only inside the module it is declared.
- Global variables are declared outside functions and can be used by only functions below their declarations in the algorithm or program.
- Global variable is one coupling method, a better coupling method is use of parameters

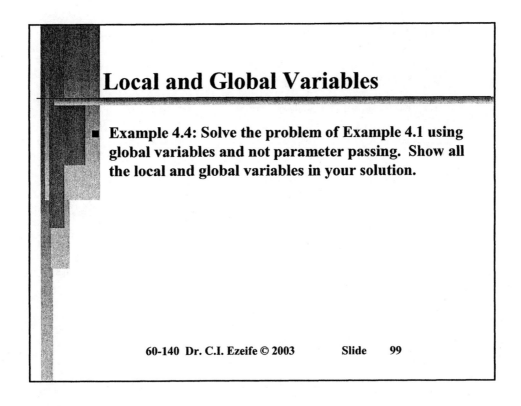

Local and Global Variables

■ **Example 4.4: Solve the problem of Example 4.1 using global variables and not parameter passing. Show all the local and global variables in your solution.**

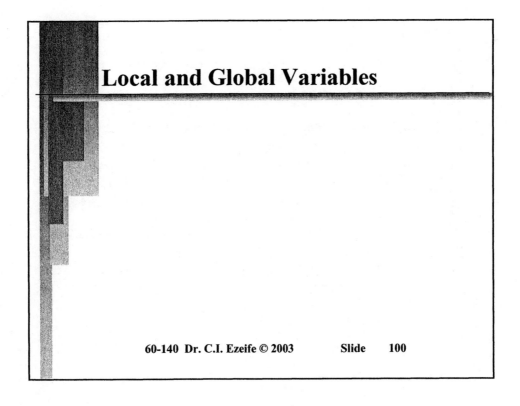

Local and Global Variables

Shortfalls of Global Variables

- 1. Side Effects: A global variable may be accidentally or wrongly altered by an incorrect or malicious module (that is, no protection of data)
- 2. No Duplication of Variable names: When an inner module declares a local variable with same name as the global variable, all changes it makes to this variable is local and it no longer has access to the global variable.

Built-in Functions

- Some common built-in functions provided by C language are:
- 1. Mathematical functions: E.g., sqrt(x), exp(x), log(x), ceil(x), floor (x), pow(x,y), fabs(x) for absolute value
- 2. String Functions: E.g., copy part of the string into another variable, find number of characters in a string. E.g., strcmp(s1,s2), strstr(s1,s2), strcpy(s1,s2), strlen(s), strcat(s1,s2)
- 3. Character Functions: For manipulating character data. E.g., isdigit(C), islower(C) for saying if C is lower case letter or not.
- 4. Conversion Functions: convert data from data type to another. E.g., used to convert a string value to a numerical value, in "C lang." atoi("2593")=2593 (integer value)

pg. 87

pg. 151-158

Built-in Functions

- 5. Utility Functions: used to access information outside the program and the language in the computer system, e.g., date and time functions.

5. Program Logic Structures

- Objectives
- 1. Program Logic structures (General)
- 2. Discuss Sequential logic structure
- 3. Discuss solution testing and documentation
- The logic structure of a program enforces the sequence of execution of instructions in the program and the main logic structures are:
  - sequential logic structure and function calls
  - Decision logic structure and
  - Repetition logic structure

Program Logic Structures

- Thus, to provide a good solution to any problem, we should proceed as follows:
- 1. Use top-down design approach when necessary.
- 2. For defining both the control module and the functions in the solution, use the relevant structure(s) among the three program logic structures:
  - a. Sequential structure (executing instructions. one after the other)
  - b. Decision Structure (executes one of many alternative instructions.)
  - c. `Repetition Structure (executes a set of instructions. many times

Program Logic Structures

- 3. Eliminate duplication of steps in parts of same program by using a module that can be re-used
- 4. Improve readability using proper naming of variables, internal documentation and proper indentation.

Problem Solving with Sequential Logic Structure

- Sequential logic structure is the most common and simplest structure
- Sequential structure asks the computer to process a set of instructions in sequence from top to the bottom of an algorithm.

Problem Solving with Sequential Logic Structure

- This is the default structure and all problems use this structure in possible combination with other structures
- #include <stdio.h>

```
void main (void)
{
    Input  variable list ;
    Output variable list;
    Instruction 1;
    Instruction 2;
       :
    Instruction n;
}
```

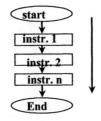

- Execution flow is Instruction1, followed by 2, 3, 4, etc.

Problem Solving with Sequential Logic Structure

- Example 5.1: Monique has some money to spend on work clothes. The type of skirt suit she likes costs $320.00, a pant suit costs the same amount. She always has enough money to buy two suits. She also wants to buy a number of shirts which cost $45 each with money left. How many shirts is Monique able to buy? Test data is $1000.00. You can assume the input data is greater or equal to $640.00. Write a C program to solve this problem.

Problem Solving with Sequential Logic Structure

Testing the Solution

- Testing the algorithm or program entails selecting test data to check the correctness of the algorithm/program.
- With the test data, stepping through the program should give the expected results
- Test data should be selected to test all possible situations that may arise (e.g. -ve, 0, +ve)
- Program testing entails pre-computation of correct result first, followed by hand simulation or tracing of the program to obtain the result produced by the program, which should be the same as the correct result.

Internal and External Documentation

- Internal documentation are remarks written with the instructions to explain what is being done in the program
- External documentation are manuals written for the user to know how to use the program
- Objective of internal documentation is to make program easily readable, maintainable and expandable by either the original programmer or another programmer.
- It includes
  - the input, output and processing information

Internal and External Documentation

- Variable usage, writer of the program and
- other acknowledgements
- Objective of External documentation is to make program easy to use.
- In solving problems, experienced problem-solvers use the sequence of steps:
  - 1. The Structure Chart
  - 2. The Algorithm or the flowchart and/or
  - 3. The program.
- Thus, a problem solver can go straight to step 3 or get to step 3 through step 1, or through both steps 1 and 2. Ultimate solution is 3 (the program).

60-140 Dr. C.I. Ezeife © 2003   Slide   113

6. Problem Solving with Decisions

- Objectives
- 1. Discussing Problem solution using both Sequential and Decision logic structures.
  - if/else and switch_case instructions

- The Decision Logic Structure has two main instructions - the If instruction and the switch_case instruction.
- <u>The if/else instruction</u>
- Meaning is IF the condition is true, we execute the TRUE part (a set of instructions), else (that is, condition is false), we execute the ELSE part (another set of instructions)

60-140 Dr. C.I. Ezeife © 2003   Slide   114

Problem Solving with Decisions

- — if (condition(s))
    {
        TRUE instructions;   }
    else
    { FALSE instructions; }

—

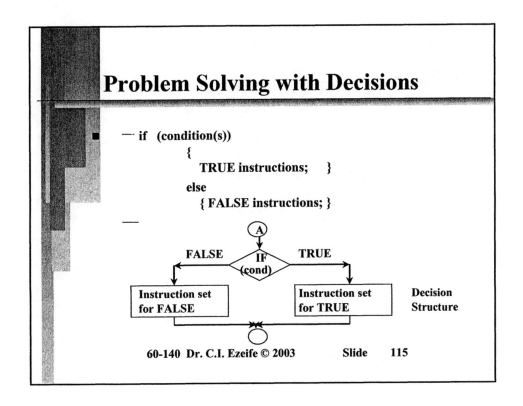

Decision Structure

Problem Solving with Decisions

- **Example 6.1: Write decision instruction to tell a learner driver when to proceed at a traffic light intersection with green, yellow and red lights, each of which can be either on or off.**

Problem Solving with Decisions

■ Example 6.2: A retail store allows part-time workers a rate of $8.00 an hour for a maximum of 20 hours of work in a week. However, a part-time worker earns $10.00 an hour for each additional hour over 20 hours. Write a decision instruction to compute a given part-time worker's wage for a week.

Decision Logic (If Instructions)

■ The if form
  • Process all decisions sequentially one after the other (no ELSE part of the instructions)
  • if (condition1)   (Draw the flowchart)
       Instructions_T1;
  • if (condition2)
       Instructions_T2;

Decision Example

- Example 6.3: Solve the problem of Example 6.2 using if instructions.
    - Num_hours   Week_wage
      hours <= 20   8 * hours
      hours > 20   (8 * 20) + (10 * (hours-20)

Decision Example

- Comparing solutions 6.2 and 6.3 of the same problem, which is more efficient and why?

if INSTRUCTION

- Now, when is it efficient to use the if form (with no else part) of the decision structure?
- With some problems where the sequence of tests are to be conducted on different variables, the only solution is if structure.
- Example 6.4:
  - Assume you want to assign a number of students (S), to different classrooms for an exam such that each room takes only 150 students and once you have got 150 students for one room you initialize S back to 0. Similarly, the GA's (G) for supervising

if/then INSTRUCTION

- the exams are assigned 10 to each room. Once you have got 10 GA's assigned, you initialize G back to 0. Write decision instructions for initializing both S and G to 0.

Nested If/else Form

- **Nested if/else form is the if instruction where either the "TRUE" sequence of instructions (first part) or the "FALSE" sequence of instructions (Else part), or both sequences contain another "if" instruction.**

Nested if/else Form

- if   (decision expression 1 is true)
  - if   (decision expression for expression1-true is true)
  - instructions for when expression of expression1-true is true;
  - else
  - instructions for when expression of expression1-true is false;
- else
  - if   (decision expression for expression1-false is true)
  - instructions for when expression of expression1-false is true;
  - else
  - instructions for when expression of expression1-false is false;
- **This structure has if instruction in both the True and else parts.**

317

Nested if/else Form

- Example 6.5:
  - In a city, the monthly bus fare for seniors 65 years or older is half the normal rate of $45.00 for adults while fare rate for kids under the age of 18 is one_third the normal rate. Write an IF instruction to determine what fare to charge a person given his/her age.
- Solution
  - Conditions

Conditions	Actions
Age >= 65	1/2 * 45
18 <= Age <65	45
Age < 18	1/3 * 45

60-140 Dr. C.I. Ezeife © 2003   Slide   125

Nested if/else Form

- For problems involving nested if instructions in only the Else or True part, they can be expressed in two ways, namely:
  - 1) Using positive logic, and
  - 2) Using negative logic.
- Positive logic writes the instruction such that some action (like assignment instruction) is executed if decision expression evaluates to TRUE but another IF instruction is executed when decision evaluates to FALSE

60-140 Dr. C.I. Ezeife © 2003   Slide   126

318

Using Positive Decision Logic

- if (Age >= 65)   (Draw the flowchart)
      Fare = (0.5) * 45.0;
  else
      if (Age >= 18)
              Fare = 45.0;
         else
              Fare = 0.33 * 45.0;

Using Negative Logic

- Process a set of instructions if condition is FALSE but process another decision if condition it TRUE.
- Can use negative logic to decrease the number of tests
- Age example with negative logic
- if (Age < 65)   (Draw Flowchart)
      if (Age < 18)
              Fare = (1/3) * 45.0;
         else   Fare = 45.0;
      else
              Fare = (1/2) * 45.0;

Logic Conversion

- May help improve on efficiency or readability of a solution
- E.g., a decision should always have instructions for the TRUE section but not necessarily for the FALSE section.
- A solution with no instructions for the TRUE section is better converted to negative logic.
- How? To convert from positive to negative logic do the following:

Logic Conversion

- 1. Write the opposite of each relational operator in every decision as:
  - operator   opposite
    - $<$ $>=$
    - $<=$ $>$
    - $>$ $<=$
    - $>=$ $<$
    - $==$ $!=$
    - $!=$ $==$
- 2. Interchange all the TRUE set of instrs. with the corresponding ELSE set of instrs.

Logic Conversion

- **Example 6.6**
  - Calculate the number of bonus air miles earned given that the bonus air miles earned by customers is 100 if traveled miles exceed 5000 in a period of time, but 60 bonus air miles are earned if traveled miles only exceed 3000 while 10 bonus air miles are earned otherwise by the customer. Write two positive logic if program/algorithmic solutions for the above problem. Then, write 2 negative logic solutions.

Logic Conversion Example

Which if Logic to Choose?

- Choose the if logic that is most efficient, and most readable
- Most efficient logic is characterized by
  - 1. Fewer tests both when you know about data and when you don't
  - 2. Easiest to maintain (modify)
- In the above example, solutions 1 and 2 are most readable with same number of tests. So, any of the two is chosen.

switch_case Instruction

- The switch_case Instruction is the second type of instruction with the decision logic structure.
  - It is made up of several or more sets of instructions, only one of which will be selected if a case label matches the label for that set of instructions.
  - switch_case instruction is used to decide which one execution path among many to choose, while IF instruction chooses one path out of two alternatives.
- Format of switch_case instruction is given below:

switch_case Logic Structure

■ **switch (EXPRESSION) {**

  case label1:instructions to execute if expression = labe11;
          break;
    case label2: instructions to execute if expression = labe12;
          break;
      :
    case label*n*: instructions to execute if expression = labe1n;
          break;
    [default: instructions to execute if expression
        matches none of labels 1 to n above;
          break;]
  }

switch_case Logic Structure

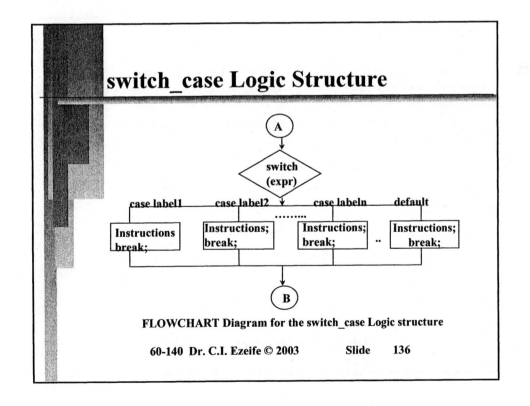

FLOWCHART Diagram for the switch_case Logic structure

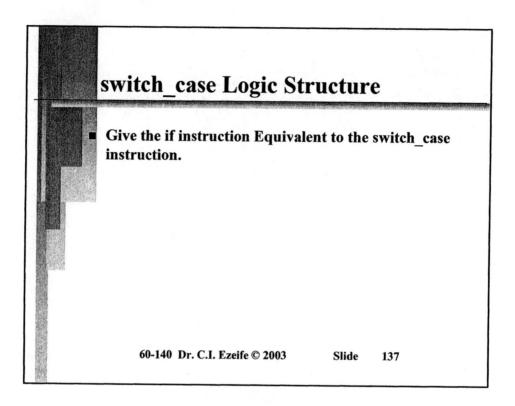

switch_case Logic Structure

- Give the if instruction Equivalent to the switch_case instruction.

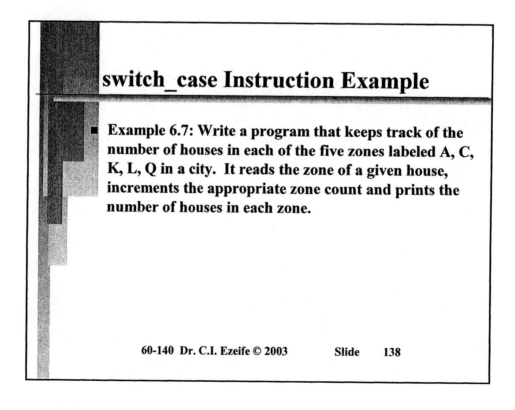

switch_case Instruction Example

- Example 6.7: Write a program that keeps track of the number of houses in each of the five zones labeled A, C, K, L, Q in a city. It reads the zone of a given house, increments the appropriate zone count and prints the number of houses in each zone.

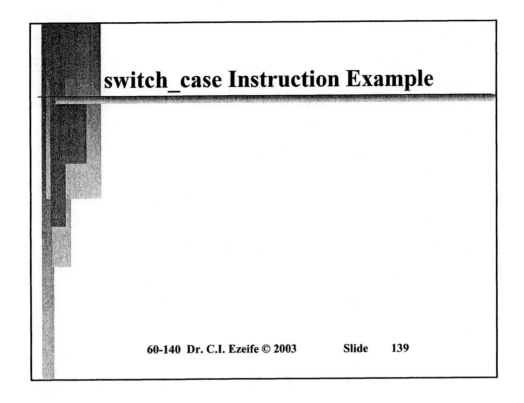

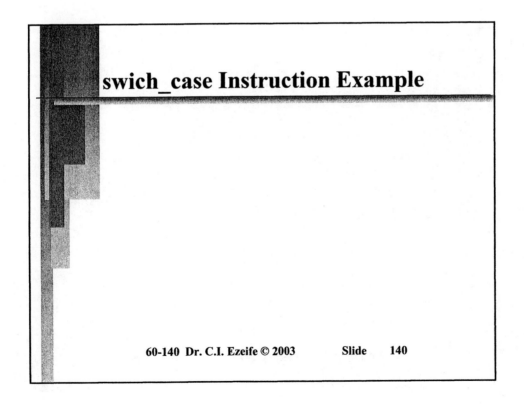

7. Repetition Logic Structure

- **Objectives**
- **1. Use three types of Loop instructions in problem solving (while, do-while, For instructions)**
- **2. Use nested loops in problem solutions touching on recursion as well.**
- **The Repetition Logic Structure**
- **Repetition logic structure allows a sequence of instructions to be executed continuously as long as a condition is satisfied.**
- **E.g. loop problems: Counting, accumulating sum**
- **3 types of loop instructions are used:**

60-140 Dr. C.I. Ezeife © 2003   Slide   141

while Instruction

- **1. while Instruction**
- **Tells the computer to (a) test a <condition> and while that condition is true (b) to repeat all instructions between the while (begin) bracket { and (end) }.**
  - **Initialization instructions;**
    ```
    while (condition(s))
    {
            INSTRUCTION;
            INSTRUCTION;
                 :
            Update Instructions;
    }
    ```

60-140 Dr. C.I. Ezeife © 2003   Slide   142

326

while Instruction

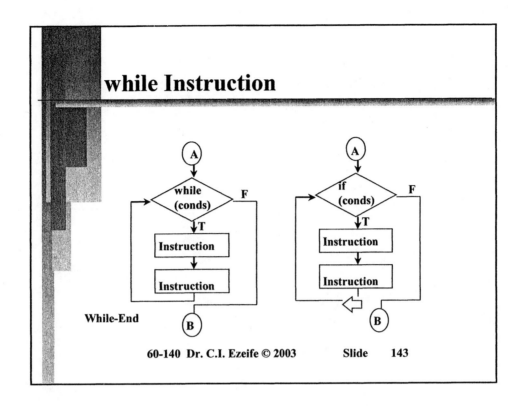

while Instruction

- While loop can be used for both event-controlled and counter-controlled loop
- Important parts of a loop structure are:
  - 1. Initialization of variables (accumulation vars) E.g., Sum = 0
  - 2. Testing of the control variables (for termination condition). E.g., while (count < 10)
  - 3. Updating the control variable (to advance to next data item). E.g., count ++

while Instruction (counter controlled)

- Example 7.1: A class of ten students took a quiz. The marks (integers in the range 0 to 100) for this quiz are available to you. Determine the class average on the quiz using a program. [Complete this rough solution]
  - 1. Declare Variables
  - 2. Init_Module {Sum=0, Counter = 0}
  - 3. while (Counter < 10)
    {
    - Read_Module(mark, sum)
    - /*reads and adds to sum   */

while Instruction Example Problem

- Counter = Counter + 1
- }
  - 4. Finish_Module /* does the following instrs. */
    - average = sum/10
    - Print_Results_Module (average)
  - 5. } /* end of main program*/
- Note that the ReadModule and Finish_Module need to be defined properly in a full program.

while Instruction With Sentinel

- **Example 7.2: Write a program that counts the number of houses belonging to each of the five zones A, C, K, L, Q in a city. The zone of each house is entered for reading and a sentinel value of '0' is used to mark the end of data.**

while Instruction Example Problem

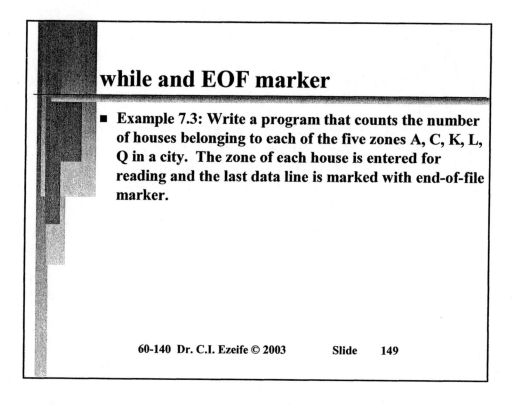

while and EOF marker

- Example 7.3: Write a program that counts the number of houses belonging to each of the five zones A, C, K, L, Q in a city. The zone of each house is entered for reading and the last data line is marked with end-of-file marker.

60-140 Dr. C.I. Ezeife © 2003　　　　Slide　149

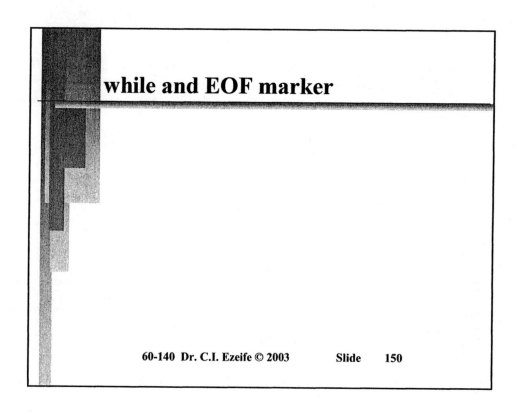

while and EOF marker

60-140 Dr. C.I. Ezeife © 2003　　　　Slide　150

(2) do-while

- Tells the computer to repeat the set of instructions between the do and the while keywords as long as the condition is TRUE.
- Difference between do-while and while instructions
  - 1. Test for loop termination condition is done at the beginning with while loop but at the end with do-while loop.
  - 2. With the do-while, the loop must execute at least once, with the while loop, zero iteration is possible.

60-140 Dr. C.I. Ezeife © 2003   Slide   151

(2) do-while

- With do-while loop,the loop instructions are processed at least once before the termination condition is tested.
- Thus, for problems that may need zero iterations (number of times the loop is processed), do-while loop should not be used (E.g., no data read)
- Format is:
  - do {
        Instruction;
        Instruction;
          :
     } while (CONDITION(S));

60-140 Dr. C.I. Ezeife © 2003   Slide   152

(2) do-while

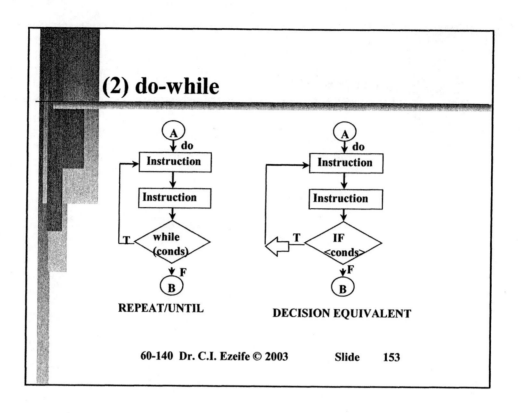

REPEAT/UNTIL   DECISION EQUIVALENT

(2) do-while

- Example 7.4: A computer class took a quiz. The scores (integer in range 0 to 100) for this quiz are available to you and the last data line is marked with a sentinel value of -1. Solve using the do-while loop structure.

do-while

(3) for Instruction (Automatic Counter Loop Control)

- This type decrements or increments the control variable each time the loop is repeated
- e.g. FOR loop
- The initialization, termination value, testing and update of the control variable all occur in the one loop instruction
- Format:
  - for (counter = begin; count (relational operator) end; counter +|- step)
    {
      Instructions;
    }

(3) for Instruction (Automatic Counter Loop Control)

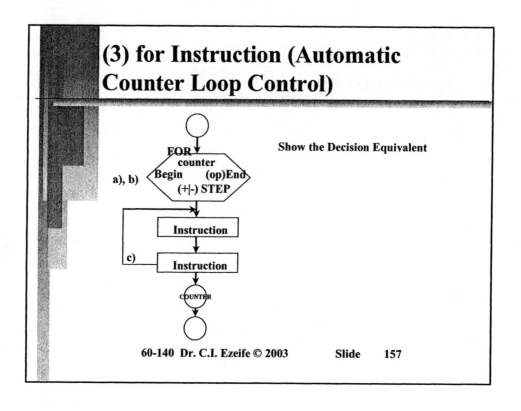

(3) for Instruction (Automatic Counter Loop Control)

- Example 7.5: A computer class of 15 students took a quiz. The scores (integers in the range of 0 to 100) for this quiz are available to you. Determine the class average on the quiz with a program.

334

(3) for Instruction (Automatic Counter Loop Control)

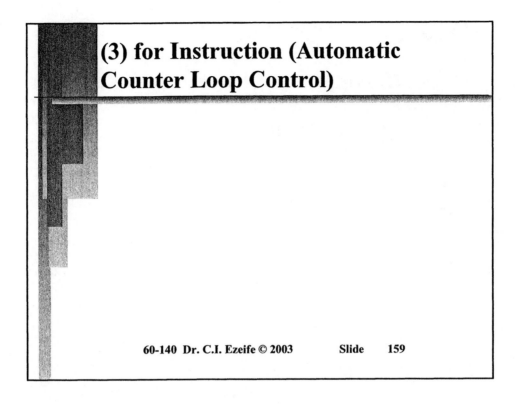

Nested Loops & indicators

- Nested loop instructions are loop instructions inside an outer loop
- Nested loops do not have to be same types of loop structures
- Event-controlled loops, programmed with while & do-while loop structures make use of *indicators*.
- Indicators are logical variables set inside a program when a certain condition occurs (e.g., end-of-file or no more data in the file, or an error occurs like invalid data)
- Indicators are also called flags, switches, dummy or trip values

Example Problem With Nested Loop

- **Example 7.6:** Write a program and a flowchart that utilizes looping to produce the following table of values:

A	A+2	A+4	A+6
3	5	7	9
6	8	10	12
9	11	13	15
12	14	16	18
15	17	19	21

Example Problem With Nested Loop

Example Problem With Nested Loop

Example Problem With Nested Loop

- **Example 7.7: Write a program and a flowchart to display the following checkerboard pattern**

```
* * * * * * *
 * * * * * * *
* * * * * * *
 * * * * * * *
```

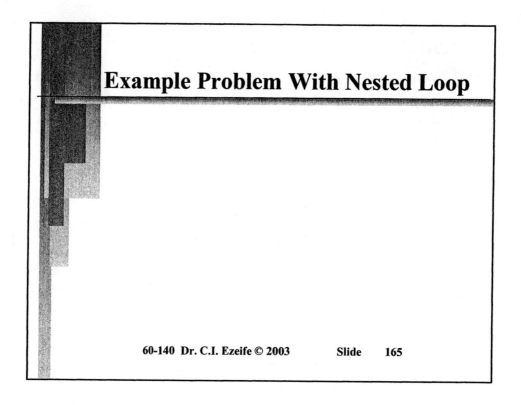

Example Problem With Nested Loop

60-140 Dr. C.I. Ezeife © 2003   Slide   165

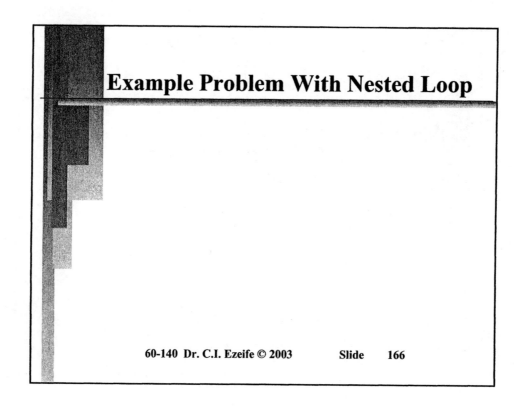

Example Problem With Nested Loop

60-140 Dr. C.I. Ezeife © 2003   Slide   166

Recursion

- Recursion is a type of loop structure where a module or a function calls itself
- Some problems are naturally recursive, e.g., factorial
- A recursive solution should have a base case for termination
- Any problem that can be solved recursively can also be solved iteratively
- Recursive approach carries more overhead in terms of memory space needed during execution and processor time.

Recursion

- So, why use Recursion?
  - For some problems that are naturally recursive, providing and maintaining a recursive solution is easier
  - In terms of performance, recursive solution takes longer and consumes more memory
- Example 7.8: write a recursive program to obtain 10!

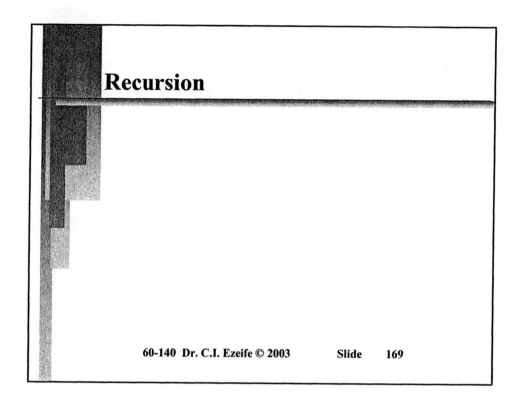

Recursion

60-140 Dr. C.I. Ezeife © 2003   Slide   169

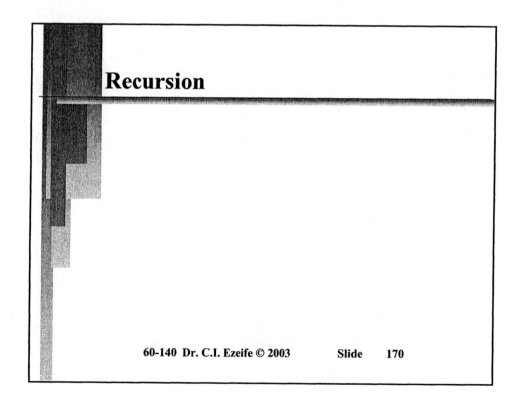

Recursion

60-140 Dr. C.I. Ezeife © 2003   Slide   170

8. Arrays

- Objectives
- 1. Develop problem solution using a more complex data structure, arrays which will enable table look-ups, sequential and binary searches and others.
- 2. Discuss file structure and search techniques.
- If we want to store 5 assignment marks for a student, we can create the variables Asn1, Asn2, Asn3, Asn4, Asn5
- If there are 10 to 20 assignments to record, this approach becomes clumsy

Arrays

- If we also have to record a matrix of 20 assignment marks for say 100 students, with a different variable for each assignment mark, we have:

    Stu1_Asn1, Stu1_Asn2, ……., Stu1_Asn20
    Stu2_Asn1, Stu2_Asn2,…….., Stu2_Asn20
    :   :   :   :
    Stu100_Asn1,Stu100_Asn2,….,Stu100_Asn20

- Approach is inconvenient and prone to error
- A way out? ---- Use ARRAY data structure

Arrays

- An array data structure allows us use the same variable name for the 20 assignment marks for one student.
- Using an array, we replace Asn1, Asn2, ...,Asn20 with a single variable Asn subscripted as: Asn[1], Asn[2], .., Asn[20].
- Thus, an array is a data structure allowing more than one memory location to be designated for a single variable.
- Each element of the array variable is referenced using its subscript

Arrays

- Arrays are useful for many data values of the same type, e.g., all ages, all grades etc.
- Arrays are easier to read and use in program statements than having different variables.
- To use arrays in a program, they have to be declared and the size of the array (number of elements) needs to be included. Format is shown below:
- E.g., to declare a one-dimensional array in an algorithm
    datatype arrayname[size];
  e.g., int assn1[7];
- ❏ Two ways to declare the size or dimension of an array

Arrays

- 1. Static Arrays: allowed by many programming languages.
  - Size and dimension declared at the beginning and never changes during the execution of the program
- 2. Dynamic Arrays: Number of array locations is a variable which can be increased or reduced during the execution of the solution (using malloc in C).
  - More flexible but more time consuming during program execution

60-140 Dr. C.I. Ezeife © 2003   Slide   175

Arrays

- The first array element (the base element) is numbered zero (has subscript 0) in some languages like C, but numbered 1 in others.
- If the base element is 0, the second element is 1; and if the base element is 1, the second element is 2.

```
            A (base 0)                    A (base 1)
A[0]    0 ┌──────────┐          A[1]    1 ┌──────────┐
A[1]    1 ├──────────┤          A[2]    2 ├──────────┤
A[2]    2 ├──────────┤          A[3]    3 ├──────────┤
 :      : │    :     │           :      : │    :     │
A[n-1]    └──────────┘          A[n]    N └──────────┘
```

60-140 Dr. C.I. Ezeife © 2003   Slide   176

343

Arrays

- By using the assignment instruction, we can assign the value of a constant, a variable, or an expression to an element.

- One Dimensional array is the simplest array structure. Conceptually, a one dimensional array represents array variable that has only one column of elements.

- E.g. of a one dimensional array: 10 assignment marks for student Maggie

Arrays

- Example 8.1: Read and print the marks for 10 assignments obtained by student Maggie as well as her average assignment marks.

Arrays

Array Variables in Functions

- An array variable can be used any where any simple variable can be used in all types of instructions including function calls.
- An array parameter in a function call simply includes the name of the array variable without specifying the dimension or size.
- However, an array's dimension needs to be specified in the function prototype and function header. Its size may also be specified if passed as a parameter.
- E.g., a function ReadData reads data into a 1-dimensional array of seven assignment marks. The function prototype and header for ReadData are respectively:
- void ReadData(int [], int);
- void ReadData(int assn [], int *size) ;

Arrays (one-dimensional parallel)

- **Example 8.2:** Write a program that computes the assignment average for assignments 1 and 2 in a small class of seven students whose names and ids are Maggie (id 1050), John (id 1051), Ken (id 1052), Joy (id 1053), Pat (id 1054), Tim (id 1055) and Tom (id 1056). The program read their ids, computes and prints the average mark obtained by each their ids.

Arrays (one-dimensional parallel)

Arrays

- Asn1[1] and Asn2[1] both relate to Student[1]; and Asn1[5] and Asn2[5] both relate to Student[5]
- To declare these three arrays, we use int Student[7], Asn1[7], Asn2[7];

Array Example

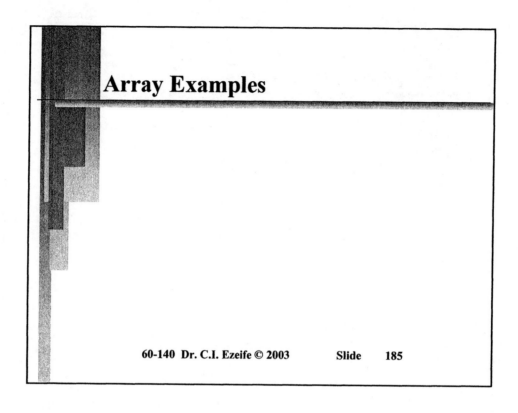

Array Examples

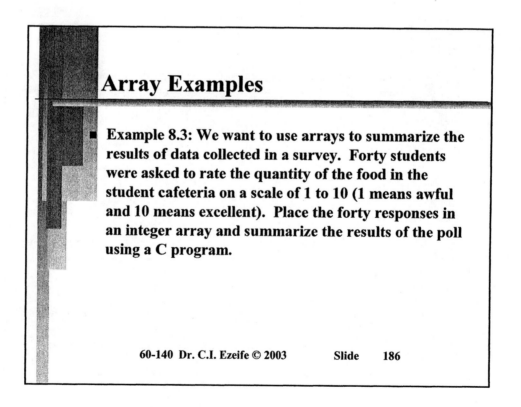

Array Examples

- Example 8.3: We want to use arrays to summarize the results of data collected in a survey. Forty students were asked to rate the quantity of the food in the student cafeteria on a scale of 1 to 10 (1 means awful and 10 means excellent). Place the forty responses in an integer array and summarize the results of the poll using a C program.

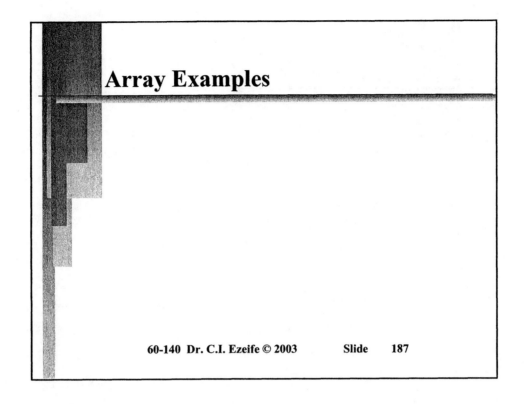

Array Examples

60-140 Dr. C.I. Ezeife © 2003   Slide   187

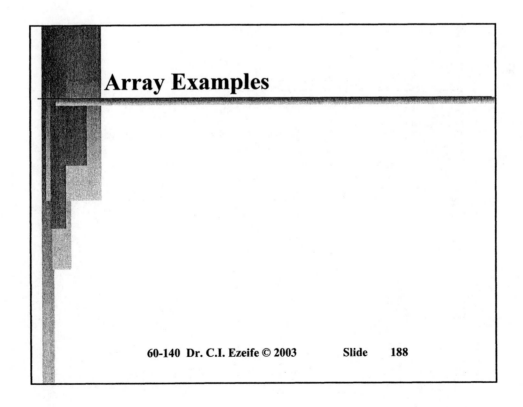

Array Examples

60-140 Dr. C.I. Ezeife © 2003   Slide   188

Two-Dimensional Arrays

- While a one-dimensional array has only one subscript indicating the number of rows, a two-dimensional array has two subscripts indicating (row number, column number).
- A two dimensional array can be used to store a table of values with more than one column (e.g. a Matrix).
- To declare a 2-dimensional array, use:

    datatype   arrayname[num_row][num_column];
- The two parallel arrays for Asn1[7] and Asn2[7] we defined earlier on, can be stored in one two dimensional array as:(write answer here)

Two-Dimensional Arrays

- Example 8.4: Write program that computes the assignment average for assignments 1 and 2 in a small class of seven students named Maggie, John, Ken, Joy, Pat, Tim and Tom. The average mark obtained by each student is also computed and printed. Solve using two dimensional array where necessary.

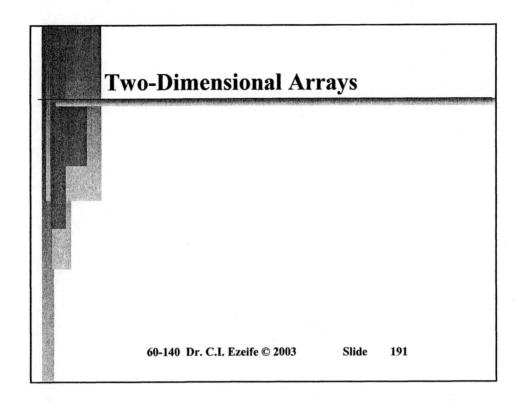

Two-Dimensional Arrays

60-140 Dr. C.I. Ezeife © 2003   Slide   191

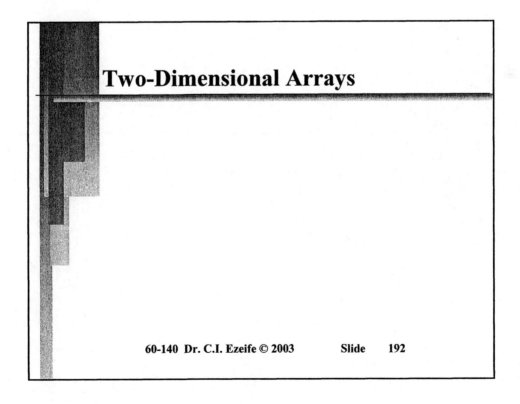

Two-Dimensional Arrays

60-140 Dr. C.I. Ezeife © 2003   Slide   192

Two-Dimensional Arrays

Multidimensional Arrays

- These are arrays with three or more dimensions
- With three dimensional array, three subscripts are needed and three nested loops are used.
- An example of a 3 dimensional array is given in the course book section 8.2
- int Cube[row][column][depth];

String Processing

- A string in C is an array of characters declared as:
  char variable[number of characters];
- The last character of the string is the null character '\0'
- Thus, a string with 20 characters has the 20th as '\0'
- E.g., char studentname[20] can hold only one student name with up to 19 alphanumeric characters.
- Now, if we want to declare a variable to hold 10 student names, it is declared as a 2-dimensional array:
  char studentname[10][20];
- Names can also be initialized at declaration as:
- char studentname[10][20] = {"John Smith", "John Adams", "Mary Goods", "Peter Kent", "Chu Lee", "Paul Best", "Okee Ndu", "Pat Madu", "Andrew New", "Mark Ogods"};

String Processing

- Library functions for string input and output include:
- gets (stringvariable);
- fgets (stringvariable, length, filepointer);
- puts (stringvariable); fputs(stringvariable, length, filepointer);
- sscanf(string_to_readfrom, format specifiers, variablelist);
- sprintf(string_to_readfrom, format specifiers, variablelist);
- Library functions for string copying, concatenation, comparisons and others include:
- strcpy(s1, s2) , strncpy(s1, s2, numchars) , strcat(s1,s2) , strncat(s1,s2,n) .
- The list of string functions in C library <stdlib.h> for I/O are summarized in section 8.4, while functions for copying and other operations are summarized in section 4.3 of book.

Searching or Table LooKup Techniques

- Searching is one important application of arrays.
- Searching entails using a value to look up another value in a table of values. For example, 100 test scores are stored in an array score[100] and you want to answer the question regarding whether there is any 96% in the 100 scores.
- You can go about this look-up in two ways
  - 1. Sequential Searching
  - 2. Binary searching
- Example 8.5: Given n test scores and a search key score, write a sequential search program to return the position of the first element in the array equal to the key score.

Sequential Search

- The program for sequential search is:

- void main (void) {
- int Score[n], key , k, I, n=10;
- scanf ("%d", &key);
  for (I = 0; I < n; I++)
      scanf("%d", &score[I]);
- k = 0;
-     while (key != score[k] && (k <= n))
            k = k + 1;
    If (k>=n) printf ("element not found");
        else printf("element %d is equal to key %d", k, key);
    }

Sequential Search

- Works well for small or unsorted arrays. Inefficient for large arrays
- In the worst case, the algorithm will search through all n elements of the array before either finding the value or not finding it at all
- In the best case, the algorithm searches through only 1 element

Binary Search

- Binary search is faster for sorted array as it eliminates half of the elements in the array being searched
- Binary search compares the mid-element of all or part of the array to the search key.
  - 1. Set the lower boundary at 0
  - 2. Upper boundary is set at the number of elements in the array less 1 (last element)
  - 3. The flag (found) is set to false. This flag is set to true when the element is found and this will cause searching to end (see solution 8.5 in course book).

Binary Search

- 4. The loop is started and will continue as long as not(found) and LB <= UB. If LB > UB, it indicates the last element has been searched.
- 5. The mid-element number is calculated (truncated to integer value)
- 6. Test to see if mid element is equal to value, if yes, found = true otherwise, loop again.
- 7. Test to reset upper and lower boundaries. If search value is greater than value of mid element number, then lower boundary is set to one more than the midpoint, otherwise it is set to one less.

60-140 Dr. C.I. Ezeife © 2003   Slide   201

Binary Search

- 8. Test if there are still elements to search. If the lower boundary is greater than the upper boundary, it means element could not be found.

60-140 Dr. C.I. Ezeife © 2003   Slide   202

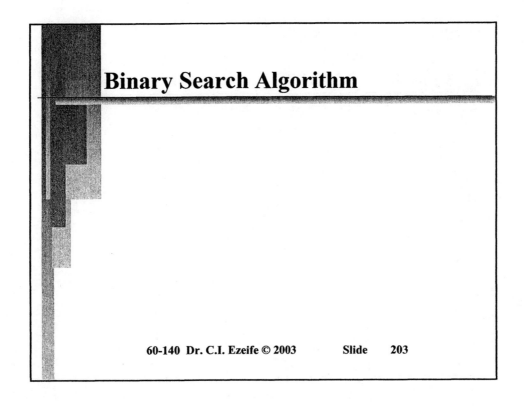

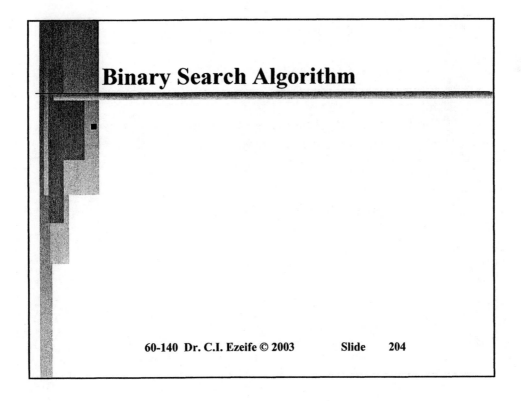

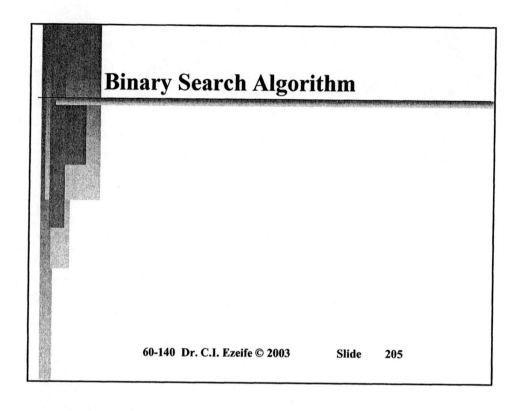

Binary Search Algorithm

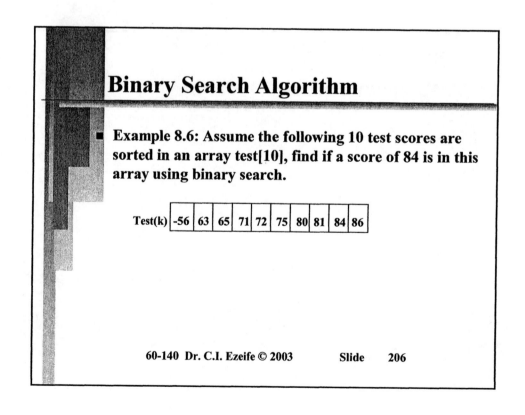

Binary Search Algorithm

■ **Example 8.6: Assume the following 10 test scores are sorted in an array test[10], find if a score of 84 is in this array using binary search.**

Test(k)	-56	63	65	71	72	75	80	81	84	86

Sorting Techniques

- Sorting is the process of putting the data in alphabetical or numerical order using a key field
- primary key is the first key by which data in a file is sorted, e.g., area code for a mailing list
- Secondary key is the second key by which data in a file is sorted within the primary key order.
- E.g., a mailing list sorted by area code can again be sorted in alphabetical order of name within each area code.

Sorting Techniques

- Sorting techniques include
  - 1. Selection Sort, bubble Sort, Quick Sort, Shell Sort and Heap Sort
- Best sorting techniques are determined by the number of comparisons and switches that take place for a file of n records in a specific order.

The Selection Exchange Sort

- To sort n records
- Maintain 2 sublists within n records
  - 1. List of sorted part (S)
  - 2. List of unsorted part (U)
- Initially number of elements in S=0 and number of elements in U = n
- 1. Find the smallest element in U and switch its position with the first element of U
  [now number of elements in S=1 and number of elements in U = n-1]

The Selection Exchange Sort

- 2. While number of elements in (U) > 1
  - Find the smallest element U and switch with first element of U. [Once switched this first element of U becomes the last element of S]
- Example 8.7: sort the following in ascending order using selection exchange sort
- 56
  80
  75
  63
  58
  79

The Selection Exchange Sort

```
{
int  score[6], num_score, I, minpos, j, temp;
  for (I=0; I < num_score-1;  I++)
  {
     minpos = I;
     for (j = (I+1); j < num_score; j++)
     {
       if (score[min] > score[j])
             min = j
     }          /* end of for j */
```

The Selection Exchange Sort

```
   if (min != I)
     {
        temp = score[I];
        score[I] = score[min];
        score[min] = temp;
     }
  }                    /* for I    */
}        /* of main */
```

The Bubble Sort

- Example 8.8: Sort in ascending order with bubble sort
- To obtain the S list from the U list, compare each element in U with the next element and switch if element is larger than next one
- 56
  80
  75
  63
  58
  79

The Bubble Sort Algorithm

```
void main (void) {
    int  score[6], numscore=6;
    int  temp, numleft ;
  for (numleft=numscore-2; numleft >= 0; numleft- -)
   {
     for  (j = 0;  j <= numleft;  j++)
        {
          if (score[j] > score[j+1])
          {     temp = score[j];
                score[j] = score[j+1];
                score[j+1] = temp;          }
        } /* end of for j */
   } /* end of for numleft  */
}   /* end of main  */
```

The QuickSort

- **Using Quicksort, sort**
  56 80 75 63 58 79

9. Pointers, Files, Records and others

- Objectives
- 1. Get introduced to more advanced data structures like pointers, files, records, stacks, linked lists and binary trees
- Pointers
- A pointer is a variable that can store only memory addresses as its value.

Pointers

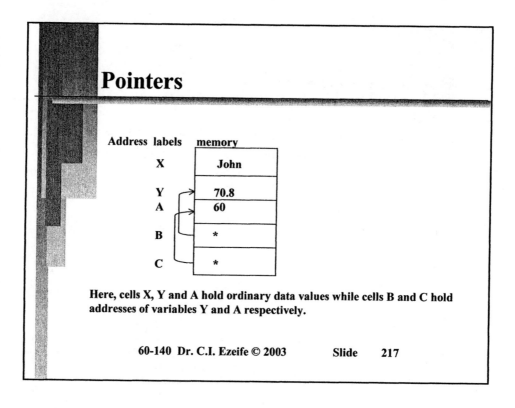

Here, cells X, Y and A hold ordinary data values while cells B and C hold addresses of variables Y and A respectively.

Pointers

- A pointer variable needs to be declared before use and the format for declaring them is:
- type_of_data_it_points_to *pointervariable;
- E.g, float *B;
- int *C;
- Operations on Pointer Variables
  - 1. A pointer variable can be initialized to 0 or null
    E.g., B = 0;
    meaning that it is pointing to nothing but it exists.

Pointers

- 2. A pointer variable can be set to point to a variable by assigning the address of the variable using address operator (&).

  E.g. B = &Y;

       C= &A;

- 3. We can read or write the data value being pointed by a pointer variable through the pointer variable by using the indirection or dereferencing operator (*).

  E.g., print (*B)   will display 70.8

    *C = *C + 10 will replace the value in A with 70.

Pointers

- 4. A pointer may be subtracted from another pointer and a pointer may be incremented with an integer value.

- 5. A pointer can be assigned another pointer variable if they both point to values of the same type.

File Concepts

- So far, we have read data from the key board
- If we write a program to process one thousand student records, reading data from the key board, then, every time we need to run the program again, we have to start typing in all one thousand records.
- Approach in this case is inconvenient and prone to error.
- A solution to this problem is to pre-type our one thousand records in a disk file, save it and tell our program to read data from a disk file and not from the standard input device which is the key board.

File Concepts

- A file structure consists of a number of records with each record representing a real life entity.
- A record is made up of a sequence of fields or attributes (e.g., student id, name, major, gpa).
- Records in a file could be accessed either sequentially or randomly.
- Sequential access files store records in some order (usually in primary key order)
- For a file to be used in a program/algorithm, the following steps should be taken:

File Related Program Instructions

- 1. Declare a file pointer variable or logical variable name. That is, declare a pointer variable to point to variable of type FILE. Format is:
- FILE   *filepointer;
- e.g., FILE *stnptr;
- 2. OPEN the file: This step associates the file pointer variable with a disk file which is to be opened for either read (r), write (w), update (r+) or append (a). Format for opening a file is:
filepointer = fopen ("disk file name", "mode");
E.g., stnptr = fopen("stnrec.dat", "r");

File Related Program Instructions

- 3. Read/Write records from/into the file:
  - Read copies the next record from disk file into the internal memory variables for processing
    Format is: fscanf(filePointer, "format specifiers", variable list to be read);
  - fprintf(filePointer, "format specifiers", variable list to be printed);
  - fscanf (stnptr,"%s %s %s %f ", studentid, name, major, &gpa);
- 3. CLOSE the file
  - tells the computer the file is no longer needed. Format is:
    Close (filePointer);
  - E.g., Close(stnptr);

File Related Program Instructions

- FILE END-OF-FILE (feof) Marker with files
- Data files contain feof marker to indicate there are no more data.
- When testing for feof marker in a file include the file pointer as parameter. E.g., while (! feof (stnptr))

- Loop structures can be used to read lines of records from a file sequentially as:
  - K=0;
    scanf(fptr,"%s %s", field1, field2);
    while (!feof(fptr)}
      {
           K++;
           scanf(fptr,"%s %s", field1, field2);
      }

Record Structure

- A record has many fields identified using one variable name but the fields can be of different data types.
- E.g., record student has fields studentid, name, major (of type string), and gpa (of type real) and can be declared as follows:
  - struct   student_type {
  -         char studentid[15];
  -         char name[20];
  -         char major[15];
  -         float gpa;
  -    }   /* of student record type */

Record Structure

- To declare a variable of record type, we need to first define the record structure type as we have done above for student record type, then secondly, we define a variable to be of this record type.
- To define a variable of student record type, we do:
  - struct student_type   studentvar;
- Now we can assign values to fields of the variable Student as follows:
  - scanf("%s %s %s %f",
    studentvar.studentid, studentvar.name,
    studentvar.major, &studentvar.gpa);

Record Structure

- Any other valid operations can be performed on these fields of the record (e.g., print, assignment etc.)
- We can also define an array of student records to store more than one student record as follows:
  - struct Record_type   record_var[size] ;
  - E.g., struct   Student-type Student[100];
  - To print the record for student number 51, we use:
  - printf ("%s %s %s %f", Student[51].name, Student[51].age, Student[51.major, &Student[51].GPA]);
- And to read a record variable from a file, we again specify the file pointer first before listing the fields of the record.
- typedef command can be used to rename a record structure.

Other Data Structures

- Data structure specifies the way data are stored in the computer memory
- Two types of Data Structures are
  - 1. Single Valued data types [or Ordinal types]
    - have ordinal values with a defined preceding or succeeding value
    - E.g. of ordinal types are char, integer, logical type
    - Real numbers do not have ordinal values

60-140 Dr. C.I. Ezeife © 2003   Slide   229

Data Structures

- 2. Structured Data Types
  - Strings, arrays and records
  - each variable has multi-values e.g., an array
- a. Stacks
- A stack is a list of numbers
- All additions and deletions are at one end (top of stack)

60-140 Dr. C.I. Ezeife © 2003   Slide   230

Data Structures

- A last-in, first-out procedure
- Operations defined on stack are
  - *Push* to add a value to the top of stack, and
  - *Pop* to delete a value from top of stack
- E.g., trace the following procedure on stack data structure and show the states of the stack before and after the procedure.
- It should be noted that before data is pushed onto stack, there has to be room to hold the data
- Also, before data is popped from stack, there is data available

Data Structures

- Push 4
  Push 5
  Push Y
  Pop A
  push 7
  Push 8
  push B

A | 10 | B | 2 | Y | 3 |

b. Linked Lists

- A linked list is a data type where each record points to its successor except for the last record
- Each record contains a field (the linking field) that contains the address of the next record in sequence.
- The link field of the first record points to the second record, that of the second record points to the 3rd record, etc. and that of the last record contains zero meaning it points to no record.
- It is easier to add or delete records from a linked list file than an array of records

Linked Lists

- With the linked list, deleted records are placed in an empty list and additions are placed in the records that had been deleted or at the bottom of the file
- Example is Figure 9.1 of course text.

Linked Lists

- Record of this type can be declared as follows:
- struct list_type
    {char id[15];
    char name[20];
    list_type   *listptr ;
    }
- struct   list_type   *listptr ;

c. Binary Trees

- A tree structure uses a top down or hierarchical structure for data
- Each record is stored as a node of the tree. E.g.

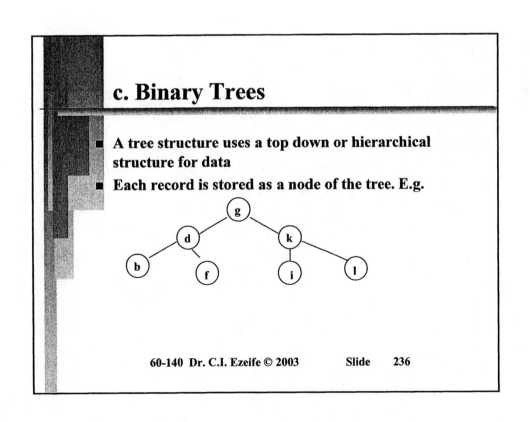

Binary Trees

- A parent node is at a higher level. The nodes at a lower level of a node are its children.
- E.g. g is the root node, d is the parent of b and f. b and f are children of d.
- A subtree consists of a chain of nodes.
- A branch is a path from root to leaf.
- A binary tree is a tree in which each node has at most two children
- Each record (a node) contains two link fields, one pointing to the left node (child) and the other pointing to the right child.

Binary Trees (Declaration

- To declare a variable of type binary tree, we do:

```
struct  btree_type {
            char node_name[20];
            btree_type      *leftPtr;
            btree_type      *rightPtr;
      } btree_ptr  (pointer to btree_type)
```

❑ struct btree_type btree_ptr;

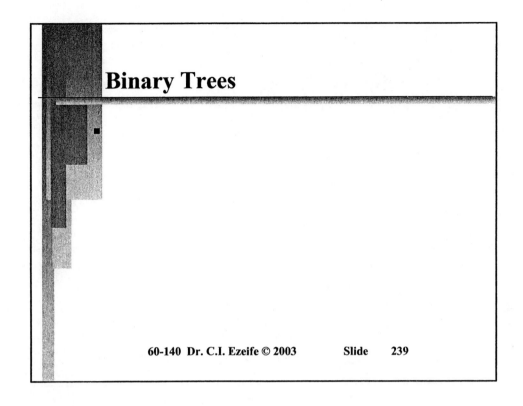

Binary Trees

60-140 Dr. C.I. Ezeife © 2003   Slide   239

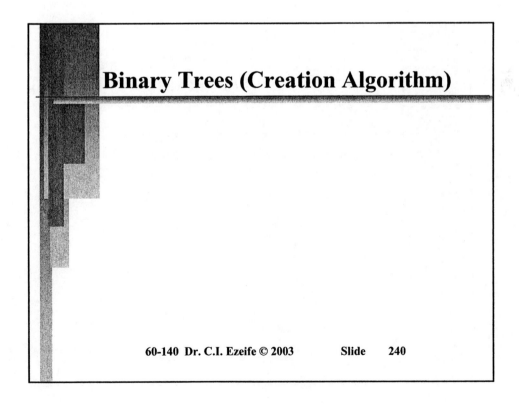

Binary Trees (Creation Algorithm)

60-140 Dr. C.I. Ezeife © 2003   Slide   240

Binary Trees (Traversal Algorithms)

- Records stored as binary trees have to be processed and printed in order
- Processing of these records can be done using tree traversal techniques
- 3 tree traversal algrorithms are used
  - 1. Preorder (N L R)
  - 2. Inorder (L N R)
  - 3. Postorder (L R N)

Binary Trees (Traversal Algorithms)

- E.g. the order of the binary tree in Fig. 14.13 when processed in each of these methods are:
- 1. Preorder: g d b f k i l
- 2. Inorder: b d f g i k l
- 3. Postorder: b f d i l k g

INDEX

T

V

W